D1551683

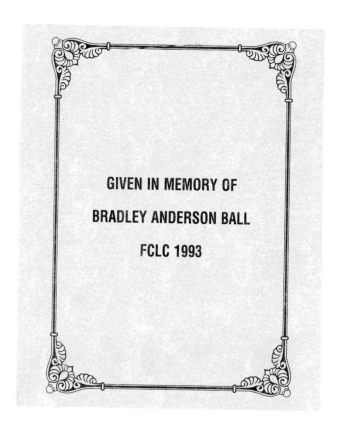

GIVEN IN MEMORY OF

BRADLEY ANDERSON BALL

FCLC 1993

FREE LOVE AND ANARCHISM

FREE LOVE
AND ANARCHISM

The Biography of Ezra Heywood

Martin Henry Blatt

UNIVERSITY OF ILLINOIS PRESS
Urbana and Chicago

© 1989 by the Board of Trustees of the University of Illinois
Manufactured in the United States of America
C 5 4 3 2 1

This book is printed on acid-free paper.

Library of Congress Cataloging-in-Publication Data

Blatt, Martin Henry, 1951–
    Free love and anarchism: the biography of Ezra Heywood / Martin
Henry Blatt.
    p. cm.
    Bibliography: p.
    Includes index.
    ISBN 0-252-01638-6 (alk. paper)
    1. Heywood, Ezra H. (Ezra Hervey), 1829–1893. 2. Anarchists—
United States—Biography. 3. Anarchism—United States—
History—19th century. 4. Free love—United States—History—19th
century. I. Title.
HX843.7.H49B57 1989
335'.83'0924—dc19
[B]   88-36734
                                                                       CIP

To Molly and Bernie Blatt
and to the memory of Clara and Henry Freund.

Contents

Photographs follow page 66.

Acknowledgments

The following persons provided intellectual support: Paul Avrich, Robert V. Bruce, James Green, Charles Hamilton, Susan Reverby, Salvatore Salerno, Charles Shively, and Taylor Stoehr. Mordechai Liebling kindly provided me with a copy of his graduate research paper on Ezra Heywood.

Several archivists provided excellent assistance in locating information used in this book. Edward Weber, director, and Kathryn Beam, manuscript librarian, of the Labadie Collection at the Hatcher Library, University of Michigan, and Martha Mitchell, university archivist at the Hay Library, Brown University, were especially helpful. The State Historical Society of Wisconsin graciously provided a microfilm copy of a complete run of *The Word*, an invaluable part of my research. Anita Woodward, former town librarian of Princeton, Massachusetts, was helpful. The staff of the Schlesinger Library, Radcliffe College, were cooperative, and David Paul of Widener Library, Harvard University, also provided assistance.

I also am deeply grateful to all those persons too numerous to mention who provided some assistance in this project.

Introduction

I chose to write a biography of the anarchist Ezra Heywood because, at significant times in my life, in which political activism has been important, anarchist ideas have seemed by far to be the most sensible. Writing this biography has afforded me the opportunity to study anarchist theory and history in depth. I selected Heywood's life because of his personality and ideas: his eccentricity, sense of humor, commitment to social change, belief in a great capacity for individuals to develop, and refusal to abandon his vision of a better world. Heywood embodies American anarchism by declaring that the individual is the core of society, that freedom is essential for human progress, and that the power of ideas can change the way we live and treat one another.[1]

Active in the New Left student movement against the Vietnam War, I found that Marxist-Leninists tended to be authoritarian and believed that there was a science of revolution, which struck me as a very silly notion. Because Marxism-Leninism appeared to be more of an obstacle than a path to social change, I began to examine anarchism and liked what I found. I was not alone in this line of inquiry. Indeed, anarchism was one of the central intellectual tenets of the 1960s' protests.[2]

In the mid-1970s, I was one of the authors of a book on draft resistance in Israel and was politically active in Middle East issues. I grew increasingly alarmed by the militarism, racism, and narrowness of all sectarian, nationalist movements, whether Arab, Israeli, or Palestinian. I began to feel that nation-states are a deformed, violent face of national expression and constitute a relatively recent phenomenon in human history. Because anarchists have been the most consistent among radical theorists in their criticism of the nation-state structure, my interest in anarchism was strengthened.[3]

Another factor that has stimulated my interest in anarchism has been my interaction with feminist men and women, activists in the second major wave of feminism in the United States. In order to change society, I have learned, it is not enough to transform large-scale social institutions. In order to truly challenge hierarchy and domination in society, each individual should respect the autonomy of others and seek to transform social relations grounded in domination and subordination in work, friendship, and love relationships.[4]

Anarchism, in my view, stands for liberty and rejects the state as violent and unnecessary as a guarantor of social harmony. The anarchist critique of society runs deeper than that posed by most Marxists. Whereas Marxism tends to focus on economic exploitation, anarchism challenges all forms of hierarchy and domination, not merely class domination. Anarchism addresses hierarchy as it exists in all social relations—in class relations but also in the family, in schools, in sexual relations, between young and old, and between races and ethnic groups.

The historian Paul Avrich asserts that the most effective way to study American anarchism is by an examination of the lives of the movement's key individuals, who brought the power of their personalities and intellects to bear upon the anarchist movement and society. The anarchist emphasis on individual freedom and responsibility has produced men and women who are idiosyncratic, colorful, unconventional, and truly distinctive.[5]

A major problem I encountered was the paucity of primary source materials, although there were significant archival materials at the Labadie Collection, University of Michigan, and at Brown University. The Labadie Collection has the largest holding of materials on American anarchism in the United States, and Brown has a Heywood Collection because Heywood attended Brown University in the 1850s. My inability to locate an autobiographical manuscript that Heywood wrote while serving his last prison term was a major source of sorrow and frustration.[6] I have relied heavily on a close reading of Ezra Heywood's reform paper, *The Word*, and a careful review of several other contemporary reform papers.

I hope that this biography can make a contribution to the growing body of feminist scholarship and to the efforts of historians to come to terms with the place of anarchism in American labor and social history. I do not believe that such a thing as objective history exists. A scholar's values determine the subjects of his or her research, shape the questions posed, and influence the themes to be downplayed or emphasized. I agree with Howard Zinn's assessment of the political commitments scholars should make: "Although obviously not remote from the pressures of business, military needs, and politics, we have just the margin of leeway, just that tradition of truthtelling (however violated in practice) which can allow us to become spokesmen for change. This will require holding up before society forgotten visions, lost utopias, unfulfilled dreams—badly needed in this age of cynicism. . . . Let the historians instruct us or inspire us, from the data of the past, rather than amusing us, boring us, or deceiving us."[7] I have attempted to write this biography in that spirit.

NOTES

1. Martin Blatt, "Why I Am an Anarchist," *Black Rose Magazine* (Fall 1979): 2–7.

2. For the relationship of anarchism and the New Left, see the following: Laurence Veysey, *The Communal Experience: Anarchist and Mystical Counter-Cultures in America* (New York: Harper and Row, 1973), p. 9; Michael Lerner, "Anarchism and the American Counter-Culture," in *Anarchism Today*, ed. David Apter and James Joll (New York: Doubleday, 1972), pp. 41–70; Howard Zinn, "Anarchist Features of the Radical Movements of the 1960s and 1980s," talk delivered at a Conference on Anarchism in America, Boston Public Library, December 4, 1982; Paul Goodman, "The Black Flag of Anarchism," in *Drawing the Line: Political Essays by Paul Goodman*, ed. Taylor Stoehr (New York: Free Life Editions, 1977), pp. 203–14.

3. See Martin Blatt, Uri Davis, and Paul Kleinbaum, *Dissent and Ideology in Israel: Resistance to the Draft, 1948–1973* (London: Ithaca Press, 1975). All the major anarchist thinkers have made excellent critiques of the nation-state. These writers include Michael Bakunin, Peter Kropotkin, Errico Malatesta, Gustav Landauer, Voltairine deCleyre, Emma Goldman, Alexander Berkman, Murray Bookchin, Paul Goodman, Dwight Macdonald, and many others.

4. A significant portion of the women in the second wave of feminism in the United States have identified with anarchist theory and history. The first wave of feminism, launched at Seneca Falls in 1848, included Ezra Heywood. In modern times, such leading writers as Grace Paley, Kate Millett, and Ursula LeGuin describe themselves as anarchists. Dozens of feminist bookstores, self-help clinics, and activist groups have named themselves after the anarchist figure Emma Goldman. See Alix Kates Shulman, ed., *Red Emma Speaks: An Emma Goldman Reader* (New York: Schocken Books, 1983), p. 4. For an interesting discussion of the relationship between modern feminism and anarchism, see Peggy Kornegger, "Anarchism: The Feminist Connection," in *Reinventing Anarchy*, ed. Carol Ehrlich et al. (London: Routledge and Kegan Paul, 1979), pp. 239–49.

5. Paul Avrich, "Preface," *An American Anarchist: The Life of Voltairine deCleyre* (Princeton: Princeton University Press, 1978), pp. xii-xiii.

6. *The Word*, September 1892, p. 3.

7. Howard Zinn, "Knowledge as a Form of Power," in Zinn, *The Politics of History* (Boston: Beacon Press, 1970), pp. 13–14.

CHAPTER 1

NEW ENGLAND ROOTS

E zra Hervey Hoar was born in Westminster in 1829 and raised in
Princeton in a hilly, agricultural region in north central Massachusetts. In order to study the lives of American radicals such as Emma
Goldman or Sacco and Vanzetti, an understanding of their foreign backgrounds is essential. Ezra Heywood, however, could trace his roots in
America back to the seventeenth century. This ancestry allowed him to
speak with authority about what was natural and just for America, and
how his contemporaries deviated from the direction set by the early
settlers who struggled for religious and political freedom.

Joanna Hoare, the widow of Charles Hoare of Gloucester, England,
came to Scituate, Massachusetts, in 1640 with five of her seven children.
Charles Francis Adams described Joanna as "the common origin of that
remarkable progeny in which statesmen, jurists, lawyers, orators, poets,
story-tellers, and philosophers seem to vie with each other in recognized
eminence."[1] Ezra Heywood often referred to his relatives, either praising
their participation in the struggle for independence or condemning their
slavishness to capital and conventional morality in his own time.

In 1659, John Hoar, one of Joanna's sons, sold his landholdings in
Scituate and moved to Concord, "where his ability, vigor, and originality
of thought and action made him one of the prominent figures in the
village." He became distinguished for his knowledge of the law. Joanna
had joined the Nonconformists, and John Hoar was "found to have been
at odds with the ecclesiastic oligarchy of the times. He was not only
independent in speech, but rashly sharp of tongue and pen, and suffered
accordingly at the hands of jealous authority." One of the legendary tales
of Princeton and its environs was about the captivity of Mary Row-
landson, the lone survivor of an Indian attack on the settlement of Lan-
caster, in 1676. John Hoar, who negotiated her release at a site later
named Redemption Rock, "protested vigorously the treatment of the
Indians in his day, and had very uncomfortable relations with the authorities."[2] Apparently, there was an independent New England spirit
far back in Heywood's ancestry.

John Hoar had three children, one of whom was Daniel, born in
1650. Daniel had eleven children. One of these eleven was Lieutenant
Daniel Hoar, born in 1680, who lived a mile east of Concord Center

and "by prudent economy and honest industry acquired a handsome fortune." Captain Daniel Hoar (the third Daniel Hoar), one of the lieutenant's seven children, was born in Concord in 1713. He moved west to Westminster and was one of its first settlers. Living there for forty-six years, he was a prominent citizen, serving at different times as town assessor and treasurer and on the board of selectmen. Most likely, Captain Daniel Hoar moved west due to restricted opportunities in Concord and greater economic chances in Westminster. The historian Philip Greven has demonstrated that many third-generation Andover, Massachusetts, men moved from that town because of economic factors and more elusive psychological factors such as breaking away from a dependent situation.[3] Similar factors may have been involved for Captain Daniel Hoar.

One of Captain Daniel Hoar's four children was Captain Stephen Hoar, Ezra Heywood's grandfather. Stephen Hoar was born in Westminster in 1758 and died there in 1810; he inherited his father's estate by will, and like him not only carried on a farm but also maintained an inn. In 1798, he built a hotel in anticipation of a new roadway; in the early 1800s, he also opened a store. William Sweetzer Heywood described him as a "man of good standing and of business ability . . . he was elected Assessor for several years." Both Captain Daniel Hoar and Stephen Hoar fought in the Revolutionary War, a fact that would help explain Ezra Heywood's strong identification with the struggle of the colonists for what they felt to be natural rights against the usurpations of the British crown.

Heywood celebrated almost any defiance of authority as a noble character trait. Although he believed in temperance, he strongly opposed laws to prohibit alcohol. Thus, he wrote in his reform newspaper *The Word* that "the free-rum Princetonian in whom Whittier found poetry, my farmer-uncle John Roper, . . . when the Maine law passed the Massachusetts House in '52, took to drinking from a sense of duty. . . ."[4]

One of Stephen Hoar's seven children was Ezra Hoar, Ezra Heywood's father, born in Westminster in 1794. Stephen died in 1810, and for the next three years the hotel he had built was run by his sons Charles and Ezra.[5] After they sold the establishment, Ezra probably worked on the family farm. Six years later, in 1819, Ezra Hoar married Dorcas Roper.

A year younger than her husband, Dorcas too was from a family that traced its New England heritage back to the seventeenth century. Several of the Ropers were killed in conflict with the Indians. Her father served with distinction in the Revolutionary War and settled in Princeton in 1791 on the northerly slope of Wachusett Mountain. The homestead, known as the John Roper place, featured a typical old-fashioned New

England farm house. It was made famous by John Greenleaf Whittier's poem "Monadnock from Wachusett." In the 1860s, Whittier came to Princeton to visit a Quaker friend who took him to the Roper farm, where he was inspired to write the poem. He characterized John Roper, Jr., Ezra Heywood's uncle, as a man who loved the farm "for his good old mother's sake who lived and died here in the peace of God." Whittier described the homestead:

> The great woods climbed the mountains at our back;
> And on their skirts where yet the lingering day
> On the shorn greenness of the clearing lay
> The brown old farm-house like a bird's nest hung.[6]

Ezra and Dorcas Hoar lived in Westminster, presumably farming the Hoar family land. Although most accounts state that Ezra Hervey Hoar was born in Princeton, he was in fact born in neighboring Westminster on September 29, 1829.[7] It is not possible to determine a precise date, but it seems that within a few years after his birth, the Hoars moved to Princeton. Ezra Hervey was the sixth of nine children. The oldest was Joseph, followed by Samuel, Dorcas, Dwight, Mary, Ezra, Fidelia, Lyman, and Alonzo. The elder brother, Samuel, who became a wealthy manufacturer in Worcester, was to have bitter dealings with his younger, rebellious brother Ezra.

However, these conflicts were far in the future when the Hoar family settled in Princeton, most likely on Roper family land. Timothy Dwight described Princeton in 1810 as "another rich grazing township, the blue hills in Milton and the waters of Boston Harbor, distant fifty miles, can both be seen here in a clear day. . . ."[8]

According to George Bumgardner, "From 1800 until after the Civil War, careful husbandry of the land and small manufactures were characteristic of Princeton. Forests were cleared, houses built, orchards and vegetable gardens planted, pastures fenced. . . . By the Civil War, the land had been cleared so much that stands of virgin forest were few and far between. The cutting of the forests opened the land for the raising of livestock. In 1831 nearly three thousand head of cattle grazed on Princeton pastures. Agricultural products rose to the value of $9000 yearly, lumber to $8000. Two tanneries were estimated to be doing $25,000 worth of business, shoe manufacturers, $33,000. The women occupied themselves in weaving great quantities of palm leaf hats." In 1855, agricultural production had the greatest value. Leading products were butter, cheese, Indian corn, hay, potatoes, apples, oats, and barley. The leading manufacturing industries in 1855 included chairs and cabinets, tanning, boots and shoes, palm leaf hats, and lumber and firewood.

The population of Princeton expanded rapidly in the latter part of the eighteenth century. From a 1790 population of 1,016, the next half century witnessed a slower growth to a total of 1,347 in 1840.[9]

Writing from prison in the 1890s and looking back several decades, Ezra Heywood remembered his father in reverent terms: "my sainted sire, Ezra Hoar, the intuitive, sedate, resolute Princeton farmer." Heywood had only positive memories of his father, whom he credited with first steering his thoughts in the direction of reform: "When six years old, a few words from my sainted sire set my mind at work on the great problems of land and labor." Dorcas Hoar also influenced Ezra's thinking. In an 1873 letter to *The Word*, she wrote: "When Labor Reform ideas come in fashion, I shall be one of the first women in society." Following the custom of the day, the Hoars worked together on the family farm. Samuel Heywood "passed his early days on the farm, swinging the scythe and doing other work about the farm. . . ." Ezra Heywood recalled a lesson in independent thinking from his father: "When 14, serving potato growth with him in the field, leaning on the shaft of his hoe, he said to me, 'Whenever you speak, say what you think, regardless of others' opinions, commands or action; the fear of man bringeth a snare.' "[10] Young Ezra would take these words to heart, never fearing to speak the truth as he saw it.

In 1845, when Heywood was sixteen, Ezra Hoar died of brain fever at the State Lunatic Hospital in Worcester. He was listed as moribund upon admission and lived only eight days after the family had him committed. Hoar's medical records indicate that he had had a history of insanity for eleven years, beginning when Ezra was five. However, the historian Barbara Rosenkrantz has asserted that "there is little indication that death under such conditions was looked at as scandalous in any way." It is difficult to determine the significance of Ezra Hoar's medical record owing to the treatment of insanity in the nineteenth century. This treatment was part of an underlying assumption that anyone, including lunatics, was perfectible and thus no illness was incurable. It was thought that the mentally ill or insane—the terms were used interchangeably—had in some ways brought their conditions upon themselves by ignoring the natural laws governing human behavior. Mental health experts listed the leading causes of disease as intemperance, overwork, and the stress of urban life.[11]

Asylum superintendents at Worcester and McLean, another Massachusetts facility, cited the following three reasons as the most frequent causes of death: the physical debility of entering patients, the frequent association of insanity with a fatal disease, and the continuous threat of epidemics imported from outside the asylum. Dr. Samuel B. Woodward, the first superintendent at Worcester and the man in charge at the time of Ezra Hoar's death, often argued that families sent their dying relatives and friends to the hospital because they had become too troublesome at home. Woodward observed: "Frequently a case is brought to our care, with delirium of fever, instead of insanity, in which the journey aggravates every symptom, and death immediately follows." Febrile diseases were often mistaken by family, friends, and even physicians for the symptoms of insanity.[12] It is entirely possible that this was the case with Ezra Hoar.

In his early years, young Ezra was primarily under the care of Dorcas Hoar while his father worked in the fields. In the winter, the workload eased and more time was available for children. During the rest of the year, especially in the busy morning hours, children under eight often attended district schools taught by women, which functioned virtually as nurseries during the planting, haying, and harvest seasons. After the age of eight or nine, boys generally attended only winter schools because they were kept at home during the rest of the year to work on the farm. Winter sessions of district schools were very different from the summer sessions. Before the 1840s, winter schools were usually taught by men of all ages and temperaments; no effective grading system existed outside of large cities; and the majority of pupils were between eight and fifteen, but often included young men up to twenty years old. Available evidence, the historian Joseph Kett concludes, suggests that disorderly conditions were the norm in winter schools. Strict discipline, featuring a combination of corporal punishment and humiliation, was the ruling force in the winter schools as teachers employed harsh measures in an effort to maintain control in a difficult environment. In all probability, such a school was the setting for Ezra Heywood's early education.[13]

Not enough documentation is available to understand exactly how the death of Ezra Hoar affected young Ezra's development. In early-nineteenth-century America, families were often disrupted by the death of one or both parents, not only because of higher mortality from disease, but also because of the length of time elapsed between the births of the first and the last child. Thus, a youth's plans could change dramatically in the face of family loss. There was no set age for leaving school, leaving home, or going to work. Whether or not a family suffered the loss of the father, it was not uncommon for a young man to work on the family farm and simultaneously, or during the slack time, involve himself in a commercial enterprise. Apparently, young Ezra displayed an aptitude for business. Robert C. Adams, a free-thought activist, recalled his youth with Ezra in a letter to *The Word*: "I well remember our Princeton acquaintance as boys; the admiration we felt for your mental culture and for the business ability evidenced when you bought out the store and sold the goods for auction. . . ."[14]

Ezra's older brother Samuel showed similar skills, and his ambition was to carry him far. In 1842, he left the farm at the age of twenty-one and went to work for E. D. and A. D. Goodnow in the general store of Princeton. The Goodnows were also manufacturers of boots and shoes, and Samuel gained valuable insight into this industry. In 1848, he decided to go into business for himself, forming a partnership with Leander W. Warren. The firm of Heywood and Warren opened a general store in nearby Hubbardston. Samuel eventually bought out Warren's interest and conducted a successful business until 1855, when he determined to broaden the scope of his enterprise and moved from small village life to the industrial city of Worcester. With E. D. Goodnow as a partner, he entered the wholesale and retail boot and shoe business. One year later he bought out his partner and maintained the retail end of the business, which he operated with much success for several years.[15]

In 1848, on the initiative of Samuel, the family name was changed from Hoar to Heywood by an act of the Massachusetts Legislature upon receipt of a petition from the family. The family was divided about the change. The older sons sided with Samuel, however Dorcas Hoar protested, but to no avail. She "refused to adopt the new name and continued to be known as Mrs. Ezra Hoar. . . . Ezra and the others were powerless to prevent the change, which was made because Samuel thought that Hoar was altogether too suggestive a cognomen." Ezra Heywood seriously contemplated retaking his father's name.[16]

Ezra related the episode in this manner: "Samuel . . . about to go into country store business . . . feared 'Hoar' would suggest 'whore' on his sign. I, with four of the other children, was then a minor accepting the name agreed upon by the three brothers and one sister of age. . . . Later thought has never revealed any good reason why the name should have been changed; deriving from him physical form I owe too much thought, life, mental growth, to my father not to respect and reverence his name." In *The Word*, Heywood printed what he claimed was a letter from the spirit of Ezra Hoar, who declared that "Heywood was not the name of your father and it does not sound as well as yours, to my ears. . . ."[17] By the time he ran this letter, Heywood was a committed spiritualist, and it is clear that he disagreed with the name change—the first serious clash he was to have with his brother Samuel.

Sometime in the middle 1840s, Ezra began attending the Westminster Academy, located in the neighboring town. Samuel Heywood had attended the academy for two terms, paying his own way while a student.

Often, farmers encouraged their sons entering adolescence to attend advanced schooling away from home or to seek a job during the winter months. In the late spring, summer, and early fall, they would return to work on the farm. Kett describes the shortcomings of the typical academy: "Although it offered a valuable opportunity for intermediate education between the district school and the college, academy students were subject to many of the same anomalies as district school pupils. One encountered in academies, as in winter district schools, students of eight or nine to twenty or twenty-five years of age with the concentration falling in the ten- to twenty-year-old category."[18] The wide age range indicates that attendance at the academy was for some the first departure from home, whereas for others it represented a respite from the demands of work.

The Westminster Academy had been established in 1830 on the initiative of the Reverend Cyrus Mann, a conservative Congregationalist minister. William Sweetzer Heywood, in his history of Westminster, recorded that one form of faith prevailed at the academy, "the faith of the Puritans, which was essentially Calvinistic." The Reverend Mann was "privileged to employ the academy as a means of directing not a few young men to careers of usefulness in the ministry and elsewhere." Ezra's plans to enter the ministry were boosted at the academy. Alfred E. Giles, a lifelong friend of Ezra's after the two were students together at Brown University, remarked disparagingly of Westminster Academy that Ezra made such preparations as he could there for college and "studied extra in college and caught up."[19]

Ezra Heywood and other sources characterized Ezra Hoar as a devout, religious farmer. Heywood wrote that his parents would pay close attention to the preaching of the Reverend Elisha Andrews in Princeton. Andrews was the father of Stephen Pearl Andrews, who would later be a colleague of Heywood's in labor and free-love reforms. Heywood likened the Baptist Andrews to Roger Williams, "the immortal exponent of soul liberty . . . Andrews took his call to preach from God within him, not from King or bishop out of him. . . ."

Heywood recalled that as a boy he did not have a great deal of enthusiasm for religion: "When a boy, living in District No. 8 of this town, we often heard Isaac Thompson speak Sunday evenings in the School-House. He was an old resident and prominent businessman, a farmer and cattle dealer, tall and homely. Prayer meetings to us [referring to himself] were an ineffable bore; when the minister and the brethren spoke we generally dozed or were disgusted; but when six feet of the angular form of this old farmer began to rise we listened, for something was likely to be said. One favorite sentence of his impressed us deeply—

'Death makes people honest.' '' In retrospect, Heywood noted that puz-
zling over this observation eventually led him to spiritualism.[20]

Despite his memories of being bored with prayer meetings, as a young
man of twenty-three Ezra decided to go off to Brown University in 1852
to prepare for the ministry. He may have been motivated by his parents'
religious devotion, along with a desire to advance himself socially. However, the key factor in his decision was the great religious ferment of
the time, known as the Second Great Awakening, which swept up Ezra
and many other young people like him. The Awakening provided the
religious context in which Ezra Heywood and many of his contemporary
social reformers first developed their notions of right and wrong and
convictions about social responsibility.

Ezra Heywood's development into a committed social reformer was
a gradual process, and much of his direct exposure to the evangelical
reform impulse came in his years in Providence, which is discussed in
detail in chapter 2. As a teenager, however, Heywood did embrace Protestantism at a time when, in the words of the historian Timothy Smith,
"the quest for perfection joined with compassion for poor and needy
sinners and a rebirth of millennial expectation to make popular Protestantism a mighty social force long before the slavery conflict erupted
into war." It was in this context that Heywood developed his religious
values.[21]

Kett describes religious crisis, often followed by conversion, as the
central ingredient in the teen years of many young people in the early
nineteenth century. In early adolescence, many began to develop deep
feelings of anxiety, characterized by sleepless nights worrying about
eternal salvation, and by morbid fears of death. Ezra Heywood no doubt
experienced some of these religious preoccupations. Precisely when he
became a believer cannot be determined, although a great number of
published autobiographical conversion narratives point to the predom-
inance of conversions between the ages of fifteen and twenty-one.[22] In
a very real sense, Heywood lived through two profound conversion
experiences, one into evangelical Protestantism and another into militant
social reform. This path was followed by many nineteenth-century social
reformers, and often led to an interesting fusion of religious and social
change language and ideology.

Ezra Heywood lived much of his later life in opposition to the church,
but this did not necessarily make him irreligious. On the contrary, the
fellow reformer Lucien Pinney correctly described Heywood as intensely
religious. This was not "the Pecksniffian cant of the Churches, their
creeds and parade of prayer," but something quite different: "The Race
perfected stands to him for Christ arisen; the Air, endowed with wisdom

and love is one of his concepts of God. . . ." Ronald Walters observes that all social reformers, including nonevangelicals and those, such as Heywood and others, who had abandoned the organized church, owed much to revivalism: "Their language was filled with its rhetoric of sin, damnation, and salvation. It gave them a way of viewing the world—even the most secular of reformers talked of 'progress' and 'civilization' in tones harkening back to millennialism and perfectionism."[23] Although Heywood was to journey far from the church in his quest for social reform, a significant part of his thinking would always retain the thought processes he developed during his first encounters with evangelical Protestantism.

Having made the decision to pursue the ministry, Ezra Heywood left his family and familiar surroundings in Princeton in 1852 and travelled to Brown University in Providence. The atmosphere at Brown was more cultured and civil than his earlier school experiences, but there was strict discipline of another kind. For example, a student could be charged with a demerit of a value from five to twenty points for missing a class without prior excuse or for failing to perform well in class; one hundred demerit points could lead to dismissal. The university convened daily morning and evening prayers, and missing prayers could entail monetary punishment. In the fall of 1854, William Dearth, who kept a diary and recorded an extensive account of daily life at Brown, wrote: "the announcement was made that students would be required, as a regular college exercise, subject if neglected to College discipline, to attend Church service twice every Sunday. . . . Monitors at the several Churches to watch. And this in the land of Roger Williams, of perfect religious tolerance!"[24] Clearly, academic and religious life were regulated closely.

Throughout his six years at Brown, Ezra Heywood lived modestly in campus dormitories, which were much cheaper than off-campus housing. He lived in University Hall for his first two years and spent the remaining four at Hope College. Because meals were not available on campus, the university's registrar maintained a list of families in Providence with whom students could obtain either board or both board and lodging.[25] Heywood took his meals at a boarding establishment that he selected from this list.

Heywood arrived at Brown when the campus was in turmoil over the introduction of Dr. Francis Wayland's "New System." Wayland had hoped to modernize Brown's curriculum in response to an American society that he perceived to be both rapidly expanding and prospering. He shortened the regular bachelor's degree program to three years, introduced an elective system with new course offerings in applied science, law, agriculture, and teaching, and redefined the master's degree by requiring that it be earned through demonstrated proficiency in advanced study. The results, however, were not what Wayland had hoped. Students of lower academic ability were attracted to Brown because of its lower entrance requirements, and several graduates found their degrees unrecognized by other institutions because of Brown's less rigorous standards. The faculty found adjustment difficult. Wayland's scheme was rolled back in 1858, but the New System held sway for most of Ezra's tenure.[26]

Despite the label "New System," much at Brown was not altered. Teaching methods "remained virtually unchanged, the method of recitation and review doing little to encourage critical or original thinking." Many of Wayland's well-intentioned reforms, such as extending the length of class periods, met with resistance from faculty and were the more easily sabotaged by students. Apparently, one hour and twenty minutes as a class period "exceeded human powers of endurance."[27]

Student life had an intimate quality at Brown in the 1850s because universities of the nineteenth century were operated on a rather modest scale. Brown had a total of ten faculty members in 1855, and Ezra's entering class numbered eighty out of a total university enrollment of 240. Heywood, who earned a master's degree in 1856, took the following required courses: each of the ancient languages (Greek and Latin) for three semesters, mathematics for three semesters, one modern language (he chose French) for two semesters, natural philosophy for two semesters, rhetoric and English literature for two semesters, chemistry and physiology for two semesters, history for two semesters, and intellectual and moral philosophy for two semesters. Heywood earned good grades; his average for a total of twenty-eight courses was 18.03 (20.0 was a perfect score). His best grades—19.76 and 19.80—were in two history courses. Other courses he elected to take included animal chemistry, didactics, and geology. After graduating in 1856, Heywood stayed on to study two more years as one of a handful of "Resident Graduates."[28]

A Shakespearean passage applied to Ezra in an 1855 mock commencement program indicates that some of his fellow students found him too scholarly:

> O! he is as tedious
> As a tired horse or a railing wife,
> Worse than a smoky house; I had rather live
> With cheese and garlic in a windmill, far,
> Than feed on cakes, and have him talk to me,
> In any summer house in Christendom.

This characterization is a marked contrast to the image that William Dearth presents in his diary. Dearth, popular in his own recollection, was designated class salutatorian by his classmates even though he constantly dwelt on fears and strategies concerning being "called up" to recite in class. He was preoccupied with his own inertia, guilt, and accountability.[29]

Heywood went into debt to his brother Samuel, who financed his education at Brown. Ezra related: "When I left S. R.'s store in 1852 he was owing me $300." Ezra had worked at Samuel's Hubbardston store and acquitted himself well. However, once at Brown, he spent the $300 and quite a bit more. Continuing his studies until February 1858, he owed Samuel $1,600, which he paid off after some years at 6 percent interest.[30]

Heywood greatly enjoyed his years at Brown. He took pleasure in immersing himself in his studies and developed a fondness for the trappings of scholarship. Reflecting his early training, future radical pamphlets contained many quotations from authoritative sources, along with dozens of footnotes. In part, Heywood could trace his future accomplishments as a radical orator to training at Brown. Junior and senior classes had regular exercises in declamation, and an original speech was required monthly of each class member.

Although Heywood had entered Brown in preparation for a career in the ministry, he became caught up in the fierce emotions of the abolitionist movement and his life veered in a very different direction.

NOTES

1. Henry Steadman Nourse, "The Hoare Family in America and Its English Ancestry: A Compilation from the Collections Made by the Honorable George Frisbie Hoar," *The New England Historical and Genealogical Register* 53 (April 1899):188; description of Joanna Hoare quoted in Daniel W. Hoare, *Digest of Ancestry and Early History of the Hoare Family and Descent of the New Brunswick Family from Charles Hoare of Gloucester, England* (n.p., 1976), p. 3.

2. Nourse, "The Hoare Family in America," p. 190; William Sweetzer Heywood, *History of Westminster, 1728–1893* (Lowell, Mass.: Vox Populi Press, 1893), p. 697; Edward Hoare, *Some Accounts of the Early History and Genealogy with Pedigrees from 1330, Unbroken to the Present Time of the Families of Hoare and Hore with All Their Branches* (London: Alfred Russell Smith, 1883), p. 63; Hoare, *Digest of Ancestry*, p. 4; George H. Bumgardner, *Princeton and the High Roads, 1775–1975* (Princeton, Mass.: Princeton Bicentennial Commission, 1975), p. 4; *Will of Charles Hoare of Gloucester, England, with Notes by George F. Hoar* (Boston: David Clapp and Son, 1891), p. 6.

3. Concord, Massachusetts, gravestone epitaph quoted in Nourse, "The Hoare Family in America," p. 197; Heywood, *History of Westminster*, pp. 499–500; see

chapter 6, "Control and Autonomy: Families and the Transmission of Land," in Philip J. Greven, Jr., *Four Generations: Population, Land and Family in Colonial Andover, Massachusetts* (Ithaca, N.Y.: Cornell University Press, 1970), pp. 125–72.

4. Heywood, *History of Westminster*, pp. 322 and 698–99; *Massachusetts Soldiers and Sailors of the Revolutionary War*, vol. 8 (Boston: Wright and Potter, 1901), p. 2; *The Word*, February 1893, p. 2.

5. Heywood, *History of Westminster*, p. 326.

6. Francis E. Blake, *History of the Town of Princeton, 1759–1915*, 2 vols. (Princeton, Mass.: published by the town, 1915), 2:251–52.

7. Ceres Heywood Bradshaw to Agnes Inglis, November 15, 1947, Labadie Collection, University of Michigan, Ann Arbor.

8. Bumgardner, *Princeton and the High Roads*, p. 24.

9. Bumgardner, *Princeton and the High Roads*, pp. 24 and 28; Francis DeWitt, ed., *Statistical Information Relating to Branches of Industry in Massachusetts, for the Year Ending June 1, 1855* (Boston: William White Printer, 1856), pp. 527–28.

10. *Lucifer*, September 4, 1891, p. 3; *The Word*, March 1890, p. 2, February 1873, p. 3, and March 1890, p. 2. In a labor reform pamphlet written in 1869, Ezra recalled receiving a boyhood lesson in the meaning of private property. As Ezra stood with his father, overlooking their mountainside home in Princeton, his father said, "Those buildings, the land and stock, custom and the courts may call mine; but I am only a trustee, holding them for others' good, not merely for the use of a family, but for the world at large, as the Lord wills." This quotation appeared in Ezra Heywood, *Yours or Mine: An Essay to Show the True Basis of Property and the Causes of Its Inequitable Distribution* (Princeton, Mass.: Co-Operative Publishing, 1877), p. 5; undated newspaper clipping, "Old Age and Heart Trouble Bring End to Life of Samuel R. Heywood—Dean of Worcester Business Men," Worcester Historical Museum.

11. Heywood's *History of Westminster* lists insanity as the cause of death for Ezra Hoar. The *Princeton, Massachusetts, Vital Records* indicates that Ezra Hoar died in a Worcester hospital, July 17, 1845, at the age of fifty-one. Barbara G. Rosenkrantz, who has conducted extensive research in the records of the Worcester State Lunatic Hospital, provided details of Ezra Hoar's commitment there; Barbara G. Rosenkrantz to author, February 27, 1980; see Gerald Grob, "Mental Illness, Indigency, and Welfare: The Mental Hospital in Nineteenth-Century America," in *Anonymous Americans: Explorations in Nineteenth-Century Social History*, ed. Tamara Hareven (Englewood Cliffs, N.J.: Prentice Hall, 1971), pp. 250–79.

12. See Barbara G. Rosenkrantz and Maris A. Vinovskis, "Sustaining 'the Flickering Flame of Life': Accountability and Culpability for Death in Ante-Bellum Massachusetts Asylums," in *Health Care in America: Essays in Social History*, ed. Susan Reverby and David Rosner (Philadelphia: Temple University Press, 1979), pp. 159–61 and 164–65.

13. See Joseph F. Kett, "Growing Up in Rural New England, 1800–1814," in *Anonymous Americans*, ed. Hareven, pp. 1–16. Because of the paucity of primary resources related to Ezra Heywood's youth, I have relied a great deal on Kett's article in helping me describe his early years.

14. *The Word*, November 1888, p. 3.

15. Undated newspaper clipping, "Old Age and Heart Trouble Bring End to Life of Samuel R. Heywood"; Charles Henry Bouley, *Biographical Sketches of the Pioneer Settlers of New England and Their Descendants in Worcester, Massachusetts* (Barre, Mass.: Barre Publishers, 1964), p. 284.

16. *List of Persons Whose Names Have Been Changed in Massachusetts, 1780–1892* (Boston: Wright and Potter, 1893), p. 120; petition dated March 20, 1848, State House Archives, Boston; *The Truth Seeker*, June 10, 1893, p. 358.

17. *The Word*, September 1892, p. 3; May 1883, p. 3.

18. Kett, "Growing Up in Rural New England," pp. 7 and 8; Bouley, *Biographical Sketches*, p. 284.

19. Heywood, *History of Westminster*, pp. 332, 337; Alfred E. Giles to Professor Poland, June 11, 1893, Heywood Papers, Hay Library, Brown University, Providence, R.I.

20. The obituary of Heywood in *The Truth Seeker*, May 27, 1893, p. 325, recorded that he was raised in "the strictest school of Calvinistic theology." Also, Benjamin R. Tucker wrote in *The Word*, August, 1878, p. 2, that Heywood was "born of religious parents, brought up religiously, educated religiously in matters of comparatively little consequence, and religiously kept ignorant of matters of vital import. . . ."; *The Truth Seeker*, October 4, 1890, pp. 628–29; *The Word*, March 1875, p. 2.

21. Timothy L. Smith, *Revivalism and Social Reform: American Protestantism on the Eve of the Civil War* (New York: Harper and Row, 1965), p. 149.

22. Kett, "Growing Up in Rural New England," pp. 5, 10–11.

23. Lucien V. Pinney, "The Man and the Woman of Princeton," *The Word*, June 1890, p. 1; Ronald G. Walters, *American Reformers, 1815–1860* (New York: Hill and Wang, 1978), p. 37.

24. *Catalogue of the Officers and Students of Brown University*, 1852–53 (Providence, R.I.: Brown University, 1853); *The Diary of William Griswold Dearth: Praeteria, Journal of Acts and Thoughts, a Portion (September 6–November 1, 1854)*, ed. Timothy Nolan (Providence, R.I.: Brown University, 1979), p. 34; *The Journal of William Dearth (November 2, 1854–September 5, 1855)*, ed. Denise Asfar (Providence, R.I.: Brown University, 1980), p. 143.

25. *Catalogue of the Officers and Students of Brown University*, 1852–53; 1853–54; 1854–55; 1855–56; 1856–57; 1857–58 (Providence, R.I.: Brown University, 1853–58).

26. See introductions to Nolan, *Diary of William Dearth* and Asfar, *Journal of William Dearth*; also, Walter C. Bronson, *The History of Brown University, 1764–1914* (Providence, R.I.: Brown University, 1914), pp. 281–82.

27. Asfar, *Journal of William Dearth*, p. ii; Bronson, *History of Brown University*, p. 293.

28. Nolan, *Diary of William Dearth*, p. ii; *Catalogue of the Officers and Students of Brown University*, 1856–57 and 1857–58. He was the only person listed in this category in 1856–57, and one of five listed for the 1857–58 academic year. (Providence, R.I.: Brown University, 1857 and 1858).

29. Passage referring to Ezra H. Heyward [*sic*], in mock program entitled "Universitas Bruin-Ensis," Saturday, May 12, 1855, Heywood Papers, Brown University. The passage is taken from William Shakespeare, *Henry IV, Part One* (New York: New American Library, 1965), act III, scene i, p. 101; Asfar, *Journal of William Dearth*, p. ii.

30. *The Word*, March 1888, p. 2.

CHAPTER 2

THE ABOLITIONIST YEARS

The question of slavery increasingly dominated national political life during Ezra Heywood's tenure at Brown University and had substantial opposition in the North. Would slavery be extended into the new territories? Should the Peculiar Institution itself be abolished? A great deal of activity centered in New England, where a significant number of the abolitionists embraced an array of social reforms. Heywood, increasingly drawn to these reformers, eventually joined with them in the fervor and agitation of the movement to abolish slavery along with other social problems. For example, Heywood defended women's rights at an early age. He recalled one of the many *"improper things"* he had done: "in 1851, when a member of the Hubbardston [Mass.] Lyceum, our boy head was metaphorically chopped off for insisting that a woman, Mrs. Emma R. Coe . . . should be heard in the lecture course." The right of women to speak to mixed audiences was a hotly contested issue within the abolitionist movement. The more radical wing, the Garrisonians, named after William Lloyd Garrison, favored equal participation by women, whereas more conservative abolitionists, typically clergymen, were opposed.[1]

Heywood's first radical mentors were two women, Phebe Jackson and Ann Whitney. He wrote in *Lucifer*: "From September 1852 to February 1858, five years and five months I studied books in Brown University . . . but more than all the books and learned Professors in College, a woman, opposite whom I sat at my boarding house table, Phebe Jackson, an adult, Baptist, maiden lady, girl-friend of Helen Benson (afterwards Mrs. Garrison) shaped my then passing and future life. Till then I was conservative; she made me a radical, gave me to read Garrison's *Liberator*, the 'craziest' newspaper of that day, started me on the line of Anti-slavery, Woman's Rights and Peace."[2]

Phebe Jackson was one of a number of religious women in New England who combined Christian piety with a commitment to social justice issues. Jackson was an activist in the cause of temperance, women's suffrage, and abolition. An 1887 eulogy offered this praise: "she labored faithfully to perform the duties that fell to her share in the great task of ministering to the needy and the poor, sparing neither time, nor strength, nor money."[3] Born in 1807, Jackson was middle-aged when she met Heywood at the boardinghouse table in Providence. Because Heywood shared her religious commitment, he was predisposed to listen to her ideas. "In her own church, as teacher of a large Bible Class and as one who could be depended on to help whenever she could, she was a power for good. In the anti-slavery struggle she was intense in her interest and active in co-operation, so much so that she subjected herself to severe criticism by her Christian friends. When it was proposed to start the Shelter, a home for colored orphans and neglected children in Providence, her sympathies were at once enlisted."[4]

Ann Whitney introduced Heywood to the notion that marriage enslaved women. When Heywood was a Sunday school teacher in the middle 1850s, Whitney was a grammar school teacher and student in his class. He recalled: "An interrogative young lady, [she] put questions that 'God's Word' did not answer; among others, this: 'If Love worketh no ill, why does human law interfere to hinder its evolution?' We spent several sessions in the light which the New Testament and our mutual wits shed on the issue. The result was that, *then*, I became a Free Lover, theoretically." Heywood visited Whitney in 1887 and related that out of her questions came his free-love tract *Cupid's Yokes*, published in 1876. Whitney responded that he had been a horrid conservative. She told him: "One Sunday when I quoted Mr. Garrison you put on a long face and solemnly said 'such Infidels as he ought not to be mentioned here.' "[5]

Befriending Jackson and Whitney and attending antislavery meetings at their prompting, Heywood was beginning to question his career decision. Were the needs of a congregation more important than serving God by contesting the evil of slavery? Heywood had first encountered the issue of slavery as a teenager. After a heated debate, he had "induced the Hubbardston Lyceum to censure a leading townsman for voting against the Personal Liberty Bill in the Mass. Legislature." Personal liberty laws, enacted in some Northern states, forbade state officials from taking part in the enforcement of the federal laws for the return of fugitive slaves, whose plight deeply affected many in the North. In Massachusetts, there was widespread disgust at the return of the fugitive slave Anthony Burns in 1854. Popular feeling was so aroused against the Fugitive Slave Law that twenty-two companies of state militia, four platoons of marines, a battalion of United States artillerymen, and Boston's entire police force were mobilized to ensure the return of this one slave.[6]

Many in the North adopted an antislavery position in response to the fugitive slave laws. If nothing else, they perceived the issue in terms of a violation of civil liberties. At his Brown graduation in 1856, Heywood demonstrated such an interest in free speech and civil liberties.

The topic of his commencement address, one of seventeen presented, was "Milton—The Advocate of Intellectual Freedom." The text of his remarks is not available, but Milton's social philosophy clearly fitted into the abolitionist framework. Milton believed that, without physical freedom, humanity enjoyed no higher, inner liberty. True freedom, for Milton, was internal and individual, the product of self-governing virtue. Liberty and human dignity were God-given, thus natural to humankind.[7]

Heywood's first encounter with the dramatic oratory of the abolitionists came in January 1855, in Providence, when he heard Wendell Phillips, a leading abolitionist, speak. Deeply moved by the brilliant Garrisonian orator, he "at once moved to elect him anniversary orator of the literary societies of Brown . . . after weeks of hard work we won, though I came near being expelled from college for it—so bitter *then* was the venom of Christians who cried 'Infidel' and of politicians shouting 'Traitor.' "[8]

Heywood's college friend Alfred E. Giles claimed that reading the works of Theodore Parker profoundly influenced Ezra's thinking. Parker, a historian and scholar who had read widely in many fields and used many sources in his writings, insisted that there was a Higher Law and an imperative obligation to obey it. Parker believed that the Christianity of Christ was not dependent upon the institutions of the church. The truths of religion could be found in the lives and faith of humanity. Parker shared with the Transcendentalists a belief in the perfectibility of humanity and the doctrine of progress.[9] Parker held that God was marching on, but that the church lagged behind. The church, he argued, was the most conservative of institutions, more concerned with ritual and dogma than with life. In the 1850s, Parker militantly asserted that the abolition of slavery was the central issue facing Americans. His strident denunciations of complacent Christianity prefigured the tone of many of Heywood's own abolitionist speeches. For example, Parker wrote in an 1840 essay: "Anointed dullness, arrayed in canonicals, presses the consecrated cushions of the pulpit and pours forth weekly his impotent drone, to be blest with bland praises so long as he disturbs not respectable iniquity slumbering in his pew, nor touches the actual sign of the time nor treads an inch beyond the beaten path of the Church."[10]

Heywood's preparations for the ministry were rather far advanced. "From '55 to '58 I was a member of the Broad St. 'dome' church orthodox, and preached in many Rhode Island pulpits. . . ." His brother Samuel wrote that "some Association gave him license to preach. I remember he supplied a Pulpit in Westerly (Rhode Island) if I mistake not, and made a very favorable impression." Alfred E. Giles recalled that Ezra intended to go to Andover Theological Institution for further study upon graduation from Brown.[11]

However, Heywood chose to remain in Providence and become more involved with the abolitionists. He had been working for some time in the fight for the rights of black children in public schools. After meeting Frederick Douglass and Charles T. Remond, Heywood increased his efforts. He voiced the slave's cause in every social group to which he belonged, including prayer meetings, Sunday schools, the Young Men's Christian Association, the Franklin Lyceum, and the university debating societies. In all of these forums, Heywood wrote, he won a "hearing for, if not an indorsement of my 'infidel-traitors,' the abolitionists."[12]

Claiming that he was "liberalized out of evangelical pulpits," Heywood decided in 1858 to leave the church to save his soul. He chose to describe his decision as a conversion experience: "In '58 I 'fell' from well-dressed and full-stomached religion to abolition 'infidelity'. . ." Of course, he believed that he had risen in grace by leaving the church. Remaining in the church, Heywood believed, would have been a risk to his immortal soul; he felt that he could only gain redemption by proclaiming his abolitionist faith. The consequences of the decision were far-reaching, most obviously in terms of the type of career Heywood would now pursue. Ezra wrote: "In abolition I lost all my church friends. . . ." His brother Samuel went to hear Garrison speak to see "what kind of 'creeturs Hervey' wrought with . . . he was so shocked to see how low *I had fallen* in being with 'that set,' he hurried home but did not sleep a wink all night!"[13]

The abolitionist movement grew out of the Second Great Awakening in the early part of the nineteenth century. The gospel of evangelical Protestantism stressed the perfectibility of humanity and the imminent coming of the millennium. The universal reformation of the world, according to this doctrine, was the path for true Christians to pursue. This road would lead to individual salvation and hasten the coming of God's kingdom on earth. The ideas of religious perfectionism—the search for perfect holiness and the notion that such perfection might be immediately possible—have been identified by historian Timothy L. Smith as "one of the nineteenth century's most persistent and socially significant religious themes."[14]

A majority of the abolitionists were religious people, often former ministers, but only a minority, based in the New England states, put forward the demand of an immediate end to slavery coupled with a commitment to nonresistance. The central figure of nonresistance was William Lloyd Garrison, for whom slavery was a sin against God and against humanity. In 1854, Garrison publicly burned a copy of the United States Constitution as a slavery document. The historian Lewis Perry contends that, among the Garrisonian abolitionists, "Slavery, government, and violence were considered identical in principle. All were sinful invasions of God's prerogatives. . . ." The logic that they employed, Perry argues, was inexorable: "to end slavery was to end all coercion; to end all coercion was to release the millennial power of God; to end coercion, again, was to secure peace and order on earth; and to secure peace was, of course, to realize the millennium." The Garrisonian abolitionists believed that self-government and divine government reinforced one another. Thus, the nonresistant Henry Clarke Wright declared: "*I regard all Human Governments as usurpations of God's power over Man.*"[15] The Garrisonians contended that nothing should intervene between God and humanity. Thus, they attacked any social institution—church, state, marriage—that in their judgment either condoned slavery or violated personal autonomy.

The perfectionist John Humphrey Noyes, founder and patriarch of the Oneida Community and a leading nineteenth-century reformer, had a strong influence on Garrison. Heywood was later greatly influenced by Noyes's theory and practice of sexual continence, which Noyes developed as part of the Oneida Community's complex marriage arrangements. Noyes wrote a long letter to Garrison announcing that he had "retracted his allegiance to the United States government and now championed the claim of Jesus Christ to the throne of the world. He depicted the government as a fat libertine flogging Negroes and torturing Indians."[16] Noyes's militant yet still religious tone anticipated the style of rhetoric Heywood was to employ.

A sense of divine purpose gave the abolitionists not only a note of urgency and sincerity, but also a tone of stridency and self-righteousness. Throughout his career, Ezra Heywood would display a deep commitment to social justice, but one often accompanied by rigidity and narrow intolerance. Richard Hildreth, an abolitionist who was active politically, wrote perceptively: "Unfortunately, this anti-slavery movement had its birth in the bosom of the church . . . they set themselves up . . . as expositors of the will of God. . . . They have come out from the church; but they have brought with them the very things in the church to which I make the greatest objections, to wit: the claim of infallibility, and the domineering, denouncing, excommunicating spirit which appertains to all priesthoods."[17]

The nonresistance of the Garrisonian abolitionists was based on their concept of the sinfulness of violence. Jesus had taught that evil should be answered with love. Because the New Testament forbids the use of force, and government is maintained by force, the Garrisonians felt that a Christian must abstain from government. Physical coercion does not change human hearts, and thus was deemed inappropriate for the holy task of moral regeneration.[18]

Ezra Heywood had come to share the abolitionists' popular belief in human perfectibility and the coming of the millennium, when God's awesome sovereignty might yet be vindicated. It was Garrison who convinced him to become a full-time abolitionist: in February 1858, "in the house of William Lloyd Garrison, 11 Dix Place, Boston, I was inducted into antislavery work. . . ."[19]

During the spring and summer of 1858, Heywood fought against segregation in the Providence schools and churches. In a letter to *The Liberator*, he attacked the churches: "The conscience of the country is in its pocket. The ecclesiastical craft take the course of the trade winds." He called for men and women of conscience to engage in direct action to stop slavery: "We want brave men and women here, willing to make themselves of no reputation, and suffer the loss of all things for truth and humanity. That is all. Agitation is the only cure for the evils with which our national life is fraught. We must have it—an agitation which has not merely a tongue, but hands and feet."[20]

In the early stage of his radical career, Heywood viewed the Republican party with anger and scorn and the Democrats in a better light. For example, in 1858 he argued that blacks in Providence received "more genuine sympathy from the Democrats than from the Republicans." Throughout his career, Heywood favored the Democrats over the Republicans, viewing the Democratic party as the more genuine standard-bearer of the American tradition of liberty. However, Heywood's thinking on the political parties was filled with contradictions. While it was true that many Republicans accepted racial stereotypes and believed that an individual's success or failure in society rested solely on personal initiative, Heywood surely must have known that the Republican party had developed a program that acknowledged the basic rights of blacks. In contrast, the Democratic party had a much worse position, consistently promoting racist policies and ideas. Indeed, at times during the 1850s, it seemed that the only significant political argument it could mount was that the Republicans were pro-black.[21] It is difficult to comprehend how Ezra Heywood could have argued that Democrats were more favorably inclined to liberty than Republicans. A further reason that Heywood might have had to distrust the Democrats was their ethnic, social character.

The majority of Democrats were urban-based, recently arrived immigrants. Heywood came from a social background that was quite different, indeed, it was closer to that of many Republicans. He often expressed fear and apprehension about the potential violence and unruliness of the urban masses. The Republicans encompassed many northern farmers, artisans, clergymen, and businessmen, people from Heywood's social background. Heywood was strongly disillusioned with a party of his peers that he perceived as a failure in the cause of liberty. In order to hold his abolitionist convictions, Heywood needed to maintain a clear separation from the Republicans and the society they represented; many abolitionists in the 1850s remained aloof from the Republican party because of its racist elements. Even after the Civil War had begun, a committed Garrisonian like Heywood had many reasons to oppose the Republicans. Heywood viewed them as a war party trampling on civil liberties and unconcerned about the plight of the blacks. Still, Heywood's stance favoring the Democrats is confusing and difficult to explain.

In 1858, scarcely nine months after he had seen his first copy of *The Liberator*, Heywood ascended the platform in the beautiful grove at Framingham to deliver his first of what would be many abolitionist addresses. He spoke as part of the annual Fourth of July celebration with Garrison, Wendell Phillips, Theodore Parker, Parker Pillsbury, and others. He began apologetically: "I say I cannot hope to give anything of interest to this vast audience. . . ."[22] However, he quickly warmed to his subject. He began by arguing that the abolitionist movement "simply reasserts the self-evident truths of the Declaration of Independence, and calls this nation to repentance of its greatest sin, and to the obedience of the Golden Rule. It does not advance any new ideas, any new principles." Like many abolitionists, he invoked the radical heritage of the Revolutionary War. The self-evident truths of the Declaration were simply that all people are created equal and endowed by their Creator with the inalienable rights of life, liberty, and the pursuit of happiness. An essential quality of liberty was self-ownership. Belief in natural rights was crucial for the abolitionists. Staughton Lynd explains: "The idea of a natural law self-evident to the common man; the idea that liberty was man's inalienable right to self-determination: these were axioms to which abolitionism added only corollaries."[23] Those that supported slavery, therefore, were seen as sinners, violators of the laws of God and nature.

Heywood continued his July 4 address by declaring that "the leading fact of the present age is the prominence of the individual." Here, he was enunciating the Garrisonian faith that the basis of society lay with each individual's conscience. However, society had gone astray: "The national energies flow in material rather than spiritual channels. . . . Now Abolitionism simply asserts the superiority of individualism over institutionalism, the inviolable sacredness of man."[24] He shared the antipathy of the nonresistants toward any institution that coerced or interfered with individual autonomy.

Heywood proceeded to discuss his ideas concerning the church and Christianity. "No man can be a Christian, and not be an Abolitionist. . . . I do not love Jesus so much because he loved me, as because he loved everybody. . . ." Heywood deplored organized religion, which he saw as based on abstractions and "seldom touches the practical life. If a man will assent to the creed, he may have free course and be glorified in all 'respectable iniquity'—war, slavery, political corruption, social antagonism, & c., to suit the now sainted sinner." He declared: "We want character more than creed, piety more than parchment, Christianity more than churchianity." Heywood was appealing to each individual to assert personal divine nature. To loud cheers, he called upon the church to act responsibly: "The only way the Church can regain her hold upon the conscience of the masses is by identifying herself with all the great moral issues before the people, foremost among which is the momentous struggle for the equal brotherhood of the race."[25] The church had a simple choice, according to Heywood: join the fight to abolish slavery to open the path for the improvement of society and the ultimate millennium, or get out of the way.

Heywood next denounced politics as a means of pursuing abolition: "Politics is the grave of Anti-Slavery sentiment. The indignant heartthrob of a single child does more to abolish slavery than the double-dealing of a great political leader." Many individuals in society making a moral commitment and acting on the basis of their beliefs would sooner lead to the end of slavery than relying on politicians in Washington. Here again he asserted the primacy of the individual over institutions and went on to attack loyalty to the Constitution and the union. "The oath to support a Pro-Slavery Constitution concedes the righteousness of slavery. . . . Death is the only cure for slavery. Liberty *first*, and Union afterwards!" Because the Constitution and the Union upheld slavery, Heywood believed they should be abolished. The Garrisonian wing of the abolitionists produced the most rigorous critique of the Constitution. They saw the main object of that document as successfully compromising the deep conflict between North and South.[26]

The Garrisonians were advocates of direct action. People should not rely on political parties, the church, or government for social reform, but rather should speak and act as motivated by personal conscience. Heywood called for agitation, "the only staff of the world's progress. This must be done by the people themselves." Wendell Phillips believed that our first duty was to God, and that people should do their duty at whatever cost. Another Garrisonian, Samuel May, claimed that the abolitionists were protected by God's truth, which would be "their shield, their helmet, their whole armor."[27] With such moral certainty, Ezra Heywood felt a total dedication and serenity in his call for action.

Heywood concluded his Fourth of July talk by praising the abolitionists, "a little knot of men, standing outside of Church and State," who had driven "those great political parties and ecclesiastical organizations before them, dashing one after another asunder, until the whole country is brought to a single alternative—freedom or slavery. . . ." He confided to the crowd that he had worried about there being "nothing left for the striplings, just let loose from school, to wrestle against." But from a closer perspective, he saw that slavery was entrenched in every part of society—pulpit, press, senate, and places of learning. He ended with a firm statement of his resolve as the audience gave him loud and prolonged applause: "Whatever others may say or do, my duty is determined. . . . Hereafter, I wish to be known as an out-and-out, through-and-through, Garrisonian Abolitionist. And I shall regard it as an insult to be called anything less."[28]

Heywood repeatedly came back to the themes that he laid out in this speech: the natural rights argument; a call to emulate the Revolutionary ancestors; the centrality of the individual and a critique of institutions; a call for direct action; and stinging rebukes to the church, the Union and the Constitution, and political parties, especially the Republicans. Overall, the tone of his speeches became harsher, but the basic substance remained unchanged. Heywood believed that the abolitionists were holy warriors, persecuted because they spoke the truth against power and false authority. He treated the older abolitionists as virtual saints, men and women who were doing Christ's work on earth. They might be maligned and abused, but the righteousness of their path would someday be seen by all. In discussing the strains of Western thought in abolitionism, the historian James M. McPherson nicely summarizes the framework of Heywood's thinking: "In America, all three intellectual traditions—the Enlightenment, Transcendentalism, and Evangelical Protestantism—were basically equalitarian. The Enlightenment produced the Declaration of Independence; Transcendentalism emphasized the innate goodness and ultimate perfectibility of man; Evangelical Protestantism taught that injustice was a sin, and that every Christian had a duty to cleanse society of its sins."[29]

Heywood's denunciations of the church were especially vehement. Having nearly committed his life to the ministry, he was particularly galled by the church's failure to act decisively against slavery. He shared this sentiment with many abolitionists. Time and again he attacked the church; for example, at an antislavery meeting in Worcester, he claimed that "the American Church, with its 40,000 speechless pulpits, is utterly faithless to the rights of the downtrodden Negro and a shameless apostate to Christ." In the following passage from a Fourth of July celebration in 1859, Ezra condemned state and church, but his comments on the church were noticeably more bitter: "Today the air reeks with fulsome adulation of heroes dead, on every virtue of whose lives the laws and religion of this people are a scandalous libel. Today, forty thousand churches go down on their knees 'amidst their brothers' blood, to offer mockery unto God!'—churches whose meat and drink is hourly to crucify four millions of Christs afresh, and put them to an open shame! If this is patriotism, if this Christianity, welcome treason, welcome infidelity!" In a final example, again from a Worcester meeting, he charged the church with "hourly crucifying the Son of God afresh" by its cooperation with slavery.[30]

Immediately following his debut on the abolitionist platform, Heywood became lecturer, and soon after, general agent for the Massachusetts Anti-Slavery Society. Heywood pursued his new calling vigorously, working at a taxing pace but lacking confidence in his abilities, as evidenced by his comments to Samuel May in 1859: "When I look back upon my utterly abortive attempt at public addresses during the past year—a vomit of words and a dyspepsia of ideas, a mess of senseless balderdash—it seems the height of presumption and impudence that I should have paraded myself before so many public assemblies. . . . You may smile at reading this, but it is just so . . . it becomes me to banish myself to the solitude of reflection, by patient and penitent brooding to hatch, if possible, an idea or two into my airy dreaming."[31] Driven by his belief in perfectibility and the urgency of ending slavery, Heywood imposed high standards on himself.

However much Heywood was plagued by doubts about his abilities, he was well regarded by his fellow abolitionists. A Rutland reader of *The Liberator* declared: "A cultivated mind and eloquent tongue, and warm heart he lays upon the altar of reform. . . .". In the summer of 1860, *The Liberator* reported that Heywood, "a young man of very marked talent and promise," spoke on "Ideas and Institutions" at the Sunday services in the Music Hall where Theodore Parker's congregation gathered. In that speech, Heywood argued that ideas had progressed in the world, not by the aid of institutions, but rather in spite of them. Ideas, not coercive institutions, had the power to alter the course of history. The article concluded that Heywood was "destined to a high position and an honored career." Garrison wrote to his friend Johnson: "E. H.

Heywood acquitted himself most creditably in his lecture on 'Common Sense' before the Fraternity. . . ."[32]

From the time he left Brown University until his death, Heywood was perpetually in financial difficulty. In the fall of 1858, he asked Samuel May to negotiate a loan for him, and he ran a notice several times in *The Liberator* to advertise his availability to speak before lyceums "to relieve himself of a debt incurred in pursuing his studies." His references included Harriet Beecher Stowe and Wendell Phillips. Heywood's lyceum topic for the winter of 1858–59 was "Individualism and Institutionalism."[33] At this time, Ezra lived with his mother in Hubbardston, a neighboring town to Princeton. He later moved to Boston for his antislavery work and then back to his native Princeton in the last years of the war.

At the urging of Wendell Phillips, Heywood took over the job of general agent of the Massachusetts Anti-Slavery Society when Samuel May fell ill. He also continued to lecture on the lyceum circuit and at antislavery meetings. From the years 1859 to 1864, more than two hundred speeches across New England by Ezra Heywood were announced in the notices of *The Liberator*. In addition, Heywood's new position made him responsible for coordinating the activities of the society. He developed his skills as an organizer, pulling together countless conventions and meetings, maintaining a voluminous correspondence, raising money and meticulously noting every dollar and cent that various agents brought in, and distributing literature. The frantic workpace that Ezra maintained may have led to his serious illness in 1861. Garrison wrote to his friend Oliver Johnson: "We have had our friend, E. H. Heywood, sick with a brain fever at our house for nearly three weeks. He is now slowly recuperating. . . ."[34]

Heywood had learned from veteran abolitionists how mobs had nearly lynched Garrison in the streets of Boston. In the winter of 1860–61, Heywood directly experienced the assault of mob action. On Sunday, December 16, 1860, Wendell Phillips addressed a crowd of 3,300 at the Music Hall. People were in every available aisle space. His topic, "Mobs and Education," was a direct response to an incident earlier in the month, when an antislavery meeting had been broken up. The meeting had been reconvened peacefully in the evening, but afterward several free blacks were beaten up in the streets and windows in their homes were smashed. Phillips was able to deliver his speech, but a near riot ensued when he left the hall. Heywood described the episode in a letter to Samuel May: "The most intense excitement prevailed here on Sunday— the service at the Hall was a complete triumph for Free Speech. Phillips was never more master of the subject. . . . He was badly hustled in the street but nothing serious occurred. . . ." *The Liberator* reported that a mob of two thousand followed Phillips to his home, hooting and yelling. Although Phillips was surrounded by a bodyguard of close friends, including Heywood, a policeman on the scene reported that two hundred police escorted Phillips home and that without them "he never would have got home alive! They would have trampled him down in the street!"[35]

Heywood's reaction to this turbulence was interesting: "Things wear a very threatening aspect—now—and it is not at all unlikely that the panic may culminate in some bloody affray on or before the annual meeting. If so I hope the blow may fall on some of us youngsters who can be more easily spared than those who for years of service in this fight are so blessedly fated."[36] His apprehensions of more violence were realistic, and, in fact, serious disruptions did occur at the annual meeting. What is striking is that Heywood expressed no fear. His abolitionist faith in the truthfulness of his course gave him a calmness akin to the spirit of *satyagraha* later espoused by the pacifist Gandhi and his followers. *Satyagraha* is a combination of two words: *satya* meaning truth, and *graha* meaning firmness. In Gandhi's words, "*satyagraha* postulates the conquest of the adversary by suffering in one's own person."[37] Heywood might have viewed the conflicts favorably because a dramatic clash of good and evil would hasten the apocalyptic resolution of slavery. His willingness to accept injury or death stemmed from his abiding religious faith in the abolitionist cause. Seeing himself as part of a small army of the righteous battling for truth, Heywood was quite willing to be a martyr for the cause. He fervently believed in the correctness of the path he had chosen. Ultimately, Heywood felt, the natural order of justice would prevail, a sentiment that would deepen as he was pilloried for his ideas during the remainder of his life.

Although nonresistance was not discarded, it was often supplanted by the doctrine of disunionism in the 1840s and afterward. Disunionism did much to weaken the foundations of nonresistance because it did not view slavery as merely one especially vile outcome of the sinful habit of governing and coercing. Rather, disunionism made slavery a sectional issue and often projected the Northern government as the representation of American liberty.[38] If the North represented liberty, then Northern violence could be viewed as righteous. Nonresistance was also weakened in yet another way. The Garrisonians had long been in a quandary over what position to take toward slave rebellions in the South. However, when the issue of violence moved out of the South, it became still more difficult. Should abolitionists take sides in the battle to determine whether Kansas would be slave or free? Was violence justified in thwarting the return of slaves to their masters? As civil war loomed, the issue of violence was to take a momentous turn when the abolitionists dealt with John Brown's raid at Harper's Ferry.

John Brown, who had led the raid in a vain attempt to launch a slave insurrection, had enjoyed the backing of some abolitionists who were not nonresistants. Garrison found a way to defend Brown and still maintain his pacifism by claiming that Brown acted only in self-defense. Thus, this argument saw Brown's most serious sin to be advocacy of violent self-defense. Garrison still argued that violence was wrong, but that cowardice was wrong, too; instead of "men wearing their chains in a cowardly and servile spirit, I would, as an advocate of peace, much rather see them breaking the head of the tyrant with their chains." According to Lewis Perry, "Harper's Ferry was truly the turning point for nonresistance as an effective voice in reform. . . . By the end of 1859 almost no nonresistant voice remained to be raised against force and violence."[39]

Ezra Heywood responded with the same spirit as his peers. He called Brown "a man of the highest faith and courage, the most perfect specimen of a true, a noble, an heroic man, that our country has yet produced." In an address celebrating the one-hundredth anniversary of the founding of Princeton, he declared: "Put your ears to the ground, and you will hear the echoing, earthquake tread of the impending second American Revolution. This very week, its Bunker's Hill was fought at Harper's Ferry." In an especially bellicose tone, he told the New England Anti-Slavery Convention that "you who believe in Bunker Hill and Lexington ought to rejoice to see the hands of every slave smoking with his master's blood, to see every bondman of the South . . . rise and break his chains over the head of his oppressor."[40]

With the outbreak of the Civil War, lines were drawn sharply throughout society, and nearly all the abolitionists opted to support the North. For the Garrisonians, this was an especially difficult decision. Many, no doubt, experienced remorse and anguish because they felt compelled to jettison long-held principles of nonresistance. However, Lewis Perry points out that "by evaluating Harper's Ferry solely in terms of individual integrity they helped explode their doctrine, and they could not respond critically as pacifists when the entire nation took to violence." The dominant theme for the abolitionists, including the Garrisonians, became that the war was "an act of God, for which the guilt of the nation rather than the decision of any man was responsible." The nation would be purified by the terrible conflict, but "even if God's government was vindicated by the nation's affliction, the war essentially transferred responsibility for abolition from reformers to human government."[41] The abolitionists, including Heywood, vigorously pushed for complete emancipation of the slaves, and many also fought for black rights after emancipation. However, the move to support the Union crippled the ability of the Garrisonians to speak and act independently.

How did Ezra Heywood respond to the war? He delivered a speech on "The Present Crisis" at the Music Hall in Boston in July 1861, a few months after the war began. He condemned the notion of a virtuous war and argued that the right to life is the basis of all other rights. He took issue with Wendell Phillips, who had argued that now the national conflict could only be settled by arms. Heywood felt compelled to reject this concession, which denied "the adequacy of the human reason to apprehend and obey the truth." Human redemption, Heywood argued, was still possible and would be the result of the ascendancy of superior ideas, not superior force of arms. Garrison printed the speech in full, but not before approaching Heywood with the page proof and asking if Heywood had better not leave out a sentence that declared "It is a graver crime to kill a man than to enslave him." Heywood replied that he could omit all the rest of the speech except for that passage. Garrison decided to print the entire speech. Heywood recalled that he "was amazed, astounded." The possibility of censorship offended Heywood deeply, but it was especially troubling to imagine that "this man whom I had revered as a god had lost his faith in truth and in human nature to example it!"[42] These lines, however, were written thirty years after this episode. At the time, Heywood was indeed striking a different chord from other Garrisonians, but had not made a dramatic break.

In fact, the remainder of the speech fitted the prevailing conventional expression of the Garrisonians. Heywood took up the argument that the war was a cleansing, purifying experience for the nation: peace would come "by Northern freemen pouring out their blood in glad atonement for seventy years of injustice to the slave. It will come by confederate armies swept like autumn leaves before the sublime wrath of the North." Further, he condemned the South's secession and called it "high treason to justice and liberty and a damnable insult to the heroes of '76."[43] Here, Heywood echoed the reversal of most Garrisonians. He stood firm with the North and the Union cause, despite the resort to violence. As the war progressed, Heywood continued, with some reservations, to support the idea that it was divinely ordained. In an 1862 address, Heywood claimed that the abolitionists were merely "the heralds of this Olympic game, the executors of God's providence. The conflict is in the nature of things." Arguing that the war was a natural apocalypse visited upon a sinful nation, Heywood won praise from Garrison for this speech.

Heywood was becoming more troubled, however, at the idea of sanctioning killing. He declared: "If the whole is greater than a part, to kill a man is a graver sin than to enslave him. . . . To men born free and equal, *life*, liberty and the pursuit of happiness are inalienable rights. Then war violates love, the divinest law of nature." A few months later, in April 1862, Ezra described what was happening in America as "the pouring out of the sixth vial of the Apocalypse, to be succeeded by the glorious Millennium." However, could the millennium be ushered in by the war method, which trampled upon the most basic inviolable right—the right to life? While still calling the war a natural collision of two social antagonisms in an address in January 1863, Heywood began to answer this question directly. Beneath politics, trade, industry—the entire fabric of society, he detected "a feeling, hidden, silent, yet inextinguishable, and to ripen into aggressive, invincible, world-wide conviction—a feeling that *war, all war, is wrong, unreasonable, unchristian, and barbarous.*"[44]

By the spring of 1863, Heywood had concluded that the abolitionist movement, in supporting the war effort, was abandoning its principles. At a convention of the Massachusetts Anti-Slavery Society, he introduced a series of resolutions upholding free speech. He deplored the arrest and trial of C. L. Vallandigham, an Ohio political figure who had been arrested and tried in military court for proposing negotiations with the Confederacy. While abohrring Vallandigham's "immoral and useless method of conciliating the Slave Oligarchy," Heywood reminded his colleagues that martial law did not hold sway in Ohio. It was wrong, Heywood declared, for the government to deny Vallandigham his "undeniable and sacred right of free speech." Further, Heywood condemned this arrest as part of a series of arbitrary arrests taking place in nonslave states. Arguing that unrestricted criticism of public men and actions is indispensable for the security and growth of free institutions, he demanded the same free speech for the opponents of abolition that the abolitionists themselves had sought.

In an argument that revealed how far the abolitionists had strayed from their prewar critique of government, the veteran abolitionist Stephen S. Foster charged that the resolutions favored Copperheadism—the disparaging Republican term for a pro-South Democrat—and said they were inappropriate for an antislavery meeting. He declared: "So long as the Government confined its violations of law to the sons of Satan, he would not find fault. But let it keep its hands from the angel Gabriel." The resolutions were tabled by a decisive vote. The historian George Fredrickson has discussed the contours of this shift among Northern intellectuals: "In the process of praising 'government' and 'civilization' as abstract ideals, Emerson's characteristic emphasis on individualism and anarchism disappeared. He now exulted in the fact that 'war organizes' and 'forces individuals and states to combine and act with larger views.'. . . The change in American thinking which occurred during the Civil War was perfectly summed up by the changing views of Emerson himself." Heywood made reference to this shift by chiding Emerson and others for the abandonment of sound principles. One intellectual outgrowth of the trend Fredrickson describes was Theodore Roosevelt's version of American imperialism. His notion of "the strenuous life" drew heavily on the example of the Civil War.[45]

Heywood clearly separated himself from mainstream Garrisonians and abolitionists with his address at the Melodeon in Boston on "The War Method of Peace" on Sunday, June 14, 1863. He criticized abolitionists for describing the nation as a first-class power, "aglow with visions of mere material supremacy." Heywood warned that they were forgetting that truth alone was the first-class power. Leaving aside the customary Biblical quotations, he instead presented lengthy passages from the Declarations of Sentiments of the American Anti-Slavery Society and the New England Non-Resistants, which he likened to the Declaration of Independence. These texts, Heywood insisted, called for impartial liberty for all and an end to militarism.

Heywood argued, again, that to kill a person is a greater sin than to enslave him or her. He now, however, unequivocally opposed the war method: "A resort to war to put down slavery is a resort to lying to put down falsehood, a resort to stealing to put down theft." He charged that war was an evil, a sin, and a crime. Noting that he had criticized war for two years, Heywood said that he had refrained from emphasizing these views because of his reverence for the abolitionists. However, at a time when many questioned the right to criticize the war at all, he felt compelled to speak out.

Heywood contended that Garrisonian abolitionism was the inheritor of great ideas and the harbinger of human advancement: "The progress of civilization . . . in Luther, Magna Charta, Puritanism, Democracy, Negro Emancipation, Non-Resistance, is the progress of mankind toward unity and fair play." However, barbarism still inspired the methods of society. Heywood said: "We have not ascended to the realm of ideas; in the fifth day of creation the world awaits man." The millennium was still possible, he believed, but the course the Garrisonians had chosen was leading in the opposite direction.

Government, Heywood declared, was only a temporary convenience to secure justice and order. It would vanish as people's ideas became unified. He saw the will of the people, not government, as natural and organic: "The elements of growth and original sovereignty forever inhere in the people, and no government can be perpetual." Heywood enunciated an understanding of democratic principles that distinguished him from most other abolitionists: "American government of the people, by the people, for the people, resides in moral power, is founded in the consent of the governed . . . peaceful secession is a moral right." The North could secede, Garrison argued, in order to preserve liberty. However, the South had seceded for the express purpose of preserving the tyranny of slavery—a fact that, Garrison maintained, justified the Union in suppressing the South. In contrast, Heywood contended that the principles of democracy and self-rule meant little if selectively applied.[46]

Although not yet identifying himself as an anarchist, Heywood elaborated a decentralist theory of social organization that was anarchistic in nature. Natural growth, Heywood argued, led to the decomposition of large nation-states into smaller, self-governing entities. "The same law of growth which radiates South America into diverse States; which makes Europe a mosaic of Nationalities; which severed these colonies from Great Britain, and will sever Canada, India, and Australia will assert its supremacy here." He envisioned the United States breaking down into a cluster of republics: one on the Pacific, one on the Gulf, one on the Great Lakes, and one on the Hudson and Connecticut.[47] Not yet identifying himself as an anarchist, Heywood used the word "anarchy," as did most abolitionists, to mean disintegration. This, he cautioned, was not what he advocated. Rather, he wished to see the great variations of human existence given free expression and autonomy: "These variegated, picturesque forms of political development are the regular and natural progress of society toward the mutual safety of persons and property, and the impartial revelation of justice."

When the South refused to abolish slavery, then separation was the only just and democratic alternative for the South and the North. The North could have declared a policy of "No union with slaveholders," and allowed the two systems to stand in mutual opposition. There was no doubt in Heywood's mind that the better social system would emerge victorious. Believing fervently in the ultimate triumph of truth and natural order, Heywood had no doubt about slavery's eventual demise: "the laws of nature which are all anti-slavery, and God who was always an Abolitionist" would take care of matters.

In Heywood's view, the effort to coerce the South by force had had only disastrous consequences. To make his point, he quoted statements of Madison and Jefferson in which both men abhorred war. Madison said that war led to armies, debts, and taxes, which accelerated political domination by the few. Jefferson felt that war generated more evils than it cured. One of the evils produced, Heywood argued, was the denial of free speech, a fundamental democratic right. Heywood declared: "This war power invoked in the service of emancipation is slavery in epaulettes. . . ." He denounced the spectacle of reformers, who were supposed to believe in liberty as a principle, advocating tyrannical measures. The issue was clear: "If it is right to speak *for* the war, it is right to speak against it." A doctrine that placed military over civil authority made the republic a despotism, Heywood contended.

Heywood raised the crucial issue that it was folly to believe a military victory could lead to a just social order. Emancipation might triumph "under the shadow of swords," with federal dragoons washing "their horse hoofs in the Gulf." An emancipation imposed by government could easily be withdrawn when it became convenient to do so. Heywood continued: "The old questions are upon you: we are two nations still." With state-imposed emancipation, "Where are the means to administer free institutions at the South? The elements of rebellion are there intensified, sullen, defiant, ready to spring to arms any moment. . . ." Heywood argued that the manner in which emancipation was achieved would be a crucial determinant in shaping the quality of life in the South for blacks and whites. Military victory for the North, Heywood argued, would not alter race prejudice in the South.

Heywood's fears proved well-grounded. When the North decided to make peace with the white leadership of the South, the result for blacks was devastating. Most were left with sharecropping—a small improvement over slave labor—and with beatings, lynchings, and the systematic denial of civil rights. Garrison, arguably the leading abolitionist, failed to anticipate these developments. George Fredrickson points out that Garrison had repudiated a basic premise of the antislavery movement: "Abolition from military necessity would not guarantee a national commitment to racial equality; it might signify no more than it did to those conservatives who viewed emancipation as a useful tactic in a war fought for conservative nationalism and the rights of authority."[48]

Garrison printed "The War Method of Peace" in *The Liberator*, but not without comment. He believed that there was " 'a time to keep silent,' as well as 'a time to speak,' and that, while the whirlwind, the earthquake and the fire of civil war are in full operation, it is not possible for 'the still, small voice' of nonresistance to be heard. . . ." Heywood had himself earlier subscribed to the belief that the war was a judgment imposed by God, but now rejected this argument: "If earthquakes are free moral agents, if earthquakes vote and join the church, that argument is in point—otherwise, it is impertinent and absurd."[49] For Heywood, the central issues of the war and of politics had become decentralism as well as the individual's rights and responsibilities. The individual acting on his or her conscience was the basis for a democratic society that valued human life, liberty, and free speech. Thus, Heywood emphasized free will and individual choice as opposed to the deterministic framework Garrison and others applied to the war.

For the remainder of the Civil War, Heywood continued his outspoken criticism of the abolitionists. For example, one of his lecture topics during the summer of 1864 was "War to restore the Union or abolish Slavery is a sin against God, disastrous to the country, and should immediately be abolished." In a letter to *The Liberator*, he denounced the military draft as a violation of personal freedom: "The right to draft men is as purely imaginary as the right to enslave them; hence, this Conscription, like the Fugitive Slave Bill, is essentially wicked and despotic, to be disobeyed and trod under foot." [50] He praised Alfred H. Love, a prominent Quaker, and John Wesley Pratt, a New England Non-Resistance Society activist, for their public refusal to cooperate with the conscription law.

Heywood severely criticized Garrison for arguing that "judging the President by the war plane on which he stands, he should have imprisoned many more Northern traitors and suppressed many more treasonable newspapers." Friends of freedom and peace, who have laid *The Liberator* next to their Bibles, were gravely alarmed, Heywood declared, that this paper "should have no protest against the great wrongs incident to the attempted settlement of the slave question by the sword." Garrison, in editorial reply to Heywood's letter, expressed his sharpest comments on Heywood yet: "we know of an exceptional non-resistant who is so unwise or so unfortunate in his treatment of the awful struggle through which the nation is passing, as to give aid and comfort to those traitorous dissemblers 'who cry peace, peace, when there is no peace.'" By the last year of the war, according to Carleton Mabee, "orator Heywood had set himself so completely against the usual abolitionist acquiescence in the war that he found himself seldom invited to speak to Garrisonian meetings any more; he was reduced to speaking independently, under his own auspices."[51]

Dismayed by the stance of most abolitionists, especially Garrisonians, and increasingly cut off from the movement, Heywood had the good fortune to meet the social reformer Josiah Warren in June 1863. Heywood recalled "resenting persecution of Democrats for denouncing war, he heard my rebuke of Garrison & Co., in Boston, for their part in the outrage, and came to Princeton to bring me more light. . . ." Warren was to have an impact on Heywood like that of Garrison: "Since '63, when I first met the Thomas Paine of coming American socialism, Josiah

Warren, the great truths he proclaimed have wrought mightily. . . ."[52] Heywood launched an intensive study of Warren's writings and the books that Warren recommended. Over the next five years, Heywood elaborated a theory of labor reform based on Warren's individualist anarchist principles.

Josiah Warren lived for two years at Robert Owen's communal settlement in New Harmony, Indiana. Subsequently, Warren formed a "time store" in Cincinnati, based on the direct exchange of commodities and services. He helped organize utopian communities in Tuscarawas County, Ohio, and Utopia, Ohio, before joining with the individualist anarchist Stephen Pearl Andrews in establishing Modern Times, a utopian community in Brentwood, New York.

Warren believed that the great mistake of all society was the compromise or surrender of the sovereignty of the individual. He envisioned a society comprised of local, autonomous communities without any government. Economic life would be regulated naturally on the basis of equitable exchange. All prices of goods and services would be determined by the actual cost to the producer. This system of labor for labor would eliminate exploitation, Warren believed, and lead to a society in which there was universal peace and security of both persons and property.[53]

Warren opposed the chattel slavery of the South but refused to take sides in the struggle between North and South, arguing that the wage slavery of the North was equally oppressive. He supported the South's right to secede but claimed that slaves, too, had the right to secede from their masters. Warren portrayed the Civil War, with its massive toll of death and destruction, as a natural consequence of patriotism, the state, and the destruction of individual personality. He condemned the war as barbaric in *True Civilization*, his most noted book, published in 1863.[54]

Besides his growing estrangement from the antislavery movement, Heywood may have concluded that Lincoln's Emancipation Proclamation left him little work to do as an abolitionist. The historian Gerald Sorin points out that most abolitionists were strongly individualistic, "with an exaggerated confidence that the black man could now make his own way." Further, their individualism militated against vigorously pursuing large-scale social planning to aid the newly freed slaves. Sorin writes that "aiding the freedmen never commanded the kind of loyalty and determination shown in the cause of the slave." Heywood, too, did little to help the ex-slaves, however he remained a committed reformer, turning his attention to the problems of laborers in the North. Many abolitionists, wearied from the war, left social reform efforts entirely, whereas others tempered their idealism as a result of the war and engaged in a more conservative, practical approach to reform.[55]

A small number of abolitionists, in addition to Heywood, including Joshua Blanchard, Adin Ballou, Alfred H. Love, and Elihu Burritt, had managed to sustain a consistent stance on peace throughout the war years. Although the Civil War left an inheritance of patriotism and a belief in the use of force, this small circle of pacifists decided to organize in order to promote their ideas. Heywood was one of the effort's leaders, and an initial conference was held in Boston on December 12, 1865.[56]

Subsequently, organizing conferences were held in Boston and Providence during the spring of 1866. At the Providence meetings, participants decided to form the Universal Peace Society (later the Universal Peace Union). A preamble and constitution, drafted by Heywood and Love, were adopted. The preamble spoke of the natural and inalienable rights of all people to life, liberty, and the pursuit of happiness; argued for the voluntary association of states and communities and the right of secession; declared that God favored nonresistance; and condemned war as a subversion of the teachings of Jesus Christ. The constitution stated that the aim of the society was to remove the causes, and abolish the customs, of war. Through lectures and publications, the organization would try to discourage all resorts to deadly force. War, the constitution charged, was "a sin against God and opposed to the best interests of mankind, and its immediate abandonment is alike a religious duty, the wisest expediency and an imperative necessity."[57]

Founded by former abolitionists, the Peace Union was composed largely of people from four religious splinter groups: the Progressive Friends, the Bible Christians, the Shakers, and the Rogerene Quakers. The union attracted four hundred active members and between three and four thousand sympathizers. The printed word was the union's chief vehicle for reaching the public; it issued a number of essays and booklets, as well as a succession of journals. The basic aim of the union, as outlined by Alfred H. Love, the Quaker who was the organization's mainstay, was to remold society in a spirit of Christian love and human brotherhood. From 1866 until 1913, the union supported conscientious objectors and encouraged unilateral disarmament.[58]

According to Peter Brock, the union "remained until the First World War the sole organized expression of radical pacifism outside the peace sects" and was in many senses the direct successor of earlier Garrisonian nonresistance. Thus, the union was significant historically despite the fact that new organizations after the Civil War based on pacifism were singularly ineffective.[59] It represented a historical bridge between Garrisonian nonresistance and the militant pacifism of the early twentieth century.

An involved member and regular participant at conferences, Heywood did not find an adequate outlet for his radicalism in the Universal Peace Union. At a conference in New York in 1867, he presented a series of resolutions calling for the repudiation of the federal war debt, which, he argued, was meant to plunder the common people. Unless it was "speedily assessed upon monopolized wealth, enlightened expediency, and religious duty will require its repudiation." Alfred Love, L. K. Joslin, and Henry Clarke Wright, all prominent figures in the union, rejected Heywood's position. Love and Wright argued that honesty required that any debt contracted must be paid. Throughout its history, the union used resolutions to advocate the emancipation of labor, but actually took few concrete steps in that direction. Love maintained that in order to "lay the axe at the root of the evil," the war spirit and the government that is largely responsible for stirring up this emotion must be corrected.[60] For Love, the struggle between the common people and monopolized wealth was not as central as it was becoming for Heywood.

Although no abolitionist, and no American for that matter, identified himself or herself as an anarchist in the 1840s or 1850s, many anarchistic or libertarian tendencies were in the abolitionist movement. A contemporary of the abolitionists, the Frenchman Pierre-Joseph Proudhon, who did describe himself as an anarchist, rejected the authority of God and the state. He envisioned as the basis of a new social order the sense of conscience and justice inherent in each individual. Proudhon denounced any individual or group claiming to represent the will of the people and condemned with equal fervor all forms of government—monarchy, oligarchy, democracy, or bureaucracy. He also emphasized liberty, responsibility, and self-respect.

Although most of the Garrisonian abolitionists clearly did not share Proudhon's atheism, they did denounce government similarly. The Garrisonians, along with Proudhon, placed the individual sense of truth and justice at the heart of the social order and would countenance no abridgement of individual autonomy. Proudhon and the Garrisonians believed in a voluntary society that was natural and organic; each individual, following the dictates of conscience, would exercise responsible self-government. In turn, an orderly society would result from the co-operation of autonomous individuals. Lewis Perry declares: "The kingdom of God, with its wonderful new harmony, could supplant both church and state. Man, in a word, could be emancipated." Libertarianism was a clear theme in the radical abolitionism of the Garrisonian abolitionists.[61]

The abolitionists were clearly anarchistic and libertarian in that the only authority they recognized stemmed from the individual. Thus, Ezra Heywood learned the fundamentals of anarchist theory in the abolitionist movement before he had ever met an anarchist or read any explicitly anarchist theory. The libertarianism implicit in abolitionist thought and action fell apart with the almost total support for the Northern cause in the Civil War. Years of support for the government war effort thoroughly eroded the libertarian impulse.

It was left for Ezra Heywood to play the important historical role, in the words of Lewis Perry, of "a direct link between Garrisonism and postwar radicalism; he was also a link with other antebellum traditions." By throwing himself into the struggle for labor reform, Heywood, according to Perry, reinterpreted Josiah Warren's message, which he took to be a restatement of the Declaration of Independence. Heywood was fond of observing in his later years that he could have become a wealthy man but his sense of truth and justice dictated another course: "if I had sailed easily along, in lyceum lecturing, with Phillips, Tilton, and the rising rest, or 'pocketed my crotchets' and gone into business with S. R. [his brother Samuel] I could now have been rich enuf to be foolish if not a knave. But what shall it profit to go for the shell and lose the egg? Whether we have souls or not, right in body, truth in what now palpably is, availeth much in the long living or dead run."[62]

NOTES

1. *The Word*, July 1880, p. 2; see Keith E. Melder, *Beginnings of Sisterhood: The American Woman's Rights Movement, 1800–1850* (New York: Schocken Books, 1977).

2. *Lucifer*, May 20, 1892, p. 3. This passage from *Lucifer* is excerpted from a series of autobiographical letters Heywood wrote while in prison from 1890–92. Although the autobiography prepared in prison was never published, the letters constitute a rich source of information.

3. *Minutes of the Thirteenth Annual Meeting of the Women's Christian Temperance Union of Rhode Island, Held in Newport, September 27, 28, and 29, 1887.* (Providence, R.I.: E.L. Freeman and Sons, 1887), pp. 27, 28. I am grateful to Elizabeth Stevens for pointing out this reference.

4. Ibid.

5. *Lucifer*, May 20, 1892, p. 3.

6. *The Word*, July 1880, p. 2; Gerald Sorin, *Abolitionism: A New Perspective* (New York: Praeger Publishers, 1972), pp. 107–8.

7. Sorin, *Abolitionism*, p. 107; "Program of the Eighty-Seventh Annual Commencement of Brown University, September 3, 1856," Brown University, Providence, R.I., 1856; William B. Hunter, Jr., ed., *A Milton Encyclopedia*, vol. 5 (Lewisburgh, Pa.: Bucknell University Press, 1979), pp. 17–23.

8. *The Word*, February 1884, p. 2.

9. See Henry Steele Commager, *Theodore Parker* (Boston: Beacon Press, 1947).

10. Quoted in Commager, *Theodore Parker*, p. 47.

11. *Lucifer*, May 20, 1892, p. 3; Samuel R. Heywood to Professor Poland, June 15, 1893, Heywood Papers, Hay Library, Brown University, Providence, R.I.; Alfred E. Giles to Professor Poland, June 11, 1893, Giles Papers, Hay Library, Brown University, Providence, R.I.

12. *The Word*, February 1884, p. 2.

13. Ibid., p. 2; September 1892, p. 2.

14. Ronald G. Walters, *American Reformers, 1815–1860* (New York: Hill and Wang, 1978), p. 27; Timothy L. Smith, *Revivalism and Social Reform: American Protestantism on the Eve of the Civil War* (New York: Harper and Row, 1965), p. 103.

15. Lewis Perry, *Radical Abolitionism: Anarchy and the Government of God in Antislavery Thought* (Ithaca, N.Y.: Cornell University Press, 1973), pp. 58–59; Wright quoted on p. 52.

16. Perry, *Radical Abolitionism*, p. 67.

17. Quoted in ibid., p. 186.

18. Ibid., p. 71.

19. Ibid., p. 45; *The Word*, December 1877, p. 3.

20. For details on abolitionists' efforts to advance the education of free blacks, see Carleton Mabee, *Black Freedom: The Nonviolent Abolitionists from 1830 Through the Civil War* (New York: Macmillan, 1970); *The Liberator*. April 2, 1854, p. 4; July 2, 1858, p. 4.

21. *The Liberator*, April 2, 1858, p. 4; Eric Foner, *Free Soil, Free Labor, Free Men: The Ideology of the Republican Party Before the Civil War* (New York: Oxford University Press, 1970), pp. 261–300.

22. *The Liberator*, July 2, 1858, pp. 4 and 2; July 16, 1858, pp. 2–3.

23. Ibid., July 16, 1858, pp. 2–3; Staughton Lynd, *Intellectual Origins of American Radicalism* (London: Wildwood House, 1973), p. 59.

24. *The Liberator*, July 16, 1858, pp. 2–3.

25. Ibid.

26. Ibid.; see Staughton Lynd, "The Abolitionist Critique of the United States Constitution," in *The Antislavery Vanguard: New Essays on the Abolitionists*, ed. Martin Duberman (Princeton, N.J.: Princeton University Press, 1965), pp. 209–39.

27. *The Liberator*, July 16, 1858, pp. 2–3; Irving H. Bartlett, "The Persistence of Wendell H. Phillips," in *The Antislavery Vanguard*, ed. Duberman, p. 112; Larry Gara, "Who Was an Abolitionist?" in *The Antislavery Vanguard*, ed. Duberman, p. 39.

28. *The Liberator*, July 16, 1858, pp. 2–3.

29. James M. McPherson, "A Brief for Equality: The Abolitionist Reply to the Racist Myth, 1860–1865," in *The Antislavery Vanguard*, ed. Duberman, pp. 176–77.

30. *The Liberator*, January 4, 1861, p. 2; July 15, 1859, p. 2; March 11, 1859, p. 3.

31. *The Word*, February 1884, p. 2; see a series of letters in 1858 and 1859 from Ezra Heywood to Samuel May, Manuscripts, Boston Public Library, for example, Ezra Heywood to Samuel May, August 21, 1859.

32. *The Liberator*, November 5, 1858, p. 1; July 6, 1860, p. 2; William Lloyd Garrison to Oliver Johnson, December 26, 1861, Manuscripts, Boston Public Library.

33. *The Liberator*, July 16, 1858, pp. 2–3.

34. William Lloyd Garrison to Oliver Johnson, October 7, 1861, Manuscripts, Boston Public Library.

35. *The Liberator*, December 14, 1860, p. 4; December 21, 1860, pp. 2, 3; December 28, 1860, p. 1; Ezra Heywood to Samuel May, December 19, 1860, Manuscripts, Boston Public Library.

36. Ezra Heywood to Samuel May, December 19, 1860; *The Liberator*, February 1, 1861, p. 3.

37. Mohandas K. Gandhi, "The Origins of *Satyagraha* Doctrine," in *The Quiet Battle: Writings on the Theory and Practice of Non-Violent Resistance*, ed. Mulford Q. Sibley (Boston: Beacon Press, 1963), pp. 36–39.

38. Perry, *Radical Abolitionism*, p. 161.

39. Ibid., pp. 259–60; Garrison quoted in Mabee, *Black Freedom*, pp. 328–29.

40. *The Liberator*, February 3, 1860, p. 2; June 10, 1859, p. 1; *Celebration of the One Hundredth Anniversary of the Incorporation of the Town of Princeton, Massachusetts, October 20, 1859* (Worcester, Mass.: William R. Hooper, 1860), p. 94.

41. Perry, *Radical Abolitionism*, pp. 268–70.

42. *The Liberator*, July 5, 1861, p. 2; *Lucifer*, June 26, 1891, pp. 2–3; *The Word*, July 1880, p. 2.

43. *The Liberator*, July 5, 1861, p. 2.

44. Ibid., January 3, 1862, p. 3; April 11, 1862, p. 4; January 2, 1863, p. 4.

45. Ibid., June 5, 1863, p. 3; George M. Fredrickson, *The Inner Civil War: Northern Intellectuals and the Crisis of the Union* (New York: Harper and Row, 1965), pp. 176–80, 217–25.

46. *The Liberator*, July 17, 1863, p. 4; Mabee, *Black Freedom*, p. 343.

47. On decentralism, see, for example, Murray Bookchin, "Toward an Ecological Society" and "The Concept of Ecotechnologies and Ecocommunities," in *Toward an Ecological Society*, (Montreal: Black Rose Books, 1980), pp. 55–71, 97–112. In the latter essay, Bookchin cites (p. 103) the tradition from which Heywood emerged as anarchistic: "The Protestant sects which were to gather together under the ample rubric of Puritan congregationalism seem to have articulated perhaps the earliest modern attempts to establish the administrative autonomy of small decentralized groups as opposed to the centralized hierarchies of the Catholic and Anglican clergy." See also, Kirkpatrick Sale, *Human Scale* (New York: Coward, McCann, and Geoghegan, 1980), a detailed account of the drawbacks of large-scale organization and the natural virtues of smallness. For a modern version of Heywood's vision of the United States, see the utopian novel *Ecotopia* by Ernest Callenbach (Berkeley, Calif.: Banyon Tree Books, 1975). *Ecotopia* takes place in 1999 and focuses on the country of Ecotopia, comprised of Northern California, Oregon, and Washington, which declared its independence from the United States in 1980.

48. *The Liberator*, July 17, 1863, p. 4; Fredrickson, *The Inner Civil War*, p. 122.

49. *The Liberator*, July 17, 1863, pp. 2 and 4.

50. Ibid., July 22, 1864, p. 3; May 6, 1864, p. 4.

51. Ibid., November 11, 1864, p. 4; Mabee, *Black Freedom*, pp. 366–67.

52. *The Word*, March 1893, p. 2; January 1889, p. 2.

53. For details on Warren, see James J. Martin, *Men Against the State: The Expositors of Individualist Anarchism in America, 1827–1908* (Colorado Springs: Ralph Myles Publishers, 1970); Ann C. Butler, "Josiah Warren: Peaceful Revolutionist," Ph.D. diss., Ball State University, Muncie, Ind., 1978; Charles Shively, ed., *The Collected Works of Josiah Warren* (Weston, Mass.: M and S Press, in press).

54. Martin, *Men Against the State*, pp. 81–82, 98–99; Merle Curti, *Peace or War: The American Struggle, 1636–1936* (New York: W. W. Norton, 1936), p. 59; Josiah Warren, *True Civilization* (New York: Burt Franklin, 1967).

55. *The Word*, April 1887, p. 3; Sorin, *Abolitionism*, pp. 156, 164.

56. See Curti, *Peace or War*, p. 73; *The Liberator*, December 22, 1865, p. 2.

57. *Proceedings of the Peace Convention Held in Boston, March 14 and 15, 1866, and in Providence, May 16, 1866* (Philadelphia: Universal Peace Society, 1866), pp. 19–20.

58. Robert W. Doherty, "Alfred H. Love and the Universal Peace Union," Ph.D. diss., University of Pennsylvania, Philadelphia, 1962, pp. 44, 48; Peter Brock, *Pacifism in the United States: From the Colonial Era to the First World War* (Princeton, N.J.: Princeton University Press, 1968), pp. 920–31; Robert Cooney and Helen Michalowski, *The Power of the People: Active Nonviolence in the United States* (Culver City, Calif.: Peace Press, 1977), p. 37.

59. Brock, *Pacifism in the United States*, pp. 923, 869.

60. *Proceedings of the First Anniversary of the Universal Peace Society, Masonic Hall, New York, May 8 and 9, 1867* (Philadelphia: Universal Peace Society, 1867), pp. 14–18; Cooney and Michalowski, *The Power of the People*, p. 37.

61. Perry, *Radical Abolitionism*, pp. 19, 43; see Edward Hyams, *Pierre-Joseph Proudhon: His Revolutionary Life, Mind, and Works* (New York: Taplinger, 1979).

62. Perry, *Radical Abolitionism*, p. 288; *The Word*, September 1892, p. 2.

CHAPTER 3

LABOR REFORM

E zra Heywood approached labor reform within the context of his growing identification with individualist anarchism, a social and political philosophy that flourished in the second half of the nineteenth century in the United States. Several individualist anarchists, including Heywood, traced their origins to old New England families. Most had been involved in the abolitionist movement. They emphasized individual sovereignty and thus opposed the invasive authority of the state and the church. They argued that no social institution had the right to place limits on individual autonomy or force obedience to a particular set of rules. Many individualist anarchists viewed themselves as spokespeople for the ideas of self-rule that Jefferson had enunciated in the Declaration of Independence.[1]

The individualist anarchists shared certain fundamental principles. Most placed primary emphasis on economic issues. They believed that men and women had the right to own what they produced with their own labor, and that a free and unregulated society of autonomous individuals could achieve a natural state of harmony based on voluntarism. Under capitalism, the state and various monopolies controlled society and prevented the free workings of the marketplace, where people could freely produce and barter. The individualist anarchists bitterly denounced not only capitalism, but also state socialism, which they felt replaced one tyranny with another by merely changing the identity of the rulers.

Many historians believe that of the abolitionists, only Wendell Phillips actively supported American laborers in their struggles. This notion is incorrect. In fact, several former abolitionists continued their efforts to improve the world with their advocacy of labor reform.[2] Ezra Heywood was a key figure in this group.

In the years following the Civil War, the number of Americans engaged in nonagricultural production rapidly approached the number engaged in farming. Independent mechanics and artisans were quickly descending to wage-earner status. The postwar worker was born into a nation of farmers, independent craftsmen, and small manufacturers, most of whom lived in rural areas. However, the same worker came of age in a nation of great capitalists and big factories located in cities. The popular belief in the self-made individual, the notion that anyone could gain wealth and improve his or her status, was confronted by the harsh social reality of burgeoning industrial capitalism. Opposed to the prevailing assumptions that the economic system was based on free labor and that all people were equal was the widespread, growing degradation of *wage slavery*, a term quite popular in the nineteenth century. *The Awl*, a newspaper published by Lynn, Massachusetts, shoemakers, warned in 1845: "Here we see a moneyed aristocracy hanging over us like a mighty avalanche threatening annihilation to every man who dares to question their right to enslave and oppress the poor and unfortunate."[3]

The burdens placed on the working class by the Civil War, especially heavy taxation and inflation, roused laborers to political and economic protest. An 1864 editorial in *The Daily Evening Voice*, published by the Boston Trades Assembly, argued that the "oligarchy of the South" was "from the very nature of things, antagonist to free labor," but added that the emerging question of the day was, "Have the laboring men of the country any rights to respect?" The years following the Civil War were tumultuous ones for the labor movement. In fact, a larger proportion of the industrial labor force joined trade unions during the years immediately before the depression of 1873 than in any other period of the nineteenth century.

The central demand during this period was shortening the working day to eight hours,[4] an idea that many groups and individuals advanced. The most significant group was the National Labor Union (NLU) which, between 1868 and 1870, held the greatest potential of providing an institution that could organize labor reform efforts on a national scale. Founded in Baltimore in 1866, the NLU, composed largely of wage-earners, adopted the Baltimore Program with its chief aim the establishment by law of the eight-hour work day. Its means to achieve this end were to be political. The following year's congress in Chicago advanced the greenback doctrine, which held that good money was anything that people thought was good money. Greenback theory attempted to tie public indebtedness and circulating currency to productivity. The NLU's early commitments to the eight-hour day, political means to achieve its ends, and "greenbackism" set the tone for the organization's subsequent history. Many middle-class labor reformers, including Ezra Heywood, joined the NLU and eventually became a significant part of the organization.[5]

Heywood committed his prodigious energies wholeheartedly to the cause of labor reform. In a speech to workingmen in the summer of 1868 at Biddeford, Maine, he declared that the labor principles of the

NLU "have been scattered over the country in many forms; I myself have issued over eleven thousand documents at my own expense during the last ten months. . . ."[6] Heywood was organizing, speaking, and writing at a taxing pace.

In the summer of 1868 labor's hopes were nowhere higher than in Massachusetts. The pivotal figure in the eight-hour movement was Ira Steward, a self-educated machinist from Boston, who, with George McNeill, had founded the Boston Eight-Hour League. The Republicans were solidly in power, with Radicals in an ascendant position, and radicalism and labor reform were closely linked. Attention focused on the race for the congressional seat from Boston's Third District. The Republican convention ignored labor's choice, General Patrick R. Guiney, Irish nationalist, Civil War hero, and supporter of the eight-hour day, and nominated a railroad president. In response, the labor caucus angrily reconvened and chose the general as a candidate of the independent Workingmen's party. At the enthusiastic meeting in Faneuil Hall to ratify Guiney's nomination, Ezra Heywood shared the platform with notables of the Boston Trades Assembly, Ira Steward, German Turners, and Irish war veterans. The program of the NLU was reviewed by its vice president for Massachusetts, then Heywood, in a lengthy speech, declared that blacks had come into politics, and the workingmen would also, even if the political parties presently ignored their cause, "Human Liberty," a cause that ultimately could not be ignored. Guiney lost the election because both Democratic and Republican workers were afraid that a vote for Guiney would aid the candidate of the major party they traditionally opposed. His candidacy was wrecked by the appeals of the old parties to workers regarding jobs and racial issues, and so the political shifts that Guiney's crusade anticipated never took place.[7]

For nine months following the Baltimore Congress and the founding of the NLU, labor reformers in Massachusetts had worked for the organization's program on every possible front. The Republicans had clearly demonstrated strict limits to their support for labor reform, and the textile corporations had beaten back their operatives' efforts to shorten the working day. Work within the legislature yielded no substantial results. However, it never occurred to Massachusetts labor reformers that any fault lay in their own reform-oriented ideology. Instead of thorough self-evaluation, they sought to continue their pursuit of the Baltimore Program through more effective tactics.

Two new ideas were presented at a large rally in May 1867. First, Wendell Phillips called upon Massachusetts workers to look to the West, where a crucial battle for the eight-hour day was then taking place.[8] Ezra Heywood put forward the rally's second new idea. Condemning monopoly interests for their thwarting of freedom, equal rights, and fair play, Heywood said that politics offered a remedy for labor's situation, but only if applied shrewdly. The workingmen of Connecticut had set an example in the recent state elections; because the Republicans had rejected their labor plank and the Democrats had accepted it, workers had given the Democratic party a majority in Connecticut's state house. Heywood declared: "The Republican Party of this state Massachusetts has turned its back upon our movement, and it is our duty to take notice of it; and when the next day of election comes off to be sure we support no man for office who does not support labor."[9] Again, as in his abolitionist days, disgust with Republican policies put Heywood in the position of de facto support for the Democrats.

The role of the middle-class reformers in the NLU grew steadily after the 1868 Congress, until by 1872 they completely controlled the organization. From 1869 on, the power base in the NLU shifted decisively from the elected officers, who were always wage-earners, to the Executive Committee, which included only one wage-earner. Heywood attended the Special Council of the NLU in the summer of 1868 and was a delegate to the New York Congress in September. In December 1868, he was listed as the Massachusetts member of the National Executive Committee of the NLU.[10]

The NLU declined during the 1870s, in part as a result of the depression of 1873–77, which had a chilling effect on all labor reform efforts. The NLU's commitment to reform through legislation was also a key factor; the political process co-opted many potential labor radicals. In addition, eight-hour laws enacted in several states proved to be worthless. Adequate enforcement mechanisms were lacking, and most workingmen were not prepared to accept the expansion of state activities that such measures would have entailed. In David Montgomery's view, another factor may have been the tendency of the middle-class reformers to try to utilize the NLU as "the springboard for rhapsodic and visionary political ventures."[11] Of course, employers' firm opposition to any labor reform was also a central factor. The NLU also foundered because Radical Republicans were not prepared to challenge the basis of inequality in American society. As David Montgomery states, "Radicalism was admirably suited for the task of erecting the equality of all citizens before the law, but beyond equality lay the insistence of labor's spokesmen that as the propertyless, as factors of production, wage earners were effectively denied meaningful participation in the Republic."[12]

Heywood did not rely exclusively on the NLU for his organizational expression. Throughout his radical career, he organized a variety of leagues dedicated to reform efforts. His first such undertaking was in Worcester, Massachusetts, in September 1867. A large group of workingmen filled Mechanics Hall for a meeting Heywood organized "in search of industrial equity." The assembled workers voted to accept resolutions supporting the eight-hour day, greenbackism, labor unions, and only candidates for electoral office who upheld labor's interest. The Worcester Labor Reform League emerged from this gathering. In a report to *The Workingman's Advocate* in June 1868, Heywood detailed the activities of the Worcester League: "We are now holding a series of meetings in an informal, social way, at private houses, conducted somewhat in the conversational style pursued by A. Bronson Alcott, the Concord seer, in his parlor gatherings for philosophical inquiries, famous in leading cities, from Boston to St. Louis. In this way artificial distinctions vanish, in that natural unity and equality most favorable to the reception of truth; and telling utterances are evoked from those having more to say than they can tell in public."[13] From Heywood's description, the league was dominated by middle-class reformers.

Deciding to expand to a regional framework, Heywood organized the New England Labor Reform League (NELRL) in 1869. He gathered together an organizing committee composed of Ira Steward and George McNeill of the Boston Eight-Hour League; Edward D. Linton, an old friend of Josiah Warren and soon to be secretary of Boston's Section 20 of the International Workingmen's Association; and Elizabeth LaPierre Daniels of the women's rights movement. The call to the organizing convention declared that with chattel slavery abolished and "the demand for impartial suffrage" for all "advancing irresistibly to general acceptance," the crucial issue facing Americans, involving the "welfare and destiny of human society, was the Labor question." All friends of honest industry and trade were asked to come to the meetings at the Tremont Temple in Boston, January 27 and 28, 1869. The convention would "explain and enforce the principles of the NLU" and organize the new league.[14]

The convention attracted quite a wide array of social reformers, including the Knights of St. Crispin (the shoeworkers' organization), eight-hour men, legislators, women's rights advocates, and veterans of the industrial congresses of the 1840s. A partial list of speakers included George McNeill, Ira Steward, Wendell Phillips and Stephen S. Foster, Elizabeth LaPierre Daniels, Josiah Warren, William Denton, S. P. Cummings, Dr. Dio Lewis, and many others. The gathering was so harmonious that everyone's ideas were incorporated into the program of the NELRL. The basic aim of the league was the establishment of a free society: "free contracts, free money, free markets, free transit, and free land." The means to achieve these ends were joining together "in associative effort" and engaging in "discussion, petition, remonstrance, and the ballot to establish these articles of faith as a common need, and a common right." Writing in *The Revolution*, Elizabeth LaPierre Daniels described the convention as a "glorious success."[15]

The harmony of the league was soon destroyed by the instability of Massachusetts' labor politics. The Knights of St. Crispin were embittered at the defeat of their application for a state charter. In order to mollify workingmen, the state legislature enacted the Eight-Hour League's proposal for a Bureau of Labor Statistics. The Crispins looked upon the bureau with distrust, seeing it at best as a substanceless effort to placate workers and at worst as an active enemy. However, the eight-hour men staffed the bureau, and the resulting antagonism carried over into the Labor Reform League.[16]

According to David Montgomery, "at its meeting in July, 1869, Heywood, supported by the Crispins, carefully planned the agenda so as to emphasize currency reform and relegate the whole eight-hour movement to a single speech by McNeill." However, *The American Workman* reported that the eight-hour men "made a mistake to suppose that the eight-hour question was not to have a fair chance, as was proved afterward, by the reading of the arrangements for the Convention, made by the Executive Committee of the League, and by the fact that the eight-hour question occupied a much larger portion of the time than any other." Writing in his journal, *Liberty*, the individualist anarchist Benjamin R. Tucker recalled that McNeill, Ira Steward, and several other "mischief-makers" had attempted to capture the league "by force of numbers, and commit it as a body to the support of the eight-hour movement." These interlopers, Tucker wrote, sought to compel league members either to leave or to accept doctrines in which they did not believe. The result of the disagreement was that the eight-hour men left the league, and the organization enjoyed close cooperation with the Crispins.[17] Although with the decline of the Knights of St. Crispin in the early 1870s, the wage-earner base of the Labor Reform League was eroded, the work of the league continued into the 1890s. Through most of the 1870s, it was one of Ezra Heywood's principal political outlets.

Heywood introduced Benjamin Tucker to labor reform, free love, and anarchism. Tucker, also a native of Massachusetts, worked with Heywood in the 1870s and then went off on his own. His journal, *Liberty* (1881–1908), which the historian Herbert Gutman called "this most important American philosophical anarchist magazine," was a forum for informed discussion of politics, sexuality, theories of social change, and the arts. Tucker translated and published Proudhon's massive *What*

Is Property?, and *Liberty* carried translations and articles from many of the most important thinkers of both Europe and America.[18] Sharp-witted, intelligent, and a keen observer of events, Tucker wrote with clarity and humor. A frequent contributor to *The Word*, he served as associate editor in 1875–76. In a handwritten autobiographical manuscript, Tucker left a long account of the Labor Reform League. His account provides a rare personal glimpse at the personalities and spirit behind the league, including Heywood.

Largely out of curiosity, the young Tucker, who had previously read reform papers and attended various reform meetings, entered Eliot Hall on Tremont Street in Boston on Sunday afternoon, June 30, 1872. Sitting well toward the front, he eagerly anticipated the beginning of the meeting. Heywood, the league secretary, made the opening remarks and presented a series of resolutions. In his firsthand description, Tucker found Heywood's speaking manner:

> very denunciatory in tone, and not of a character to convey to a newcomer a clear idea of the League's purposes, which were set forth in a much calmer and more orderly fashion in another set of resolutions offered by Edward D. Linton. Mr. Heywood's manner, on the other hand, was not at all violent. On the contrary, it was very attractive. He was a tall and rather lank New Englander, with a fine profile and a full blond beard and flowing hair. A little angular in his movements, his presence on the platform was easy and almost graceful. His delivery was slow and measured, but without hesitancy, and his appearance was that of a scholar and gentleman.

While Heywood was speaking, Tucker wrote that "my eyes fell on a simple old man seated two rows in front of me, whose Socratic features wore an expression of shrewdness and good humor. Suddenly, Mr. Heywood indicating this figure with a gesture, referred to the presence in the hall of Josiah Warren, notable for his forty years' pilgrimage through the wilderness of American transgressions. From that introduction dates the real beginning of my career."[19]

Tucker was sufficiently impressed with Sunday's proceedings to want to return on Monday. He provides an interesting account of Colonel William B. Greene, who helped found the league and co-authored with Heywood the league's *Declaration of Sentiments and Constitution* and also provided financial support for some of Heywood's projects. Greene fought during the Indian Wars in Florida and in the Fourteenth Massachusetts Infantry during the Civil War, and was subsequently often referred to as Colonel Greene. However, he progressively became more disenchanted with the military mindset. Greene had become a Unitarian minister in 1845, and was a strong advocate of free speech, women's rights, and labor reform. After living in Europe and befriending Pierre-Joseph Proudhon, Greene returned to the United States and was active in the abolitionist movement. By the time he met Heywood after the Civil War, Greene was a veteran reformer, and his advocacy of Proudhon's mutualism greatly influenced Heywood. Mutualism was a social and economic theory that held that the individual maximizes personal autonomy to the extent that he or she joins with others in various voluntary associations for specific ends.[20]

Before the opening of the Monday morning league session, Tucker wrote, "a man came walking down the aisle whose presence would have made him notable in any company. He was tall; of large frame, though not especially stout . . . about 65 years old. His hair, beard, and moustache were white and smoothly trimmed, and he had a very high forehead, a decisive mouth, and eyes that were twinkling as well as wonderfully piercing. He was strikingly handsome, and wore a black velvet coat that became him remarkably." For several years, Greene served as president of the league and chaired its meetings, for good reason, as Tucker related: "Col. Greene's courtly manner and polite banter always carried the day. Of the art of decision without offence he was a master. His light irony disarmed. One forgot the firmness of his chin under the charm of the twinkle in his eye."[21]

Tucker reported that Heywood prepared league resolutions the Saturday evening before a convention at Greene's home, which was "in the earlier years a fine house at Jamaica Plain (a Boston suburb), and in the later years a suite of rooms at the Parker House in Boston. The little gathering passed for a meeting of the executive committee, but the members were not summoned, those attending being Heywood and myself, sometimes accompanied by William Ben Wright [Tucker's friend and fellow lodger at that time]. We were treated sumptuously, but the chief treat was Col. Greene's conversation. Sometimes, for a few moments, his wife or daughter was present. The former had been Ann Shaw, known in her youth as 'the belle of Boston.' She belonged to an old family of abolitionists. To see the stately, but unassuming couple enter the Parker House restaurant, arm in arm, was a sight for the gods, who, however, did not monopolize it, for I sometimes enjoyed it myself."[22]

League meetings were wide-open affairs. Anyone who wished to speak would be heard, and resolutions were presented but neither accepted nor rejected. Tucker, recalling how this developed, wrote that the league's early meetings:

> had been conducted on the usual democratic plan, any resolutions that were presented being submitted to the vote of the audience present, regardless of membership. The method was soon found to be incautious

and disastrous. Eight-hour advocates and trade unionists attended in force; and introduced and passed resolutions not at all in keeping with the purposes of the League's founders. It became necessary, therefore, to adopt a new plan. The League existing for propagandism rather than political action, it was decided that resolutions should be offered for discussion only, and that no question should be put to vote. Resolutions were desirable for the reason that being carefully considered in advance and presented in the form of proof slips, they were generally given in full by the newspapers, while speeches suffered from condensation and misrepresentation. In the long run the new plan proved workable, but was very shocking at first to those accustomed to determining the truth or falsity of a proposition by a counting of noses.[23]

Always vigilant for the rights of the minority, Heywood explained that the league rejected the "majority swindle" and declined "to coerce the minority by votes." He welcomed all opponents of the league to the platform. Writing in the influential free-thought paper *The Index*, the individualist anarchist Sidney H. Morse found the league meetings in 1873 "extremely interesting." He thought that the absence of a vote contributed to a positive, evolutionary process of change. Morse wrote that after an issue had "received its many-sided presentation, it is remanded to the intelligence of each private mind. In this way it is hoped that a new and wiser public sentiment will in good time prevail." Not everyone agreed with this sentiment. Writing in *The Word* in 1874, John Gray of Boston stated that he enjoyed the last convention very much, but one "clownish fellow went on for ten minutes. The good of the Cause you advocate does not make it obligatory on your chairman to tolerate every clown who is propelled by no other motive that the inordinate vanity of his untutored mind to thrust his senseless balderdash on unwilling ears."[24]

Tucker recorded that Heywood "fixed the dates of the conventions, which invariably began on a Sunday." This was done as a direct, conscious affront to the church. Heywood's antipathy to the church dated back to his abolitionist years, when he and other Garrisonians had arraigned the church for failure to act against slavery. Now, he lambasted the church for failing to embrace labor reform. For example, at a NELRL convention in New Bedford, Massachusetts, he charged that the churches did not investigate labor reform and true religion, which were bound together in his mind. He declared that they were hired by the establishment and upheld official sin, the worst kind.[25] The New England Labor Reform League basically operated in the context of its conventions. It did not actively seek to organize workers into a specifically working-class organization or garner support for already existing labor groups.

The league seldom attempted to intervene directly in the public arena, although it did unsuccessfully introduce free banking resolutions into the Massachusetts legislature.

In 1871, in New York City, Heywood, in concert with key members of the NELRL, organized a national organization, the American Labor Reform League (ALRL). Its roster of personnel and range of activities were remarkably similar to those of the NELRL. The ALRL did have a heterogeneous nature that was reflected in its officers; William B. Greene was president, and vice presidents included John Orvis of the Sovereigns of Industry and Fourierist socialist Albert Brisbane. Elizabeth Cady Stanton, the individualist anarchist Stephen Pearl Andrews, free-love activist Victoria Woodhull, and the land reformers J. K. Ingalls, Lewis Masquerier, and Henry Beeney all held honorary posts.

Tucker maintained that the organizational forms of both the NELRL and the ALRL, which encompassed "formidable lists of vice presidents, secretaries, treasurer, and executive committee, were mere facade. . . . The two boards consisted largely of the same men and women, distributed in a different order. There was no sham about it, since all the officers authorized the use of their names; but, in reality, so far as activity and management were concerned, the secretary, Ezra H. Heywood, was 'the whole show.' " Tucker claimed that all the pretense involved in the show of organization "may not have been unpardonable, since it was necessary to the securing of a hearing. Thus heralded, a convention drew an audience that a single name, unless that of a great celebrity, would have failed to attract, and apparently few felt defrauded, since many came again."[26]

Heywood believed in setting up voluntary organizations established to promote ideas held by like-minded individuals. The many leagues he helped initiate were modelled after the old antislavery societies. Persuasion by means of the written word and speeches and debates at the frequent conventions were his chief weapons in the struggle to change society. Heywood maintained that social change would result from men and women thinking in new ways; hence, he emphasized debate and the promotion of ideas rather than an explicitly activist program geared to the attainment of certain specific ends. Assessing the New England Labor Reform League in the pages of *Liberty*, Tucker observed: "The League was founded by a little body of earnest men and women interested in the labor movement, for the purpose of holding conventions for its public and free discussion. Most of them had definite convictions of their own, but no one in joining the League was committed to any belief. The purpose was not to vote principles or measures down or up; but to compare and study them in the interests of truth and justice."[27]

Heywood lived in the industrial city of Worcester, Massachusetts, from 1865 until 1871, when he moved back to his nearby hometown of Princeton. There he launched his own newspaper, *The Word*, published from 1872 until 1893, and his own publishing venture, the Co-Operative Publishing Company. These two projects provided Heywood with the means to express his individualist anarchist politics, with its emphasis on the values of Jefferson and the Transcendentalists, to a national audience.

Heywood began publication of *The Word* in May 1872. The paper, a four-page broadsheet issued monthly, was dedicated to basic economic change and individual freedom. The prospectus stated:

> *The Word* favors the abolition of speculative income, of woman's slavery, and war government; regards all claims to property not founded in a labor title as morally void, and asserts the free use of land to be the inalienable privilege of every human being—on having the right to own or sell only his service impressed upon it. Not by restrictive methods, but through freedom and reciprocity, *The Word* seeks the extinction of interest, rent, dividends, and profit, except as they represent work done; the abolition of telegraphic, banking, trades-union, and other corporations charging more than actual cost for values furnished, and the repudiation of all so-called debts the principal whereof has been paid in the form of interest.

The Word regularly carried a section called "The Opposition," featuring writings of Heywood's critics. The paper usually carried articles by Heywood, his fellow anarchists, labor reformers, and free-lovers, as well as reports of reform conventions and notices of upcoming meetings. *The Word* also printed a lengthy, lively letters section where reformers of all shades of opinion expressed themselves. A greater proportion of items in *The Word* dealt with sexual reform as Heywood became more involved in this area after the mid-1870s. Heywood believed that by the mid-1870s, *The Word* was a "recognized fact in social reform," and although the paper was not yet self-supporting, he hoped to make it so, as well as to enlarge its format and issue it weekly.[28] Plans for expanding *The Word* existed for several years, but Heywood was never able to realize his goals because of his chronic indebtedness.

Heywood established the Co-Operative Publishing Company in order to publish his own works as well as those of other individualist anarchists and writers concerned with labor and sexual reform. Most of the booklets Heywood wrote were twenty-four pages long and sold for 15 cents. He wrote a series of booklets specifically on economic issues, as well as essays on suffrage, sexual reform, and temperance. Heywood distributed his newspaper and publications at lectures and conventions and through agents of his various reform leagues who travelled across the country. It is extremely difficult to gauge the influence of Heywood's writings on labor and economic issues. His writing style was scholarly, and it is possible that his prose, choice of vocabulary, and frequent, lengthy footnotes made him inaccessible to many. No doubt his writings on free love, which achieved much greater notoriety, had a far wider, although still limited, impact. The title pages of Heywood's booklets frequently noted a figure in the thousands that probably represented the amount in print; his home in Princeton was always stacked with boxes of unsold booklets.

Ezra Heywood based his notion of labor reform on individual freedom and the free market. Private monopolies and their chief accomplice, the state, were the principal roadblocks to the realization of his social vision: a society rooted in freedom of choice and personal responsibility, with cooperative enterprises based on voluntary association. Heywood condemned the great concentration of wealth in the hands of the few as another version of slavery. He declared: "What slave oligarchy was to republicanism,—that our profit-system is to legitimate enterprise."[29]

Heywood believed that each worker was entitled to the fruits of his or her own labor. He subscribed to Josiah Warren's doctrines that the cost of production of goods and services should be the sole determinant of price, and that each man, woman, and child should exercise sovereign control over personal time, labor, and property. Thus, the cost of goods and services would be set by each individual producer as a system of barter would be established. Warren suggested that each individual issue labor notes for his or her own work, and that these notes would supplant money. This program could only have worked in a small-scale social environment where mutual trust could be developed among a group of people. The laissez-faire philosophy of a natural and free society that Heywood advocated called for the elimination of all privileges, the equalization of all opportunities, and the freeing of human energies for the greatest mutual benefit of all society's members.[30]

Heywood vigorously condemned the terrible working and living conditions that the majority of American men and women faced. The founding document of the NELRL clearly articulated the social critique of the individualist anarchists. Their goal was the "abolition of class laws and false customs, whereby legitimate enterprise is defrauded by speculative monopoly," and the reconstruction of society on the basis of justice and reciprocity.[31] Echoing Proudhon, Heywood termed interest, rent, and profit to be varieties of thievery. He felt that the private accumulation of great concentrations of wealth could only be accomplished with the willful aid of the state and at the expense of individual autonomy.

Although Heywood defined labor reform as a revolt against class rule, his aim was not to destroy the capitalist system. Rather, he sought to free capitalism by restoring the law of supply and demand, which Heywood believed would naturally regulate society. Heywood often maintained that there was no natural conflict between labor and capital. Both Marxists and communist anarchists rejected this contention, arguing that capital had to be displaced forcefully in order for labor to assume its rightful position. Ezra Heywood was invoking the image of a rapidly vanishing America, a rural society of farms and small workshops. Because labor reform was an enterprise that concerned the rights and interests of all people in society, Heywood argued, then the movement was open to all who embraced its aims, including laborers and manufacturers.

Heywood defended the rights of working people and focused on their plight, yet he profoundly distrusted city dwellers. His Yankee heritage, rural upbringing and prejudice, and conservative social vision of restoring the nation to its finer, agrarian origins all combined to instill in Heywood a fear and contempt for recently arrived immigrants. Heywood argued that immigrant working people were degraded by intemperance, lust, and other vices. He warned that the finest expressions of civilization might be "undergulfed by a fiery tide of barbarism" unless "new principles and methods of order are speedily introduced."[32] This fear and lack of understanding of urban workers stands in sharp contrast to the collectivist anarchists of the late nineteenth and twentieth centuries, who lived and worked in urban centers. These activists developed schools, unions, cultural centers, and foreign-language newspapers that addressed the social reality of urban workers.

During Ezra Heywood's tenure with the NLU, he was torn between his individualist anarchist distrust for political action and his commitment to the general plan of action of the NLU. With the demise of the NLU, Heywood moved the NELRL away from conventional political activities on behalf of labor.[33]

In his 1877 booklet *Yours or Mine*, Heywood articulated a clear anarchist position. If labor reform were to succeed, the state must be destroyed because the state and private wealth reinforced each other at the expense of individual freedom. He declared: "If laws were not made, and enforced in the interests of theft, if the State were not one great embodiment of speculative piracy, Astor, Vanderbilt, and Stewart, would have to run for their lives, or cease to steal. Since legal sanction makes stealing popular, respectable and possible, the great anti-theft movement, known as labor reform, involves the abolition of the State."[34]

Ezra Heywood's deepening commitment to anarchism led to his eventual break with eight-hour activists. In his pamphlet *The Labor Party*, he warned that the achievement of the eight-hour day would not mean victory, but only a limited gain, one step in the long struggle to gain justice. He saw the campaign as a useful recruiting device with which to involve people in the general labor reform effort. Caught in a contradictory stance in the late 1860s, Heywood called for eight-hour legislation while simultaneously arguing for free contracts and strict limits on government. By the early 1870s, however, Heywood had developed a sharp critique of the eight-hour movement. He warned that he was not apologizing for the real evils of the factory system or taking the employers' side. He contended that workers had the right to determine their own hours and to strike, if necessary, for a reduction in hours. Heywood could envision a reduction of the work day to six, or even four, hours as a result of unmediated direct action by working people. What Heywood resolutely opposed was any governmental regulation, which he saw as interference with natural society.[35]

Heywood also changed his views on trade unionism and greenbackism. A supporter of trade unionism while active in the NLU, Heywood declared in a debate at an NELRL meeting in 1871 that "trades societies as now organized, are monopolies." Advising workingmen that he was criticizing "in a spirit of friendship," he stated: "If there is any right sacred, it is the right to acquire knowledge, and especially mechanical knowledge, because that is one great means of providing the necessaries of life. Trades unions . . . are a hindrance to the spread of knowledge." Heywood declared in *The Labor Party* that trade unions, eight-hour associations, and cooperative societies are "necessary steps toward right, but not its enactment." Arguing that workers should be free to negotiate their own terms regarding hours, wages, apprentice programs, and the like, Heywood opposed what he saw as these organizations' attempts at monopolizing workers and dictating working conditions. Heywood had backed the greenback solution when it was advanced by the NLU. However, by the mid-1870s, Heywood had come to reject what he termed "the greenback delusion," which sought to base currency "on the property of the nation, which has no property to speak of, and would use the American people's property without their consent."[36]

In addition to the individualist anarchism of Ezra Heywood and his associates, another group of nineteenth-century anarchists in the United States, foreign-born radicals and some native Americans with a collectivist orientation, played a far more significant role in working-class agitation. In the 1880s, according to the historian Paul Avrich, "anarchism became a distinct power within American labor, particularly within the German speaking segment." These activists initiated their own organization, the International Working People's Association, as well as newspapers, cultural activities, and tumultuous street demonstrations. The centers of the movement were major industrial cities with large working-class, immigrant populations including New York, Philadelphia, Chicago, and St. Louis.[37]

Most of these urban laborers called themselves social revolutionaries. They had first been involved in socialist agitation, but had become disenchanted with this approach. Committed to issues of class struggle, they continued to think of themselves as socialists, but, Avrich writes, "socialists of a distinctive type, anti-statist, anti-parliamentarian, and anti-reformist. . . ."[38] In contrast, the individualist anarchists celebrated the yeoman farmer and the artisan. Still, these groups had certain ideas in common. The social revolutionaries shared with the individualists a concern for individual liberty, a belief in free association, and the conviction that society would change only when individuals had transformed themselves. Both groups opposed the state and private monopolies and also sought a decentralized society.

However, there were serious disagreements. In 1883, the social revolutionaries combined anarchism and revolutionary unionism in their enunciation of the "Chicago idea," so named because it was elaborated by the Chicago anarchist, working-class leaders Albert Parsons and August Spies. Parsons, a leading social revolutionary and in 1886 one of the eight Haymarket defendants, called the union "the embryonic group of the future 'free society.'" The social revolutionaries sought an anarchist society where industry would be organized for the public good. The individualists refused to accept the notion that social cooperation and respect for the individual could be equal components in a radical program, fearing the loss of individual freedom. They did not support the forcible redistribution of wealth and property and were hostile to large-scale organizations. Most eschewed the language of class struggle and any advocacy of violence. The anarchists were able to agree among themselves that if the state socialist system of Karl Marx were adopted, it would end, in the words of Benjamin Tucker, in a "state religion, to the expense of which all must contribute, and at the altar of which all must kneel."[39]

The distinctions between the individualists and the social revolutionaries, and especially between socialism and anarchism, were not sharply defined in the nineteenth century. Although the term *anarchism* was neither common nor clearly defined in Heywood's time, there is no doubt that Heywood considered himself an anarchist. In later years, he asserted that his address "Ideas vs. Institutions," which he had delivered before Theodore Parker's Society in 1862, pronounced anarchist beliefs that he then developed for the remainder of his career. Heywood declared that individualist anarchism was rooted in the American democratic tradition: "Democracy, as taught by Paine, Jefferson, Franklin and Adams, collective order that recognizes and *guarantees* Personal Liberty, this is Anarchy, natural order, fruitful association, private and public felicity." The individualists rooted their anarchism in the natural rights philosophy of freedom and individual liberty of their revolutionary ancestors. Like the social revolutionaries, Heywood at different times referred to himself as an anarchist and a socialist. The term *socialism* was often used in this period as a generic word for radicalism. Different activists used it to describe their own activities. Thus, Heywood offered classes in socialism that focused on his particular concerns, labor reform and free love. Socialism, for Heywood, respected the claims of all and invaded no one's rights.[40]

Of all the individualist anarchists, Heywood was most willing to support a broad range of radical groups. In 1872, he praised the International Workingmen's Association, founded by Marx and Michael Bakunin, for preaching a new gospel proclaiming that "human beings have an inalienable right to life, to land, and the fruits of their industry." He hailed the organization's "tendency to obliterate national lines and abolish the most stupid and barbarous of virtues, patriotism." However, he warned, "It is not pleasant to see Dr. Marx and other leaders of this great and growing fraternity lean so strongly toward compulsory policies. . . . If the International would succeed it must be true to its bottom idea—voluntary association in behalf of our common humanity." In 1877, Heywood published a manifesto in *The Word* that was written by a group of nineteen imprisoned Italian anarchists. Claiming that their program was parallel to that of the NELRL, Heywood called their doctrines "the animating life of steadily growing numbers of conscientious people. . . ." However, he rejected their collectivist ideas. Instead, he proposed his Labor Reform League's "American method of liberty, which, banishing compulsive authority, proclaims *the inherent right of all citizens to be governed by the laws of nature* AS INTERPRETED BY THEMSELVES INDIVIDUALLY."[41] He hoped that collectivists, whether Marxist or anarchist, would come to see the necessity of basing radical action on individual sovereignty.

Heywood extended his support to the communist anarchists. He was the first person in the United States to print an English translation of Michael Bakunin's writing. Bakunin, perhaps the most noted figure in communist anarchist history, helped launch the First International with Karl Marx and inspired significant groups of followers in southern and eastern Europe as well as in the United States. Heywood also had warm words for Alexander Berkman, Emma Goldman's lover and a key figure in the communist anarchist movement in the United States. In 1892, Berkman attempted to assassinate the industrialist Henry C. Frick in retaliation for Frick's ordering assaults on striking workers and their families at the Carnegie steel works in Homestead, Pennsylvania. Heywood wrote that Berkman's twenty-two-year sentence was "retaliative vengeance such as slew Nat Turner and John Brown."[42]

In the 1880s, Heywood printed several of Johann Most's speeches and letters in *The Word*. The most notorious of the social revolutionaries and Emma Goldman's political mentor, Most was a dramatic, fiery speaker. He urged that "the war of the poor against the rich" was the only way exploited workers could free themselves from oppression. The workers were enslaved, he declared, and their only choice was to kill or be killed. Therefore, he called for "massacres of the people's enemies." Despite Most's oratory and the fact that he printed bomb-making instructions in his paper *Freiheit*, there is no evidence that he ever employed violence in his actions. Although convinced that violence would be necessary in toppling the ruling order, he insisted that tactics should not be confused with principles. He maintained that anarchism, calling for an end to compulsion and the establishment of freedom, was the very antithesis of violence. With the violence of the state and existing society eliminated, he felt, people would discover ways to live that did not institutionalize violence.[43]

Ezra Heywood and Benjamin Tucker differed in their views of Most. Heywood called Most "a modest, refined gentleman, in courage genuine intelligence and moral power few living men may match. . . ." Although Heywood was critical of Most's collectivist tendencies, he saw libertarian impulses in his vision of a cooperative, decentralist society. In a letter to *The Word*, Most was enthuiastic: "I rejoice that you have struck the right keynote in your resolutions branding as you do 'the present robber rule' and urge 'association to abolish government'. . . . Be anarchistic in philosophy; be aggressive in your propaganda, and the American Republic may yet become truly 'the home of the free, the land of the brave.' " Tucker intensely disliked the tone and substance of Most's pronouncements. An article in Tucker's *Liberty* stated that "it is perfectly true that the enforcement of Communism partakes of the nature of the State, and in espousing it Most proves himself at heart a Stateist." The anarchism that *Liberty* espoused totally rejected the "compulsory equality of Communism."[44]

The activities of the social revolutionaries culminated in a general strike for the eight-hour day in May 1886. The effort was based in Chicago, where the social revolutionaries had their greatest strength. At a rally in Chicago's Haymarket Square on May 4, a bomb was detonated in the middle of a police contingent. That explosion precipitated the first major red scare in American history. Eight leading anarchists were arrested, tried, and convicted, although the Chicago police never identified or brought the actual bomb-thrower to trial. Four of the men were executed; one committed suicide in his cell to prevent his execution; and three served lengthy prison terms.[45] Heywood visited the Haymarket anarchists in prison in Chicago and found them to be "noble men. . . guilty of serving Labor, Liberty, and Justice too well." Tucker supported them in their fight against authority. However, he called them "rash, but noble men," whose calls to arm working people were wrong and foolish. Tucker thought that they were mistaken to believe that dynamite had become a panacea for social ills.[46]

A critical issue that divided Heywood from Tucker and other individualists was his willingness to offer substantial support for the revolutionary violence, or at least the violent rhetoric, of the social revolutionaries. For example, Heywood proclaimed in 1885, "The issue is Right or dynamite." Although still professing a belief in conquering evil by good, clearly Heywood had altered his pacifism considerably.[47]

Heywood changed his thinking during the 1870s. The first major public indication was a clash with Josiah Warren, Heywood's mentor. The aging Warren had moved to Princeton in 1873 to live with Heywood. There he wrote and printed his last work, Part 3 of the *True Civilization* series. According to his biographer William Bailie, "at Princeton typography occupied part of the veteran's time, while his leisure was frequently beguiled by music. He sang and performed on the violin for the entertainment of his friends." Warren spent his last months at the home of Edward Linton, a colleague of Heywood's, and died there in 1874.[48]

While in Princeton, Warren became disturbed with the tenor of Heywood's labor reform politics and expressed his disagreements in a long letter. Warren criticized Heywood's "wholesale denunciation of ordinary businessman as 'thieves and robbers' because they live on profits." Heywood, Warren felt, was alienating "many of the best of men" who "might gladly assist in the saving revolution required." Warren questioned how Heywood would accomplish the restoration of "all existing wealth to its proper owners" without resorting to violence. Warren exclaimed: "This, coming from an Anti-war-under-any-circumstances-man, defies all rational criticism."[49] Although Heywood, like Warren, opposed violent social change, Warren's criticism had a degree of accuracy. In *The Word* and on the Labor Reform League platform, Heywood had been projecting a militant, confrontational stance that Warren felt was unwise.

Heywood's militancy deepened with the coming of the Panic of 1873 and subsequent depression of 1873–77, which took a heavy toll on the lives of many working people. As Heywood grew increasingly impatient and angry at circumstances he could not control, his rhetoric became more belligerent. For example, at an ALRL meeting in New York in May 1874, Heywood denounced the leading bank and railroad magnates as "financial swindlers. . . , backed by chronic mobs called governments." Working people, Heywood advised, must do their own thinking because they would "not get the truth from pulpit, press, or other paid advocates of their enemies." In the winter of 1877, Heywood asked a rhetorical question in an editorial in *The Word* about the recently deceased Cornelius Vanderbilt, the millionaire railroad magnate. Why, Heywood asked, did the president of a railroad get so much more money than an engineer or a brakeman? The answer, he felt, was that Vanderbilt's facilities to steal were greater than those of the more honest, useful employees of the road.[50]

The year 1877 was the worst of the depression and the year that witnessed the most intense conflict between working people and their employers, who were backed by the state. Ezra Heywood expressed his views on these conflicts in a booklet entitled *The Great Strike*, which was originally published as an article in Benjamin Tucker's short-lived journal *The Radical Review* in November 1877, and then reissued in an expanded form by the Co-Operative Publishing Company in 1878. Heywood wrote *The Great Strike* specifically in response to the events of the summer of 1877. A pay cut on the Baltimore and Ohio Railroad provoked a work stoppage at Martinsburg, West Virginia. Because wage rates on all the major lines had been cut considerably during the previous three years, the strike spread rapidly and spontaneously to nearly every important rail center in the country. Local militia units were called out to move the trains, but these efforts failed. Often, these forces refused to carry out orders and instead fraternized with citizens. The efforts that they did make were blocked by large crowds composed of strikers and many others in community after community. The strike included much violent conflict; in Pittsburgh, soldiers fired on a demonstration, killing twenty and leaving many wounded. The movement became much more than a railroad strike, as general strikes developed in several locations. The federal government and railroad owners viewed the unreliability of local militias as a serious problem. The railroads came to rely on the use of thousands of federal troops, working away from their home areas, and special police forces to finally break the back of this first mass strike in American history. In the strike's aftermath, the federal government established the system of armories and national guard service precisely to deal with the problematic nature of local militias.[51]

In *The Great Strike*, Heywood stated in the strongest language he had yet used that capital and labor were implacable foes. He wrote that between "capital and labor there can be no truce and no compromise. . . ." Heywood argued that "capital at every point was the aggressor" in the 1877 strike. The employers and their governmental accomplices who suppressed the strike "represented the existing financial, commercial and political power of the strong to plunder the weak. In siding with capital against labor in such an issue, government reveals its own despotic, felonious character." In contrast, the strikers were simply asserting their "natural rights to live by their labor, and a just claim to ownership in, at least, a part of their earnings." These workers were upholding the proper "claims of labor and also the morally defensible rights of property."[52]

Ezra Heywood significantly qualified his pacifism in *The Great Strike*. He drew a qualitative distinction between the violence of the oppressor and the violence of the oppressed. Heywood termed the strikers lawful belligerents engaged in justifiable defensive action to protect their natural rights. He wrote: "Personally a non-resistant, I would not take another's life to save my own. . . . But as our sympathies are with the Colonial right to self-government against British invasion, with slaves against masters, so impartial observers recognize the Pittsburgh strikers as morally lawful belligerents, and concede to them all the rights of defensive warfare."[53]

Heywood drew two major lessons from the strike. First, he stated that "property held to the injury of others thereby becomes contraband in the war of capital on labor, as in other wars." Second, he rejoiced that a significant number of militia refused to fire on people during the strike. He praised the *"Non-Resistant Soldier"* and asserted that "it is not only the privilege, but the duty, of soldiers to decline to support capital against right."[54]

Ezra Heywood was coming to a clearer understanding of the depth of workers' frustrations and anger that often led to violence. His analysis of the 1877 conflict closely paralleled that of Albert Parsons. Both stressed the subservience of the press to capital, the active cooperation of government with capital, and the parallel between chattel and wage slavery. Viewing the lessons to be learned from the strike as momentous, Heywood made extensive lecture plans. His projected lecture topics for the fall and winter of 1877–78 included "The Great Strike: Its Relations to

Labor, Property, Government" and "Nonresistant Soldiers; or, The New Order, Which Refusing to Fire on the Strikers, Heralds." In *The Word* of January 1878, Heywood deplored the fact that the "July strikers" were being tried "singly and in lots . . . by courts which administer fraud and oppression in behalf of capital." However, Heywood's plans were interrupted: "Just as we were planning a lecture campaign in Pennsylvania cities, and other insurgent cities on the Great Strike, we were restrained of our liberty by religio-sensual despotism."[55] Following his arrest for free-love advocacy, Heywood would decide to dramatically alter the priorities of his reform agenda.

The individualist anarchists as a group did not have a major impact on American workers. Most were middle-class reformers who did not labor in the factories of the growing American cities. Language barriers and cultural differences further separated the individualists from many working people. The individualist anarchists were farmers, lawyers, editors, and small manufacturers who often lived in small towns or rural areas. They envisioned a society based on the Jeffersonian model of independent farmers and artisans.

Heywood and his colleagues feared the consequences of urban industrialization. They blamed greedy capitalists for the oppressive working and living conditions many working people faced, but they also deplored what they saw as the dangerous, uncontrollable urges of working people themselves. They felt that the seething masses in the cities, who drank excessively, brawled among themselves, and overindulged in sex, could quite possibly revolt in cataclysmic violence that would not only overturn the injustices of capitalism but also threaten civilization. Although Heywood believed in the need to overhaul the capitalist order, he also thought it essential for working people to drastically alter their behavior and develop a more self-regulated lifestyle.

Despite these antagonistic attitudes, a significant part of Heywood's thinking echoed deeply held working-class ideas regarding artisan republicanism. Heywood believed that a worker possessed natural rights, including the right to be independent, to be industrious, and to control what he or she produced. These rights were increasingly under attack. Under these circumstances, workers had a natural right to self-defense. Workers, Heywood argued, who fought for their social and economic rights were merely upholding their absolutely legitimate claim to property and the fruits of their own labor.

Artisan republicanism was a widespread, popular concept among American workers throughout the nineteenth century. The historian Sean Wilentz writes that for working-class artisan republicans, equality connoted "the right of all independent, virtuous citizens—including the artisans—to exercise their will without interference from a nobility of privilege, wealth, or title. . . ." Workers reasoned, according to Wilentz, that if property was in fact sacred, then bosses were guilty of theft because they exploited the labor of their employees. Working people articulating artisan republicanism, like Heywood, were addressing the same fundamental question: "Did metropolitan industrialization and the transformation of wage labor into a commodity enhance the independence and mutuality of the Republic itself?"[56]

Indeed, Ezra Heywood's labor reform ideas were well known among Crispins and many NLU activists. Middle-class reformers influential and active in labor circles, including former abolitionists, spiritualists, and women's rights advocates, were familiar with Heywood's ideas. Samuel Gompers and the American Federation of Labor espoused a philosophy of "voluntarism." Gompers argued that unions should never "seek at the hands of government what they could accomplish by their own initiative and activities." Voluntarism, the historian James Green writes, reflected a "desire to keep workers dependent on the unions, rather than the government, for the regulation of wages and hours, the provision of social insurance, and so on." Yehoshua Arieli and other historians make the arguable claim that the labor reform philosophy of the individualist anarchists had a significant impact on working-class movements in nineteenth-century America.[57]

Still, Ezra Heywood's vision of labor reform did not adequately address the growing urbanization, industrialization, and concentration in American life. More and more, society was being divided into distinct, hostile social classes, and Heywood's approach was inadequate to meet this challenge. Heywood's economic program was based on an implicit ethical assumption that human beings were inherently honest and capable of cooperation. From his abolitionist training, Heywood retained the perfectionist notion that people's capacity for development and improvement was infinite. The common denominator of human integrity, Heywood argued, would thrive under conditions of freedom. With a soil composed of freedom and independence, Heywood believed, a self-regulated society based on voluntary cooperation would flourish.

David Montgomery argues that "passionately, vainly," Heywood and other labor reformers were "attempting to impart to the emerging industrial order some values other than purely commercial ones, to impose moral order on the market economy."[58] Heywood and his fellow individualist anarchists looked back in history to an earlier, less complicated, society in which face-to-face exchanges could facilitate social agreement about the nature of honest versus exploitative economic activity. They hoped for a nation wherein capital and labor might cooperate freely in a land of abundant, unlimited wealth. The individualist anarchists sustained the optimistic spirit of progress embodied in perfectionism. With hard work and the absence of restrictions, they believed, each individual could achieve prosperity and happiness. The attempt of the individualist anarchists to impose a moral sensibility on American industrial capitalism may have been unrealistic. However, their dedication to social justice was a firm ethical position, based on enduring values rooted in the American Revolution, which pitted them against the rich and powerful.

NOTES

1. For detailed treatment of the individualist anarchists, see James J. Martin, *Men Against the State: The Expositors of Individualist Anarchism in America, 1827–1908* (Colorado Springs: Ralph Myles Publisher, 1970); William O. Reichert, *Partisans of Freedom: A Study in American Anarchism* (Bowling Green, Ohio: Bowling Green University Popular Press, 1976); Rudolf Rocker, *Pioneers of American Freedom* (Los Angeles: Rocker Publications Committee, 1949).

2. David Montgomery, *Beyond Equality: Labor and the Radical Republicans, 1862–1872* (Urbana: University of Illinois Press, 1981), pp. 123–24.

3. Montgomery, *Beyond Equality*, pp. 26–31; Milton Meltzer, *Bread and Roses: The Struggle of American Labor, 1865–1915* (New York: Random House, 1973), pp. 4–5; *The Awl* cited in Norman Ware, *The Industrial Worker, 1840–1860* (New York: Quadrangle Books, 1964), p. xvi.

4. Montgomery, *Beyond Equality*, pp. 113, 140.

5. Ibid., pp. 170, 176–77; Walter T. K. Nugent, "Money, Politics, and Society: The Currency Question," in *The Gilded Age*, ed. H. Wayne Morgan (Syracuse, N.Y.: Syracuse University Press, 1970), pp. 119–20, 126.

6. "A Speech by Ezra H. Heywood—President of Labor Reform League, Worcester—Emancipation of Labor—Delivered at Biddeford, Maine, Monday Evening, August 31, 1868," four-page sheet, Manuscripts, American Antiquarian Society, Worcester, Mass.

7. Montgomery, *Beyond Equality*, pp. 265–66 and 272–75; James R. Green and Hugh Carter Donahue, *Boston's Workers: A Labor History* (Boston: Boston Public Library, 1979), pp. 50–51; *Daily Evening Voice*, October 12, 1866, p. 3.

8. Montgomery, *Beyond Equality*, pp. 294–95.

9. *Daily Evening Voice*, May 16, 1867, p. 2.

10. Montgomery, *Beyond Equality*, pp. 400–1; Martin, *Men Against the State*, p. 106; *Workingman's Advocate*, January 16, 1869, p. 3.

11. Montgomery, *Beyond Equality*, p. 397.

12. Ibid., p. 446.

13. Ezra Heywood, editor's preface, William B. Greene, *Mutual Banking: Showing the Radical Deficiency of the Present Circulating Medium and the Advantage of*

a Free Currency (Worcester, Mass.: New England Labor Reform League, 1870), p. 1; *Workingman's Advocate,* October 12, 1867, p. 3; June 20, 1868, p. 2.

14. Montgomery, *Beyond Equality,* pp. 412–13; Bailie, *Josiah Warren,* p. 97; *The Revolution,* January 7, 1869, p. 10; the same text announcing the convention appeared in *The Workingman's Advocate,* January 16, 1869, p. 3.

15. *The Revolution,* January 21, 1869, p. 33. Later in the year the May meetings featured a similarly wide range of speakers, including the anarchist Lysander Spooner, Ralph Waldo Emerson, A. Bronson Alcott, John Orvis, Benjamin Butler, Julia Ward Howe, and several others (*Workingman's Advocate,* May 22, 1869, p. 2); Montgomery, *Beyond Equality,* p. 413; Ezra Heywood and William B. Greene, *Declaration of Sentiments and Constitution of the New England Labor Reform League* (Boston: Weekly American Workman, 1869), p. 6; *The Revolution,* February 11, 1869, p. 84.

16. Montgomery, *Beyond Equality,* p. 413.

17. Ibid.; *American Workman,* July 3, 1869, p. 4; *Liberty,* December 12, 1885, p. 1.

18. For information on Tucker, see Reichert, *Partisans of Freedom,* pp. 141–70; Martin, *Men Against the State;* Herbert Gutman, introduction to *Liberty* (Westport, Conn.: Greenwood Press, 1970); Martin Blatt, "Ezra Heywood and Benjamin Tucker" in *Benjamin R. Tucker and the Champions of "Liberty",* ed. Michael Coughlin, Charles Hamilton, and Mark Sullivan (St. Paul, Minn.: Michael Coughlin, Publisher, 1987).

19. "The Life of Benjamin R. Tucker—Disclosed by Himself in the Principality of Monaco at the Age of 74," handwritten manuscript, pp. 75–84, Benjamin R. Tucker Papers, Rare Books and Manuscripts Division, The New York Public Library, Astor, Lenox and Tilden Foundations.

20. For details on Greene, see Martin, *Men Against the State,* pp. 125–38; Reichert, *Partisans of Freedom,* pp. 100–16.

21. "The Life of Benjamin R. Tucker," pp. 86, 88.

22. Ibid., p. 89.

23. Ibid., pp. 86–87.

24. *The Word,* December 1873, p. 2; *The Index,* June 21, 1873, p. 246; *The Word,* October 1874, p. 3.

25. "The Life of Benjamin R. Tucker," p. 89; *The Word,* December 1873, p. 4.

26. Ibid., June 1872, p. 1; "The Life of Benjamin R. Tucker," pp. 88–89.

27. *Liberty,* December 12, 1885, p. 1.

28. *The Word,* May 1872, p. 1; March 1874, p. 2.

29. Ezra Heywood, *Yours or Mine: An Essay to Show the True Basis of Property and the Causes of Its Inequitable Distribution* (Princeton, Mass.: Co-Operative Publishing, 1877), p. 20.

30. Yehoshua Arieli, *Individualism and Nationalism in American Ideology* (Cambridge: Harvard University Press, 1964), p. 117.

31. Heywood and Greene, *Declaration of Sentiments,* p. 7.

32. Ezra Heywood, *The Labor Party* (New York: Journeymen Printers' Co-Operative Association, 1868), p. 12.

33. Martin, *Men Against the State*, p. 108.

34. Heywood, *Yours or Mine*, p. 23.

35. Heywood, *The Labor Party*, p. 12; *The Word*, June 1877, p. 2.

36. *Workingman's Advocate*, May 27, 1871, p. 1; Heywood, *The Labor Party*, p. 12; *The Word*, March 1876, p. 2.

37. Paul Avrich, *The Haymarket Tragedy* (Princeton: Princeton University Press, 1984), pp. 79, 84.

38. Avrich, *The Haymarket Tragedy*, p. 55.

39. Ibid., pp. 72–73, 89; Benjamin R. Tucker, *State Socialism and Anarchism and Other Essays*, ed. James J. Martin (Colorado Springs: Ralph Myles Publisher, 1972), p. 15.

40. Charles Shively, "Introduction," in Stephen Pearl Andrews, *The Science of Society* (Weston, Mass.: M and S Press, 1970), p. 21; *Lucifer*, April 3, 1891, p. 3; *The Word*, February 1880, p. 2.

41. *The Word*, May 1872, p. 3; July 1877, p. 2.

42. Bakunin's article "Gospel of Nihilism" appeared in *The Word*, April 1880, p. 1. I am grateful to Paul Avrich for indicating to me that Heywood was the first publisher of Bakunin in English in the United States. For information on Bakunin, see *Bakunin on Anarchy*, ed. Sam Dolgoff (New York: Vintage Books, 1972). See also Dolgoff's revised collection, *Bakunin on Anarchism* (Montreal: Black Rose Books, 1980); *The Word*, January 1893, p. 2.

43. Reichert, *Partisans of Freedom*, pp. 376–78.

44. *The Word*, December 1887, p. 2; February 1888, p. 3; *Liberty*, July 20, 1889, p. 5.

45. For the most complete account of the Haymarket episode, see Avrich, *The Haymarket Tragedy*. See also David Roediger and Franklin Rosemont, *Haymarket Scrapbook* (Chicago: Charles H. Kerr, 1986), which contains my essay "Ezra Heywood and the Chicago Martyrs."

46. *The Word*, April 1887, p. 2; Avrich, *The Haymarket Tragedy*, pp. 311, 166.

47. *The Word*, February 1885, p. 2; June 1881, p. 2.

48. William Bailie, *Josiah Warren: The First American Anarchist* (Boston: Small, Maynard, 1906), p. 97.

49. Warren's letter appeared in *The Word*, September 1873, p. 3. It was also printed as "Letter to Ezra H. Heywood," four typeset pages, Josiah Warren Papers, Labadie Collection, University of Michigan, Ann Arbor. In *Josiah Warren*, pp. 127–35, Bailie includes it as an Appendix and labels it "letter to a friend," but it is basically the same letter cited above.

50. *The Word*, June 1874, p. 1; February 1877, p. 2.

51. For details on the strike of 1877, see the following: Robert V. Bruce, *1877: Year of Violence* (Indianapolis: Bobbs-Merrill, 1959); Jeremy Brecher, *Strike!* (San Francisco: Straight Arrow Books, 1972), pp. 1–24; Howard Zinn, *A People's History of the United States* (New York: Harper and Row, 1980), pp. 240–46; Meltzer, *Bread and Roses*, pp. 85–94.

52. Ezra Heywood, *The Great Strike: Its Relations to Labor, Property, and Government* (Princeton, Mass.: Co-Operative Publishing, 1878), pp. 4, 14, 11.

53. Heywood, *The Great Strike*, p. 13.

66 *Free Love and Anarchism*

54. Ibid., p. 20; for an example of local officials aiding strikers before 1877, see "Trouble on the Railroads in 1873–74: Prelude to the 1877 Crisis" in *Work, Culture and Society in Industrializing America*, ed. Herbert Gutman (New York: Vintage Books, 1977), pp. 259–320.

55. Avrich, *The Haymarket Tragedy*, p. 37; *The Word*, September 1877, p. 2; January 1878, p. 2.

56. Sean Wilentz, *Chants Democratic: New York City and the Rise of the American Working Class, 1788–1850* (New York: Oxford University Press, 1984), pp. 93, 242, 388.

57. James Green, *The World of the Worker: Labor in Twentieth-Century America* (New York: Hill and Wang, 1980), p. 48; In his book *Individualism and Nationalism in American Ideology*, Arieli claims (pp. 295–96) that Heywood and the NELRL were instrumental in disseminating Josiah Warren's anarchist views directly to the American labor movement. Lillian Symes and Travers Clement in *Rebel America: The Story of Social Revolt in the United States* (1934, reprint, Boston: Beacon Press, 1972), pp. 79–80, argue that the theoreticians of greenbackism were strongly influenced by the anarchism of Josiah Warren. Ronald Creagh, a French historian at the University of Montpellier, has argued that anarchist ideas influenced the Knights of Labor. When the Knights adopted the preamble and platform of the Industrial Brotherhood, Creagh points out, they made particular changes manifesting an anarchist sensibility. For example, instead of the phrase "the blessings of the government bequeathed to us by the founders of the republic," they substituted "the blessings of life." See Norman J. Ware, *The Labor Movement in the United States, 1860–1890* (1929, reprint, New York: Vintage Books, 1964), p. 377. More research is needed to establish the role and influence of anarchism, both individualist and collectivist, in the labor movement, a topic that has been neglected by historians. See Paul Buhle, "Anarchism and American Labor," *International Labor and Working Class History* no. 23 (Spring 1983): 21–24.

58. Montgomery, *Beyond Equality*, p. 445.

Ezra Heywood, ca. 1860 (Labadie Collection)

Ezra Heywood, ca. 1878 (Labadie Collection)

Angela Heywood, 1880 (Labadie Collection)

Hermes Heywood, 1880 (Labadie Collection)

Josephine S. Tilton, 1878 (New York Public Library)

Lucy M. Tilton, Angela
Heywood's mother, 1875
(New York Public Library)

A. H. Simpson and J. Flora Tilton, 1910
(New York Public Library)

Laura Kendrick (New York Public Library)

William B. Greene (Labadie Collection)

Benjamin R. Tucker, ca. 1887 (Labadie Collection)

Moses Harman (From Victor Robinson, *Pioneers of Birth Control in England and America*. New York: Voluntary Parenthood League, 1919)

Dr. E. B. Foote, Sr. (From Robinson, *Pioneers of Birth Control*)

Dr. E. B. Foote, Jr. (From Robinson, *Pioneers of Birth Control*)

Pamphlets by Ezra Heywood (Brown University)

Josiah Warren (From William Bailie, *Josiah Warren: The First American Anarchist.* Boston: Small, Maynard, 1906)

Stephen Pearl Andrews (From Stephen Pearl Andrews, *The Science of Society*, ed. Charles Shively. Weston, Mass.: M & S Press, 1970)

Anthony Comstock (From Heywood Broun and Margaret Leech, *Anthony Comstock: Roundsman of the Lord*. New York: Albert and Charles Boni, 1927)

Victoria C. Woodhull, ca. 1873 (From Emanie Sachs, *"The Terrible Siren": Victoria Woodhull*. New York: Harper and Brothers, 1928)

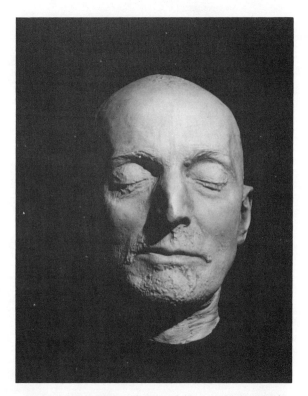

Death Mask of Ezra Heywood (Brown University)

CHAPTER 4

———⪻◉⪼———

THE REFORMING IMPULSE

E zra Heywood believed that the world could be perfected, a conviction he carried with him from his abolitionist days; he also believed that the millennium would be achieved only with a lot of hard work on several fronts. Therefore, labor reform was one of several reform efforts Heywood pursued. The historian Hal Sears argues that the three great "infidelisms" of this period were mutually supporting: feminism, the infidelity to male supremacy; spiritualism, the direct communication with the spirit world; and free love, the infidelity to the social institution of marriage. In an apt description of Heywood, Sears writes, "A true social radical of the time often worked simultaneously for all three causes, and, perhaps, leavened the mixture with abolition, phrenology, and hydropathy."[1]

For most of his radical career, Ezra Heywood had a partner in his efforts to change the world. Heywood had moved to Worcester because of his love for the abolitionist Angela Tilton, a Worcester native. They married on June 5, 1865, at the Old South Church in Boston. Writing in 1877, Heywood confided that if he could retrace his steps, he would have "tread underfoot the forms of repression," namely, marriage. In marrying, he claimed not to endorse the institution; rather, he felt compelled to marry just as he was forced to endure the invasiveness of taxes.[2] At any rate, Ezra and Angela Heywood together shared a commitment to spiritualism, labor reform, free love, and a host of reform issues.

Angela Heywood was raised in a radical household. Her mother, Lucy M. Tilton, was an abolitionist, labor reformer, and free-love advocate. Lucy N. Colman, herself a veteran reformer, in 1892 attended the eighty-fifth birthday party of her long-time friend, Lucy Tilton. She described the party as a gathering of reformers "of every shade of thinking. . . labor reformers, Anarchists, Nationalists, and Socialists, all earnest thinkers and doers, as they understand duty." Angela's two sisters, Flora and Josephine, also radical activists, hosted the party. Colman wrote that she was welcomed by these "excellent and heroic women, as though I were indeed their mother."[3]

Angela Heywood wrote that her parents operated a large, fine farm that was, however, "slowly devoured by usury, assisted by hostile fire, grim death and taxes." She related that her parents did not have wealth to bequeath, and "poverty afterwards looked us point-blank in the face." The scanty evidence available indicates that Lucy Tilton was a widow for most of her life. Her entry in daughter Josephine's autograph book indicated that she thrived on hard work: "Work has been and is my Salvation." In the words of Stephen Pearl Andrews, she was "what the world would call a fanatical opponent of books, literature, schools, intellectual culture, and what the world deems the higher enlightenment of education." However, Mrs. Tilton, despite her hatred for "the learned and their paraphernalia of books and bookishness . . . with an admirable inconsistency, reads everything and keeps up with the times." Andrews called Tilton "an apostle . . . of persistent, useful, skilled labor, and a model teacher of every part and parcel of female industry in the family, which she has faithfully taught her daughters. Born into the consciousness of being a person of more than ordinary native powers, and being deprived by conditions from acquiring book-learning in any large way, the supercilious assumption of superiority by the literary aristocracy burnt into her soul, until she came to hate the learned class as a set of snobs and tyrants, to denounce and degrade whom, in comparison with the workers, is her special mission."[4]

In a letter from prison in 1892, Ezra Heywood described his mother-in-law as a "Grand Mother . . . a radical who taught and wrought anarchism long before the meek conservatives who now mouth the noble word were born. She says 'learned' men and 'refined' women who don't even know the names of their sex organs are so ineffably idiotic that she has to keep herself hid for disgust of them." In another letter, he recounted that Lucy Tilton was a student of sexual issues from girlhood and imparted this sense to her daughters. "When her children were young the family lived on a farm where a stallion was brought one day when a mare was coming there to be served. Mrs. Tilton arranged the chairs at the window for all her little ones to witness the spectacle, and stood beside them explaining carefully what had occurred. So you see that Mrs. Heywood and her sisters went to school young in these matters." Angela Heywood recalled that her mother "taught us little children from infancy to respect and study sex."[5] Throughout her long life, Lucy Tilton was a strong supporter of Ezra and Angela Heywood's reform efforts, serving as an officer of the New England Labor Reform League for many years.

Angela Tilton was born in Deerfield, New Hampshire, and raised on the farm of Daniel and Lucy Tilton until the farm failed. She spent some of her girlhood years working as a servant in the home of a clergyman. Like Ezra Heywood, as a young person she was a religious believer; she joined the church at the age of eighteen, starting prayer meetings and teaching Sunday school. Also like Heywood, the preachings of Garrison, Phillips, Parker, and other abolitionists converted her from the church to the antislavery movement, where Ezra and Angela met.[6]

Angela Tilton faced greater economic hardship in her youth than did Heywood. Stephen Pearl Andrews wrote that her revolt against the "literary and 'cultured' class," inherited from her mother, was "intensified by her experience as a shop-girl. . . . Also deprived of the opportunity of a literary education to the classic expression of the thoughts with which her observant and active brain was teeming, she was noted and marked as a distinctive and representative girl, well known in the old anti-slavery ranks, courted and sought for, for her bright, original, daring manifestations of genius." After marrying Heywood, her whole life, according to Andrews, "settled down into a devoted championship, first of the skilled-labor class as a whole, secondly, of the women especially of that class; finally, and especially, of the working-girl." He characterized her spirit as "not of the grim order, but lively, jovial and entertaining." Regarding her attitudes on sexuality, Andrews commented: "Her natural and inherited revolt against a pretended sanctity, propriety and culture on the part of the polished hypocrites, men and women," had led to her "determination that folks shall hear openly talked about what in secret they dwell on as the staple of their lives; that the hypocrisy shall be exposed; that the inflated pretense of virtue which does not exist shall be punctured and collapsed."[7]

Angela Heywood's sisters, Josephine and Flora Tilton, were committed individualist anarchists dedicated to labor reform and free love. They were the most efficient and energetic sales agents in the field for the Co-Operative Publishing Company. Ezra and Angela Heywood utilized many women agents not only as a practical matter—someone had to do the selling—but also as a way of expanding and dignifying women's role in society. Ezra Heywood editorialized in *The Word* in 1875 that working women were the "worst cheated victims of the present male politico-financial system." However, Fate was "silently ordaining among them evangelists of the labor gospel" who would emerge at labor reform conventions. To girls and women, Heywood wrote, "we are under especial obligations for their especial public advocacy of labor ideas, and also for inestimable service as canvassing agents for the sale of books. . . . They earn good wages, acquire health, experience, knowledge, self possession beyond what anything else would yield. . . ."[8]

The Tilton sisters, a remarkable trio of women, all became radical activists. Angela Heywood recalled that her mother was "compelled by poverty to send me and my sisters out into the world as a flock of

chickens to pick our way. . . ." Lucy Tilton instructed her daughters to
look for radical solutions, and all three responded to her teachings. For
example, Josephine Tilton wrote: "Wendell Phillips secured me a situation on the *Liberator* to learn the art of compositor; I was the last
apprentice on that paper. . . ." On the day of the execution of the Haymarket anarchists, she sent a telegram to one of the condemned men,
Albert Parsons. Quoted in part in a *Liberty* editorial, the telegram declared: "Not good-bye, but hail, brothers. From the gallows trap the
march shall be taken up. I will listen for the beating of the drum."
Josephine Tilton never married and Flora Tilton, even though she eventually married her longtime companion, the anarchist Archibald H.
Simpson, consistently maintained an independent spirit. Although married to Heywood, Angela, too, never backed off from an argument where
she believed her principles were involved. Writing in *The Word*, J. H.
Swain claimed that Josephine and Flora Tilton had distributed the paper
widely as well as getting out to the public "hundreds of thousands of
short essays [publications of the Co-Operative Publishing Company]."
Ezra Heywood called the two women "sisters in Love and Labor . . .
devoted to . . . active, aggressive *work* for the abolition of Usury, Marriage, Taxation, and other relics of barbarism."[9]

Angela Heywood was an articulate social critic. She argued that women
were doubly oppressed—by the economic system and by male domination. Women, she asserted, were forced to sell their bodies in exchange
for physical security because they were paid much less than men for
doing the same work. She wrote: "The power of poor pay to force girls
into the physical embrace of men is a stupendous and appalling fact.
Girls' lives are not matters of choice, but of persuasion and compulsion."
Angela Heywood strongly influenced the tenor and direction of the New
England Labor Reform League, which consistently spoke out on the
particular economic plight of women and general women's rights. A
central aim of labor reform, Angela Heywood argued, should be to
ensure that women's wages would allow women a position of
independence.[10]

Heywood developed a sophisticated critique of male cultural domination. She wrote that "wars between men's and women's eyes and
ideas will become unique and renovating," leading to profound changes
in social institutions. "Religion will repent of the subjection it has imposed on women; learning will confess its ignorance of us; books (simply
because they are *he* [sic] books) will move forward from their alcove
shelves and come down ashamed longer to be books; and male science
will dissolve itself to escape from the infamy of its rude and savage
treatment of us." For social change to be genuine, woman must be able

to "take her rightful place in religion, literature, art, and philosophy." For Angela Heywood, a privileged position for men had to be abolished: "After this play of masculine force, down through the centuries, which has hitherto ruled and depraved life, the social, religious, and moral world, by natural law and necessity, must change its vital essence and aspects." She envisioned a future where men and women would live in equality and looked forward to the "glad spectacle of men and women working together, impelled by love, not compulsion."[11]

Angela Heywood's thinking on women's economic and social rights had a deep impact on Ezra Heywood. The two spent countless hours discussing the circumstances of women's oppression and developed a common analysis. Although in basic agreement, there were times when Angela Heywood felt that Ezra had not gone far enough, and she did not hesitate to call him to task. For example, at a meeting of the NELRL in May 1875, Angela Heywood criticized her husband for being "very negligent of the girl side of labor." Sometimes she wished to "stone or scalp him to make him wake up to the claims of working women. Their conditions are prearranged for them by men who deny them the natural right to be and do as they think best."[12]

The social controversy surrounding Victoria Woodhull was perhaps the most important episode polarizing people around free-love issues in American history. Ezra Heywood's involvement with Woodhull deepened his commitment to free love. A spiritualist and outspoken free-love advocate, Woodhull had a varied career. She worked as a spiritualist medium and later became the nation's first woman stockbroker with the aid of her lover, Commodore Vanderbilt. For a time, she was allied with the International Workingmen's Association organized by Karl Marx and Michael Bakunin in 1864 and became the dominant personality in its leading American section, Number Twelve. She and Stephen Pearl Andrews were responsible for the first American publication of the English translation of *The Communist Manifesto* in *Woodhull and Claflin's Weekly* on December 30, 1871. After Bakunin and the anarchists had been driven from the International, Marx personally expelled Woodhull and her Section Number Twelve from the International Workingmen's Association in 1872. He denounced them for elevating the women's question over the issue of labor and for organizing around such issues as suffragism, dress reform, free love, and spiritualism.

In January 1870, Woodhull addressed the House Judiciary Committee in Washington, D.C., on women's suffrage. She argued that the Fourteenth and Fifteenth Amendments to the Constitution already guaranteed women the right to vote. Although Congress did not accept her shrewd argument, it won her temporary entry into the ranks of the suffrage leadership. Along with her sister Tennessee Claflin, Woodhull published *Woodhull and Claflin's Weekly* from 1870–76, a paper that carried articles on the rights of labor, women's rights, free love, free speech, and much more. Woodhull lived in a palatial New York mansion in an unconventional household that included her parents and children; her sister; her lover and companion Colonel James Blood; her former husband, Dr. Canning Woodhull, ill and in need; and, occasionally, Stephen Pearl Andrews.[13]

Andrews, who was a significant figure in the individualist anarchist movement and a close associate of Ezra Heywood, was born in Massachusetts. He boldly opposed slavery while living in Texas from 1835 to 1843 and resolved that Josiah Warren's ideas were the basis for social change. In a debate with Henry James, Sr., and Horace Greeley in the pages of the *New York Tribune* in 1852, Andrews announced that "freedom in love was . . . the culminating point, toward which all other reformers tend," and declared himself "a Free Loveite." Ezra Heywood recalled that one day in 1861 he found *Love, Marriage, and Divorce* (the debate had been put in book form) in the office of the Massachusetts Anti-Slavery Society. Heywood wrote: " 'Who is Stephen Pearl Andrews?' I asked of C. K. Whipple, one of Garrison's quills. 'He is a scoundrel,' replied Mr. Whipple. A book worthy of such wrath I was bound to read, *then*, but I never met Mr. Andrews until he, Horace Greeley, Mrs. Woodhull, John Orvis, Josiah Warren, and many other reformers were with us in the great labor Reform convention in New York in 1871." Andrews wrote *The Science of Society*, which faithfully presented Warren's principles, and helped, along with Warren, to found Modern Times. He was also an active participant in several conventions of the American and New England Labor Reform Leagues, deeply involved in the women's rights movement, and worked as an editorial partner for *Woodhull and Claflin's Weekly*. Some historians argue that Andrews and Colonel Blood drafted many of Victoria Woodhull's speeches and writings. He developed a new science called Universology; a practical sociology, Pantarchism, or the Pantarchy; and a universal language, Alwato; he also pioneered the development of shorthand.[14]

For a short time, both Elizabeth Cady Stanton and Isabella Beecher Hooker regarded Victoria Woodhull as a likely standard-bearer for women's suffrage. However, Woodhull's outspoken advocacy of free love and her flamboyance did not endear her to most suffragists. For example, when she ran for president of the United States in 1872—the first woman to do so—she declared in one speech: "Yes, I am a Free Lover. I have an *inalienable constitutional* and *natural* right to love whom I may, to love as *long* or as *short* a period as I can; to *change* that love *every day* if I please. . . ." Most social commentators of the day subjected Woodhull to a blistering attack. A Thomas Nast cartoon in *Harper's Weekly* depicted Woodhull as Mrs. Satan holding a placard declaring "Be Saved by Free Love." Harriet Beecher Stowe, in her novel *My Wife and I*, introduced a character, Audacia Dangereyes, who bore an unflattering resemblance to a caricatured Victoria Woodhull. The Beecher sisters, Catherine Beecher and Harriet Beecher Stowe, also regularly attacked Woodhull.[15] Woodhull's response to her attackers was to continue her free-love efforts, but she grew increasingly defensive, angry, and frustrated.

In May 1871, Woodhull had learned in conversation with Elizabeth Cady Stanton that the Reverend Henry Ward Beecher, distinguished pastor of Brooklyn's Plymouth Church, was having an affair with one of his leading parishioners, Elizabeth Tilton, wife of Theodore Tilton. Woodhull tried unsuccessfully to blackmail Beecher into introducing her at a lecture meeting in New York in exchange for her remaining silent about his affair. Beecher refused and instead of Beecher, Theodore Tilton presented her the night of November 20, 1871. Tilton and Woodhull initially met in May, with Tilton seeking to prevent her public disclosure of Beecher's affair with his wife. The two became close acquaintances (the exact degree of intimacy became a subject for much later debate), and his last-minute decision to introduce her forestalled for the moment any action by Woodhull. She wrote to and met with Henry Ward Beecher on different occasions, and her letters to the press contained thinly veiled references to knowledge of the affair. Woodhull may have sought to extract money from Beecher, or perhaps she only applied pressure on the loftier level of ideas. A correspondent in the *Boston Globe* claimed that Woodhull and her sister demanded money from more than thirty men against the threat of printed exposure of sexual activities. It has also been reported that she threatened to expose certain leading suffragists and was willing to resort to blackmail, but the truth of these charges remains unclear.[16]

By the summer of 1872, Woodhull faced great pressures on different fronts. She was confronted with the prospect of financial ruin: she and her entourage had been evicted by a series of New York City landlords, her office rent had been raised considerably, and she faced several lawsuits for debts. In May, she also had been cast out of the ranks of the suffrage movement when she organized the People's party and ran a spirited but politically marginal campaign for president, with Frederick Douglass as her vice-presidential running-mate. In the course of her split with the suffragists, she had alienated Theodore Tilton, a development that removed one major impediment to her going public with the Beecher story. Beecher's biographer reports that she tried to sell the story to several newspapers without any success.[17]

In September 1872, tired, worn, and discouraged by her financial situation and distance from significant portions of the labor and women's movements, Woodhull attended the convention of the National Spiritualist Association in Boston and broke the Beecher-Tilton scandal. The November 2, 1872, issue of *Woodhull and Claflin's Weekly* also carried the news of "The Beecher-Tilton Scandal Case." In part, she sought vengeance against her detractors, notably Catherine Beecher and Harriet Beecher Stowe, and against Henry Ward Beecher himself, who was respected as a solid citizen while she was pilloried in public. She was furious with Beecher for not capitulating to her efforts at coercion, and she may also have hoped that this dramatic revelation would generate revenue via lectures and increased sales of her flagging paper. Woodhull endorsed Beecher's having the affair because she saw it as the application of her free-love concepts. What drew her ire was the hypocritical secrecy with which Beecher practiced in private what she preached in public.

The scandal held the public interest for three years and eventually culminated in the Tilton-Beecher trial in 1875, which lasted nearly six months before ending in a hung jury.[18] Woodhull and her sister were charged, in November 1872, with transmitting obscene literature through the mail, specifically, the November 2, 1872, issue of the *Weekly*. The paper was temporarily suspended, and Victoria Woodhull was incarcerated for four weeks without trial in Ludlow Street Jail in New York City. After her release on bail, the case was eventually dismissed because the judge ruled that the 1872 obscenity statute applied only to books, pamphlets, and pictures, and not to newspapers.[19]

A devout Christian, Anthony Comstock, who brought the obscenity charge against Woodhull, was sincere, fanatical, and unrelenting in his efforts to enforce social purity. Comstock also dogged the steps of Ezra Heywood, pursuing him at every turn in his free-love proselytizing efforts over three decades. Comstock was a man of massive proportions—broad shoulders, with large biceps and a bull neck—who did not back off from a physical encounter with the enemy. According to the historian Ralph McCoy, "his ginger-colored mutton-chop whiskers became a cartoonist's symbol of the stolid but humorless reformer." Comstock fervently believed that he was battling in the service of God; he was obsessed with the issues of sex and temptation. As he wrote in his book *Frauds Exposed*, "Lust defiles the body, debauches the imagination, corrupts the mind, deadens the will, destroys the memory, sears the conscience, hardens the heart, and damns the soul." Heywood Broun and Margaret Leech write that, to Comstock, "passion was, like rabies, a disease. One touch of lewdness could make the whole world mad." Comstock was haunted by the devil and believed that through evil literature, Satan was shaking the pillars of society: the family and the state. In *Traps for the Young*, he declared: "I unhesitatingly declare, there is at present no more active agent employed by Satan in civilized communities to ruin the human family and subject the nations to himself than EVIL READING. . . . The world is the devil's hunting-ground, and children are his choicest game. All along their pathway the merciless hunter sets his traps, and they are set with a certainty of a large return. To corrupt a boy or girl, he knows lessens the chance of a pure man or woman."[20]

Comstock had grown up in rural Connecticut, and returned to his hometown of New Canaan in 1865 after serving in the army. However, the Comstock family farm was in disarray and he moved to New Haven, finding work as a clerk and bookkeeper in a grocery store. The young Comstock's dream was that he might some day own a large drygoods business in New York City. In the late 1860s, he moved to New York and found work in a series of drygoods establishments. In 1871, while working as a drygoods salesman, he fell in love with Margaret Hamilton, a woman ten years his elder, described by Broun and Leech as a "faded, sweet, and self-effacing woman." The couple lived in Summit, New Jersey, for most of their married life. While Comstock worried about his flagging drygoods sales, he delighted in his orderly life with his wife, entertaining guests in their home, and church activities.[21]

In his late twenties, the intensely religious, poorly educated Comstock longed to "live nobly, to do his duty," in the words of Broun and Leech. Comstock had been distressed at the interest shown by his fellow workers in erotic books and pictures; in 1868, he had gone so far as to have two bookdealers arrested. In 1871, he engaged in a protracted, successful struggle to close down a saloon violating the Sunday closing law. With the entrapment of the bookseller Conroy in this same period, he began his long career of suppressing "corrupting" literature. Wherever Comstock turned in New York City, he over and over perceived the degenerating influence of moral corruption at work. Broun and Leech confirm that obscene books and papers were said "to have been sold on the streets at that period as freely as roasted chestnuts."[22]

The social fabric of New York City provided the spark that ignited Comstock's passion to do the Lord's work in pursuit of evil. American cities had experienced rapid growth in the aftermath of the Civil War. A growing influx of immigrants led to the spawning of urban slums.

The depression of 1873–77 heightened the level of poverty and crime and deepened the gulf between the wealthy and the poor. Commercialized vice flourished, writes Ralph McCoy, and prostitution was practiced on a grand scale.[23]

In this environment, many Protestant Americans recoiled at the disorder and sexual license they perceived the immigrants brought to urban life. One response was the rise of the disparate social purity movement, which aimed to preserve American society and to uplift the urban immigrants. The historian David Pivar observes, "Former abolitionists dominated the leadership of the crusade against prostitution and exercised substantial control over the social purity movement as it turned to more universal reform."[24] Comstock represented a repressive component of purity efforts that had nothing to do with universal reform. He aimed his wrath at the pornographer, not the prostitute, believing that the sins of thought led to sinful behavior.

Comstock vigorously pursued pornography publishers and dealers, carefully orchestrating his actions to maximize exposure in the popular press. Impressed by his free-lance efforts, the New York Young Men's Christian Association (YMCA) began to provide him with a salary in 1872 to back his efforts to stamp out vice and to secure federal and state anti-obscenity legislation. The YMCA Committee for the Suppression of Vice included such men as financier J. P. Morgan, copper baron William E. Dodge, and soap magnate Samuel Colgate. Because some YMCA leaders felt Comstock was involved in such dirty activities, the committee divorced itself from the YMCA and became an independent Society for the Suppression of Vice in 1873. Similar vice societies were established in cities all over the United States.[25]

In 1865, in response to reports that soldiers were receiving obscene materials through the mail, Congress enacted the first law to deal with obscenity in the mails and in the printed word. An 1872 amendment provided little additional enforcement strength. Supported by his influential backers in the YMCA committee, Comstock went to Washington in the early months of 1873 to lobby for a stronger bill. Presented to a corrupt Congress in the midst of the Credit Mobilier scandal, the vice society's bill finally passed at 2 a.m. in a rowdy session on Sunday, March 2. Perhaps, writes Hal Sears, Comstock's traveling exhibit of pornography had suitably impressed the lawmakers.[26]

The Comstock Act, as it came to be called, provided up to ten years' imprisonment for anyone who knowingly mailed or received "obscene, lewd, or lascivious" printed and graphic material. One section forbade the mailing of contraceptive and abortifacient materials and information, along with any "thing intended . . . for immoral use." The law, writes

Sears, was silent on two crucial points: first, it offered no definition of obscenity; and second, it did not specify whether it aimed to establish a civil post office censorship separate from any criminal provisions of the law. The courts regularly discounted First Amendment arguments, leaving defendants with little but technical arguments for defense. As Sears observes, "Using methods that bordered on entrapment and with government authority and respectable public opinion behind them, Comstock and the vice societies won an impressive majority of their cases." Further, Sears writes, the Post Office Department assumed independent powers of censorship and confiscation based upon the Comstock Act. With no due process, postal officials prohibited, confiscated, and in some cases destroyed without remuneration any mails that they found to be objectionable.[27]

The effect of the Comstock Act intensified as state governments, influenced by efforts of vice societies, enacted "little Comstock" acts, laws prohibiting commerce in "obscene" items such as suggestive books and birth-control devices. The act had also created the position of post office special agent to inspect mail and to track down violators. Sears notes, "Although it appears that Comstock did not lobby for his personal appointment, he was an obvious choice, and he expressed pleasure at being duly appointed. He declined to accept his government salary, however, until the year 1906." He received a regular salary from the Society for the Suppression of Vice.[28]

With the backing of the YMCA, vice societies, and the federal government, Comstock was endowed with moral and legal authority. The federal obscenity statute of 1873 threatened free expression, effectively banning sexual discussion and the exchange of information on matters ranging from abortion to criticism of Christianity. According to Comstock's own account, when he began his work the library of obscenity was comprised of 165 publications. By 1876, the printing plates of 160 of the original publications had been destroyed. However, Comstock extended his reach by attempting to stop the publication of any material that remotely touched upon sex. Leech and Broun write: "The frequent statement that Anthony Comstock could not discriminate between a frankly pornographic book and a sociological or medical publication of educational character was fair criticism. To the vice-hunter reference to the body or its functions was always sinful." Comstock and the vice-suppression societies cast a very wide net and either managed to censor or silence a broad range of publications dealing with medical information and unorthodox social views. Indeed, they broadened their targets to include the pursuit of quack advertising, swindling schemes, dime novels and story papers, gambling, and horse racing.[29]

Comstock viewed himself as constantly under attack for his love of purity and for his protection of the innocent young. His campaign to thwart Satan permitted him the freedom, he thought, to utilize any tactic, no matter how cruel or dishonest. Constitutional guarantees of freedom of thought and speech should not be respected, Comstock maintained, if they permitted filthy publications and activities. Thus, Comstock used decoy letters, espionage, and all types of subterfuge to snare his potential victims. D. M. Bennett, prominent free-thinker and one such victim, wrote: "He has simply acted the part of a despicable spy and detective. Falsehood, deception, traps, and pitfalls for the un-wary have been the agencies he has employed in the prosecution of his nefarious business." Comstock went so far as to celebrate the deaths of opponents. Ezra Heywood quoted a letter Comstock sent to C. L. Mer-riam on January 18, 1873: "There were four publishers on the second of last March; *today three of these are in their graves, and it is charged by their friends that* I WORRIED THEM TO DEATH. BE THAT AS IT MAY, I AM SURE THAT THE WORLD IS BETTER OFF WITHOUT THEM."[30]

Comstock pursued his crusade for purity into the second decade of the twentieth century. Although Comstock died in 1915, writes Hal Sears, not until the 1930s did the federal law that popularly bore his name become redefined. Some states, according to Sears, still have lin-gering Comstock legislation on the books in the form of laws prohibiting or restricting birth-control devices. Leech and Broun write that many viewed Comstock as "the strong arm raised against pictured and written indecencies. Good folk were on his side, the Christian laymen, many of the clergy, mothers and fathers, school-teachers—all right-thinking peo-ple, in fact."[31]

Comstock faced considerable opposition from those who valued free speech and a free press, however. The small free-love community, of which Ezra Heywood was a prominent member, bitterly attacked him. Heywood accused Comstock of waging a relentless war upon "honest writers and publishers who favor theological and social reform," called him "the hound of the labor robbery and lecherous Church and State," and warned of the immensely serious threat Comstock posed to social freedom: "masked under federal law and the sacred forms of religion, we have here incarnate intolerance, to which neither pro-slavery sav-agery, Puritan bigotry, nor high-church proscription—nothing this side of medieval inquisitions—will furnish a parallel." Heywood insisted that social critics had a natural right to discuss physiological and sexual issues openly and frankly. As Broun and Leech observe: "Anthony Comstock may have been entirely correct in his assumption that the division of living creatures into male and female was a vulgar mistake, but a conspiracy of silence about the matter will hardly alter the facts."[32]

Upon her release from prison in 1872, Victoria Woodhull wanted to speak in Boston on "Moral Cowardice and Moral Hypocrisy, or Four Weeks in Ludlow Street Jail." However, Governor Claflin of Massachusetts feared she might "repeat the vile stories about Mr. Beecher or even attack some of us in Boston. . . . She is no better than a panel thief or a common street walker, and I will see that she doesn't open her vile mouth in the city which was so recently honored by Mr. Beecher's presence." Such treatment of Woodhull was not limited to Boston. Spiritualist and free-love advocate Laura Cuppy Smith, also known as Laura Kendrick, chaired a meeting on January 3, 1873 at New York's Cooper Institute, where Comstock had banned Woodhull from speaking on "The Naked Truth." Smith announced that Woodhull could not speak "lest she be thrust again into an American bastille. . . ," but Woodhull disguised herself and slipped past the United States marshals. Mounting the platform and dramatically throwing off her disguise, she was able to make her speech without interference or arrest. Free speech was clearly under attack, however.[33]

Ezra and Angela Heywood did not observe these developments passively. Ezra had met Victoria Woodhull in 1872 while in New York for a convention of the American Labor Reform League. Reflecting his views on the Beecher-Tilton affair, he printed an article from the *Oneida Circular* in *The Word* that called the episode "an important chapter in the Trial of Marriage." Many free-love activists imagined that the Beecher-Tilton affair, if properly explained, would help hasten the end of the marriage institution. Heywood termed the whole affair a "quarrel between two slave masters. . . . 'Respectable' people who say, 'Such revolting facts should never have been made public,' thereby concede that the marriage system will not survive criticism." Angela Heywood denounced Beecher's hypocrisy: "Are we not morally responsible for every pleasure which it pleases our natures to accept? . . . There is no love under heaven, that can be justified privately, which one should be ashamed to have publicly known." Ezra Heywood termed Tilton, the self-proclaimed legal owner of his wife, the incarnation of jealousy and the marriage spirit. In an 1875 issue of *The Word*, he cited Woodhull's definition of free love on the first page: "Free Love is the regulation of the affections according to conscience, taste, and judgment of the individual, in place of their control by law, which, since they are of natural and not of legal origin, can have no rightful or proper dominion over them."[34]

In the January 1873, issue of *The Word*, Heywood declared: "Virtuous Boston shuts its Halls against Woodhull to avoid contamination" and offered the platform of the Labor Reform League. Mayor Henry Pierce and the city council of Boston, as well as Governor Claflin, used all their powers to prevent her from getting a hearing. According to Benjamin R. Tucker, "In this critical situation Mr. Heywood and Colonel William B. Greene, the president of the League, determined that free speech should be upheld in Boston." Tucker related that Tremont Temple was secured for the next league convention, scheduled to begin February 23, 1873. When the league issued publicity announcing that Victoria Woodhull would speak, the owners of the hall cancelled the contract. Threatened with a suit for damages, they paid a considerable sum to the league to avoid court proceedings. Tucker continued: "The League then secured several smaller halls for a convention lasting three days. The authorities threatened all sorts of interference, but the convention was held nevertheless. . . . In all, Woodhull addressed the convention four times, including two set lectures, and the authorities were powerless to intervene."[35]

The evening session of the second day was devoted entirely to Victoria Woodhull's presentation of her "Suppressed Speech." According to *Woodhull and Claflin's Weekly*, "the hall was crowded to its fullest capacity with ladies and gentlemen" well before the speech began. Although there was tension in the room as she rose to speak, "the audience preserved a perfect quiet during the evening and Mrs. Woodhull spoke with comparative ease and freedom." It was necessary to repeat her speech the next evening because many who had purchased tickets for the lecture had been unable to get into the hall. Rather than repeat herself, Woodhull gave her talk the next day on "The Naked Truth."[36]

Woodhull began her "Suppressed Speech" by reviewing the history of her paper and the attacks upon it. She declared herself for freedom, "holding it is simply nobody's business what anybody eats, drinks, or wears, and just as little who anybody loves, or how he loves, if the two parties to it are satisfied. In other words, self-ownership is inalienable, it can neither be sold, bartered, or given away." Woodhull also argued for basic changes in the economic system, but her emphasis was on the necessity for woman to be emancipated from sexual slavery. She attacked Anthony Comstock and warned that freedom of speech and the press were threatened. Comparing several passages of the Bible to the issue of her paper charged with obscenity, she inquired whether or not the Bible was obscene. Woodhull branded latter-day Christians "the most consummate hypocrites." Clearly referring to the Reverend Henry Ward Beecher, she said that "whatever a person really is, it is best for himself and society to be known as that and not as something else, which he is not." She concluded by vowing to continue to wage war upon the infamies of the social system. This warfare will be sustained, she declared, until the "old, worn-out, rotting social system will be torn down, plank by plank, timber after timber, until place is given to a new, true, and beautiful structure, based upon freedom, equality and justice to all—to women as well as men; the results of which can be nothing else than physical health, intellectual honesty, and moral purity."[37]

Victoria Woodhull applauded the courage of the New England Labor Reform League, which she called "perhaps the most radical and thoroughgoing body of reformers in the direction of industrial equity that there is in the world. . . . Free speech was vindicated by the actions of the League. All honor to them!" Writing in *The Index*, the influential free-thought journal of the Free Religious Association, the individualist anarchist Sidney H. Morse observed that Victoria Woodhull had delivered her "Suppressed Speech" and "Boston still lifts its head above the sea! . . . Much of the prejudice against her is itself 'vulgar,' and I have heard far more 'obscenity' uttered about her than escaped her lips . . . she has a philosophy in which she believes *desperately* and Garrison himself was not more determined to be heard."[38]

Heywood had many problems with Victoria Woodhull's politics outside of her free-love advocacy. Basically, he rejected her call for a strong state apparatus. He opposed her for supporting "compulsory education, licensing prostitution, state currency, schools, nurseries, majority despotism. . . . everything except love is to come under the nose of conventional supervision." When in later years she abandoned her free-love principles and called the marriage laws "most divine," Ezra Heywood said: "Our friends so anxious to 'get religion' and respectability have yet to learn that living Conscience is better than dead Gods or despotic laws." Liberty, he asserted, was "the bride of order and the guarantee of moral responsibility. . . . Women who cling to the marriage law as a necessity are as seriously mistaken as Southern negroes who thought themselves 'protected' by the slave system." Woodhull and her sister Tennessee Claflin left the United States for England in 1877. The death of Commodore Vanderbilt, who had financed their brokerage firm and paper, had led to a disputed will. Rumors indicated that their trip was subsidized by William Vanderbilt, who sought to forestall the sisters' testimony in open court. In England, both sisters married wealthy, respectable men, and Victoria Woodhull busily set about the task of rewriting her genealogy and denying her past. Benjamin Tucker, who had had an affair with Woodhull in the 1870s, sharply rebuked her for the attempt to repudiate her past radicalism.[39]

One major result of the Labor Reform League's sponsorship of Victoria Woodhull as a speaker was the founding of the New England Free Love League (NEFLL). A few radicals met immediately after the closing of the NELRL convention and decided to form a new group whose immediate purpose was to sponsor a series of talks by Victoria Woodhull throughout New England. The long-range goals were "the abolition of legal and compulsory marriage and all other institutions, laws and customs, whereby the sexes are bound and fettered in their relations in any form or degree, and the substitution therefore of such a social system as shall guarantee to all individuals the power to exercise their right of freedom at their own cost in matters of love." Benjamin Tucker was the corresponding secretary and general agent, while Angela Heywood was one of the vice presidents. The Executive Committee included Ezra Heywood, Tucker, and L. K. Joslin of Providence.[40]

Joslin, who served for several years as president of the organization, declared that with the abolition of slavery, legal marriage remained the last form of human slavery. He called for "protest against unnatural, forced, and deathly sensual relations. I would rather wield the lash of a slavemaster than force an unwilling wife or mistress to my embrace. . . ." Free love, Joslin maintained, was the "newest and most important reform of the ages. Love is of the divine; freedom is our birthright. With freedom for every human being to love with their own life and in their own way there will come to men the kingdom of heaven on earth." Joslin, like Heywood, believed that freedom in matters of love would naturally lead to monogamous relationships.[41] Varietists, who emphasized total sexual freedom as did Victoria Woodhull, were a minority within free-love circles. Having achieved an end to slavery in the South, free-lovers now viewed the sexual slavery of women as the leading social issue. Free love meant opposition to marriage and that women had the right to control their sexual activity. Free-lovers felt their cause was divinely inspired, a movement whose victory would usher in the millennial era of well-being for all.

Ezra Heywood's espousal of free love and women's rights did not, in his view, mean abandonment of labor reform. He saw these issues as interdependent. Ezra and Angela Heywood emphasized that women should receive equal pay for equal work and should be able to work at any job a man had. They sought *"the liberation of woman from the special financial thraldom,* in which she is now held *by man;* by which, as compared with man's wages, she is defrauded of fifty percent of her rightful earnings. Were the whole profit system . . . destroyed, the special fraud now practiced on woman by man would continue . . . to perpetuate this odious financial aristocracy of sex." Linking sexual reform with labor reform, Ezra Heywood declared that "marriage restrictions, usury, and the exceptionally low wages of women are the chief causes of 'prostitution'; that sexual excess, privation, disease, and antagonism will continue until the nourishing sources of Social Evil, marriage and usury, are swept away."[42]

Several labor reformers did not share Ezra Heywood's enthusiasm for linking free love with labor reform. In 1873, Heywood charged Josiah Warren with evasion of the marriage question. In turn, Warren thought Heywood's focus diverted attention from the central ideas of individual sovereignty and the exchange of labor for labor. Worse still, Warren felt, Heywood was alienating many potential sympathizers. Warren's participation in the Modern Times colony provides evidence that he may not have disagreed with Heywood's substantive views on free love; however, it is clear Warren viewed Heywood's free-love activities as ill-advised. In 1876, Heywood denounced those "select" (he did not indicate a number) labor reformers who withdrew from the Labor Reform League after notice of a NEFLL meeting was read. The individualist anarchists Warren and William Greene, and Benjamin Tucker after the 1870s, disagreed with Heywood's manner of insistently raising the question of marriage and free love and linking these issues to labor reform. Heywood saw himself dissenting from the dissenters and seeking to reform the reformers "a painful task, of which we have had our full share since 1861."[43] Still, he was committed to speaking the truth as he understood it, no matter what the consequences.

The New England Free Love League held its first public convention in Boston on March 26 and 27, 1876. The sessions of the convention were crowded, with several hundred people turned away. The league publicly affirmed that its goal was the abolition of marriage; league members contended that lovers have the natural right "to make and dissolve their own contracts as they think best."[44]

Ezra Heywood presented a series of resolutions that constituted his individual opinions but also represented the ideas of the league. He condemned the marriage institution for denying liberty and destroying love, and established his connection between free love and labor reform. Repudiating society's efforts to make people chaste by statute, he called for the unconditional repeal of the laws against adultery and fornication. Believing in self-control versus regulation by church or state, he argued that "the sexual instinct may be inspired by intelligence and brought within the jurisdiction of reason and conscience." Asserting his commitment to the natural rights doctrine, Heywood declared that the league was dedicated to human rights and sought "the emancipation of men as well as women from the demoralizing sway of marriage." He argued that "to suppose Free Love dangerous in its tendencies is the old plea of despotism that liberty is unsafe." He contended forcefully that women have the right to participate as equals with men in all aspects of social life: "the insinuating assertion that girls and women cannot associate and do business with men without having sexual intercourse with them is a lewd falsehood . . . women have an equal right to receive money or estates from men, to walk, ride, dance, or pray with them as men have with each other. . . ." Heywood concluded by hoping that the day would soon come when the marriage system would join "slavery, piracy, and its other kindred abominations of the past."[45]

Spiritualism was a widely diverse pseudoscientific movement that became vastly popular in the United States and Europe in the nineteenth century. Spiritualists believed in communication with spirits through human mediums. This communication was a means of finding stability in the midst of great change. American life in this period featured unsettled conditions—social mobility, large-scale immigration, and expanding industrialization. Many Americans viewed science and technology with much excitement, but also with fear. The new developments in society led many to feel a need for compensatory spiritual revelation. The spiritualists sought to apply the spirit of science—optimism, progress, limitless expansion of opportunity—to their own lives. Spiritualism functioned as a surrogate religion for many.[46]

By no means was every spiritualist a free-lover, but almost all free-lovers were spiritualists. In the 1850s, spiritualist ranks were swept by the doctrine of spiritual affinity, based on Charles Fourier's theory of passional attraction and the harmonial philosophy of Andrew Jackson Davis, which held that certain individuals were natural mates, drawn to one another because of complementary spiritual auras. The idea of natural mates was a powerful argument against marriage. Spiritualists also believed in everlasting cosmic progress, which for many meant actively attempting to overcome the injustices of slavery and marriage. Disregard for church authority and an emphasis on individual conscience and rights often moved spiritualists to argue against marriage and for women's rights. Significantly, the professional life of public mediums provided many women with an opportunity for travel and sexual adventure that was unattainable for most women in society. It was claimed that women's rights was the most popular cause of the spirits.[47]

The goals of antebellum reform helped shape the attitudes of spiritualists. In the early 1850s, many millennialist reformers interpreted "rapping sounds" as signalling the coming of an age of harmony. Like the abolitionists, spiritualists believed reform was rooted in individual change. Thus, spiritualist ideas about reform did not seek a uniformity of opinion, but rather encouraged the removal of all artificial restraints on individual development.[48]

Spiritualism constituted a threat to orthodox Christianity. Ministers of the leading Protestant denominations feared that investigation into important theological questions without the guidance of the Scriptures or any church would lead to the dissolution of established church authority. Ezra Heywood described spiritualism as a "world-embracing, irresistible power because it is based on liberty, not authority; on mediumship, constant appeal to Personal sense of Truth." Spiritualism represented a consummation of two primary forces in American life—Protestantism and individualism—in that it permitted every person to communicate with the hereafter without the benefit of clergy or religious dogma.[49]

In his novel *The Bostonians*, Henry James, Jr., connected feminism with spiritualism and condemned both, a common attitude. There was indeed a link among feminism, spiritualism, and other reforms. For example, Victoria Woodhull was president of a national spiritualist organization. The historian R. Laurence Moore relates that "spiritualist editorials throughout the 1870s and 1880s argued along with Woodhull for fairer treatment of American Indians, the abolition of capital punishment, prison reform, equality for women, higher wages for workers, and the right of labor to organize for cooperative goals."[50]

Ezra Heywood's conversion to spiritualism was gradual; in contrast, Angela Heywood was a dedicated spiritualist as a young woman. In 1863, Ezra Heywood claimed in *The Liberator* that, although not a spiritualist, "their theory is the only one I know of which approaches an intelligent explanation of these interesting and marvelous phenomena [rappings, spirit communications, etc.] . . ." As late as 1874, he still was not a "first-class believer," although he criticized free-thought activist Horace Seaver for doubting the existence of spirits. He wrote that "not seeing electricity and doubting thus its existence, is it right to call the electric telegraph a hoax?"[51]

Stephen Pearl Andrews described Angela Heywood as "in a very high degree mediumistic, inspirational, and prophetic." She was the key in moving Ezra Heywood toward a more committed spiritualist viewpoint. Several letter-writers to *The Word* praised her spiritual utterances.[52] The reformer Lucien Pinney wrote that Angela Heywood communicated with the dead: "She has visions, hears voices, and dreams dreams. . . ." For example, she wrote her friend Elizabeth Denton in 1884 that she had had "some long and wonderful dreams about Mr.

Denton. Talked with him so plain. . . ." A geologist, free-thinker, and friend of the Heywoods, Denton had died in New Guinea in 1883.

Ezra Heywood openly declared himself a committed spiritualist in an 1875 editorial, "Abolition of Death," in *The Word*. He wrote that spiritualism, "the successful application of scientific methods of investigation to religious facts and phenomena," was destined "to sweep all other religions into oblivion." He affirmed the authenticity and importance of clairvoyant medical practice, materialization (spirits manifesting themselves), and communication with departed spirits. Heywood wrote enthusiastically: "Unimpeachable evidence accumulates to show that Spiritualism, fulfilling the prophecy of St. Paul, has 'destroyed the last enemy-Death.' " Here was a faith in progress and perfectibility that held that death itself need no longer be dreaded. Death was yet another human imperfection that could be overcome.[53]

Heywood actively promoted his spiritualist ideas and linked them to his reform efforts, a connection he saw as natural. For example, an announcement in *The Word* related that he would speak one Sunday morning and afternoon in East Princeton. His topics were "Anti-Death—or Immortality of the Human Soul Viewed in the Light of Modern Spiritualism," and "Labor as Related to Property and Usury." At the eight-day Radical Spiritualists' camp meeting at Lake Walden, Massachusetts, topics of discussion included finance, labor and capital, social reform, spiritualism, and materializations. These gatherings, which attracted large groups of people, featured daily speeches, music, and dancing. Heywood spoke on the day finance was considered.[54]

In 1878, Ezra and Angela Heywood and spiritualist friends founded their own organization, the New England Anti-Death League. Death, Heywood declared at an 1880 convention, although seemingly irresistible, was "not a fact in the Nature of Things." Rather, it was a transient illusion, "born of limited mentality, but transcended by Life and Immortality revealed in convincing evidence of immaterial Intelligence," the spirit world. Much worse than physical death was the moral death, Heywood charged, "of falsehood, intrigue, dishonesty, theft, usurpation, and murder which underpin and perpetuate Church and State. . . ." Making his case for anarchism, he argued that "until citizens, as discoverers and exponents of truth, favor anarchy, the natural society which transcends government, they are death-stricken, conservative perverts rather than converts to Spiritual Life. . . ." Heywood's resolutions also called for women's rights, an end to marriage, and the overthrow of the existing economic system. In a millennialist tone, Heywood wrote that the Anti-Death League was evolving "new morality and religion fore-lighting the New Heavens on a New Earth."[55]

Ezra and Angela Heywood believed in a range of practices—mesmerism, phrenology, homeopathy, and the like—which successfully rivaled more respectable scientific doctrines for public attention, and then defended these disciplines against attacks from physicians and scientists. Practitioners of these "psuedosciences" believed they could overcome evil and promote perfection in the world. The Heywoods were among the many reformers who used the language of phrenology regularly. Phrenologists believed that the thirty-seven diverse elements that comprised individual character, temperament, and ability were each controlled by a different, definable area of the brain. The size of each cerebral organ indicated its functioning power and could be increased by exercise, and thus human improvement was limitless. Some of the areas of the brain included "agreeableness," "combativeness," and "approbativeness." Sexual desire, or "amativeness," was thought to originate not in the genital organs, but in a region of the brain[56]—a crucial distinction for the Heywoods, who often referred to amativeness. Tracing the origins of sexual desire to the brain meant that desire could be controlled by rational self-discipline.

Besides the psuedosciences, the Heywoods gave their time and energy to a number of reform efforts including dress reform, the abolition of taxes, and life insurance schemes. Benjamin Tucker served as secretary of the American Free Dress League, and Olivia Shepard, another officer, was a frequent contributor to *The Word*. These critics of women's fashions of the period pointed to health hazards and denounced the use of women as objects of sexual display, an important issue for women's rights advocates. Both the leading suffragist papers, *The Revolution* and *Woman's Journal*, gave considerable space to dress reform.

While working as associate editor of *The Word* in 1875, Tucker was arrested and spent a few days in jail for refusing to pay town taxes. Tucker, Heywood, and others formed the Worcester County and New England Anti-Tax Leagues. For Heywood, the issue was between "voluntaryism and Collective Intrusion." Heywood also joined with others to set up the New England and American Mutual Life Relief Associations, nonprofit life insurance plans based on mutual cooperation.[57]

The Union Reform League was the creation largely of Heywood and Stephen Pearl Andrews. The league sought to unify all reform efforts into one grand organization for social change. One of the organizers, John M. Spear, declared: "The time has come for blending all shades of opinion and the union of all *Schools of Reform* on one common platform." The league constitution, adopted at the founding meeting in 1879, stated that the league's purposes were "to repeal legislative restrictions of natural rights, to diffuse knowledge for the promotion of individual and social improvement, and to encourage cooperative action in all progressive movements." The league included a wide array of social reformers and championed a panoply of causes, including women's suffrage, repeal of all obscenity laws, a new world language, and many more. League members decided that it should become an "Individual Sovereign Auxiliary" of the Pantarchy, Stephen Pearl Andrews's organization. Pantarchism, Andrews modestly explained, was to become the "practical orchestration of all Human Affairs." Pantarchy was the social institution that would administer whatever was dictated by the science of Universology and the philosophy of Integralism, further creations of Andrews's creative imagination.[58]

Heywood did not particularly care for the name "Pantarchy" or its authoritarian implications. The Pantarchal constitution described the "Head of the Pantarchal State" as a self-elected individual who was "powerless except as he is voluntarily acknowledged and obeyed." That individual, not surprisingly, was Andrews. The Pantarchy, a universal government, was supposed to result in a government that would usher in the millennium. Pantarchy suggested hierarchy to Heywood and, in its place, he proposed "Wordocrasy," from his newspaper's name. Heywood was capable, like Andrews, of making himself the center of attention; to him, Wordocrasy meant intelligent, spontaneous association.[59]

After living together in Worcester for six years, Ezra and Angela Heywood moved in 1871 to Princeton, where they based their reform activities. Still an agricultural community, Princeton had become a popular summer resort for visitors from Boston, Worcester, Providence, and New York. Because of easy access by railroad, spectacular mountain views, and a more comfortable climate than the cities, Princeton's hotel business peaked in the years 1860–80. Guests and summer residents would amble through the countryside or amuse themselves with daily games of tennis, croquet, and bowling at tenpins. Existing hotels were expanded, and new facilities built. The typical hotel was a rambling frame building with wide porches that featured rocking chairs.[60]

In 1871, the Heywoods built Mountain Home resort, which they hoped would be a profitable hotel where reformers of all kinds could enjoy a relaxing vacation. The Mountain Home stood opposite the northwest edge of the Princeton town common. Mrs. Houghton, a Princeton native whom Kenneth Davis interviewed in 1967, described the house as fairly large "with a mansard roof" and "an L-shaped wing at one side of the main body of the structure." The paying summer guests were a key source of Heywood family income, although in *The Word* Ezra Heywood indicated that his publishing efforts were profitable. The publishing business, based in the Mountain Home, was a consuming task. Davis related that the family all worked. "All the writing, editing, mailing, and correspondence was handled in their home. Mrs. Houghton tells me that the house they lived in could have accommodated comfortably some fifteen summer guests, but many of the rooms were piled high with Co-Operative Publishing Company materials and so could not be rented." Heywood also employed assistants from time to time to aid with *The Word* and the publishing company, and they often stayed at the Mountain Home. Ceres Heywood Bradshaw, daughter of Ezra and Angela Heywood, maintained that the Mountain Home was always the principal source of family income. Angela Heywood, according to her daughter, worked hard and "upon her efforts the financial end of the home depended. The reform movement never paid in any surplus and often went into debt. The Mountain Home was a forty-two room house and for three to four months in the summer brought in the income. The children all learned to work and there were four of us." The summer season generally ran from late May until sometime in October. *The Word* regularly carried a notice for the Mountain Home; an 1872 announcement stated "Mountain Home—A newly fitted House, with Large Airy Rooms, commanding a wide prospect. Those seeking a quiet, healthy summer resort can address Angela T. Heywood."[61]

The Heywoods did not interpret women's rights to mean that Ezra Heywood should share in the cooking and cleaning. In this sense, they shared the Victorian attitude of women's proper role. They did, however, see housework as serious work for which women should be compensated, an attitude that was uncommon. From time to time, Ezra Heywood expressed his regret that housekeeping and family chores prevented Angela Heywood from writing more articles. For example, he wrote in 1888 that an article on "Motherhood" was delayed; Angela Heywood is "affluent in ideas," Heywood stated, but " 'much serving' hinders their getting on paper."[62]

Angela Heywood was a tireless housekeeper, and the Mountain Home won many accolades. Elizabeth Dudley Doughty wrote that it was a pleasure "to go through her house so well-kept and orderly. I thought she worked too hard, but it was her pleasure to do so." Stephen Pearl Andrews observed that "as to her domesticity, she prides herself upon being the 'drudge,' the 'Bridget,' the mere housewife, the working woman. She provides elegant parlor accommodations for her boarders, for the reformers, for other lady visitors, yet keeps herself secluded in the basement, doing more work than three ordinary women. . . ." Jay Chaapel described the Mountain Home: "The large airy rooms, abundant, wholesome fare, the neatness and quiet, and the attractive hospitality, are such, not only to promote health, but mental and spiritual, recreation, rest, and reinvigoration."[63]

Competition for summer boarders was serious with other Princeton hotels and nearby establishments, but nonetheless the Mountain Home prospered in its early years. Benjamin Tucker wrote in 1873: "Judging from the number of Radicals who intend to visit your town this summer, I think Princeton bids fair to become the New Jerusalem." Four years later, Ezra Heywood wrote: "Reverend J. M. L. Babcock, editor of *New Age*, Stephen Pearl Andrews, Pantarch, Henry Appleton, and other prominent radicals are visiting at Mountain Home; other distinguished reformers to come during the season; drift of Seers and Thinkers—as visits of Whittier, Emerson, Thoreau, and Henry James years ago—bids fair to make Princeton erelong a Parnassus of Inspiration, as it is now a much frequented mountain resort for seekers of Health and Recreation."[64]

Ezra and Angela Heywood were able to purchase Mountain Home resort in 1871 only because Ezra's brother, Samuel Heywood, was willing to guarantee the mortgage. Samuel Heywood had become a wealthy boot and shoe manufacturer in Worcester. President of the Heywood Boot and Shoe Company, he also was a director of the Central National Bank, and later president of the People's Savings Bank. In addition, he was an active member of the Republican party, was elected to various public offices, and contributed financially to the United States Senate campaign of George Frisbie Hoar, a collateral relation.[65]

Like many small-property owners, Ezra Heywood was hurt by the depression of the 1870s. Despite the national economy, the hotel and the book trade generated some income. Heywood claimed to have earned more than $1,100 from sales of *Uncivil Liberty* alone; between 1871 and 1877, he shipped more than five hundred thousand books from Princeton. Thus, he was able to carry the debt owed to his brother, "paying from 700 to 1,000 dollars interest a year, without much trouble until 1875 or 6," when mortgage payments became more difficult to maintain. Finding himself "heavily in debt with only a depreciated property to show for it," Ezra Heywood met with his brother several times in 1876 and 1877, seeking "how, as men and brothers, could we unload, with the least possible loss. . . . In 1876 he said if I would drop reforms, 'pocket your crotchets,' and go to work for him, it would be worth $1,500 a year and expenses on the road as a salesman." Ezra considered the offer for several days and decided to accept, but by then Samuel had decided not to hire him, and so nothing came of it. Heywood's indebtedness to his brother continued over the years to be a troublesome issue between them.[66]

The Heywood brothers were very different. In 1876, Ezra Heywood caustically referred to his brother as "an Orthodox deacon and a leading capitalist of Worcester." They shared two common characteristics: each stood well over six feet, and each worked very hard. Dee Heywood, Samuel Heywood's granddaughter, recalled that he was dedicated to his business. He would walk to work everyday dressed entirely in black, with his Homberg hat, Chesterfield suit, and shirt with batwing collar and stiff cuffs.[67]

The rest of the Heywood family was involved in diverse activities. Samuel Heywood sent his brother, Alonzo, to Denver to establish a retail shoe outlet, but he died there in 1870. Two Heywood sisters, Mary and Fidelia, lived in Princeton all their lives. Dee Heywood remembered Mary as a "tough, crotchety New Englander," and Fidelia as a "sweet woman." Samuel Heywood looked after the two women, and upon his death in 1913 left a trust fund for their benefit. Joseph H. Heywood, another brother, cast his lot with Ezra Heywood in the reform movement. He was a strong supporter of *The Word* and occasionally contributed articles. He helped organize a series of lectures by Ezra and Angela Heywood in Boston in 1878 and a mass meeting for the Russian Leo Hartman in 1881. In 1888, Ezra Heywood received an appeal from his brother, Dwight H. Heywood, who wrote as president of the Anti-Monopoly and Settlers' Rights Association. He, too, had become a radical.[68]

Ezra and Angela Heywood lived together for twenty-seven years and raised four children. They had two daughters—Vesta Vernon, born in 1869, and Psyche Ceres, born in 1881—and two sons—Hermes Sidney, born in 1874, and Angelo Tilton, born in 1883.[69] According to Stephen Pearl Andrews, the Heywood offspring exceeded the other children in town "in learning, in demeanor, and in a certain reserved and distinguished bearing." The Heywoods invested much energy in their children. Besides serious home training, they did all they could with their limited resources to provide a good education. Distrustful of state-administered schools, they sent Hermes and Vesta to a Quaker facility in Providence, Rhode Island, and later to a school in Wellesley, Massachusetts. They obtained part of the necessary funds from an appeal in *The Word* by a long-time supporter, Abbie Knapp, who wrote that Vesta had an "intense desire to obtain substantial education." Knapp proposed to be "one of fifty or one hundred who would pay a share of expenses. Mrs. W[illiam Lloyd] Garrison's children received such aid; Anna Dickinson was aided by Lucretia Mott."[70]

The Heywood children often stayed home, playing with one another or their parents or getting lessons. Ceres Heywood Bradshaw recalled: "Our mother never taught us any 'liberal' ideas but always dwelt on conscience and our ability to see the right and do it. She was a devoted student of Emerson and in her religious sense she was like a Universalist. She discussed the Bible freely and never shut us out of any type of information." Angela Heywood had grown up working hard, and, according to Stephen Pearl Andrews, had trained her children "in the most laborious, painstaking, housewifely artistic way." She gave her children explicit sex education lessons. Angela recorded: "By my special request Vesta and Hermes were either present at or called in soon after the birth of my two later children, in order that they might have palpable evidence, and individually sense, at what Cost human beings are produced. To the minutest particulars, both before and later, I informed them of what takes place on such occasions and how; of the methods, experiences, processes *involved* in creating them."[71]

Andrews observed that the Heywood children "are welcome guests at all the neighboring houses, but seldom go." Mrs. Houghton remembered "one day in school when the teacher asked for a show of hands from pupils who had ever seen the inside of a prison. Poor Hermes was the only one who held up his hand; he had visited his father in the penitentiary."[72] There was much that separated the Heywood children from other children in Princeton.

Indeed, a large gulf stood between Ezra and Angela Heywood and the residents of Princeton. Harry C. Beaman, a Princeton neighbor, recalled: "He minded his own affairs and had little to do with town's people." The Heywoods' reform leagues, *The Word*, and the publishing operation were consuming projects aimed at regional and national audiences, not necessarily local people. A good example of this gap was the Union Reform League, which held its annual meetings in Princeton. Informal discussions among Mountain Home guests had sparked the formation of the league. Suffragists, labor reformers, free-lovers, and many others streamed into Princeton for several days in the summer to discuss social issues, pass resolutions, and enjoy the country environment, featuring food and lodging at the Mountain Home or another Princeton resort. Beaman described league members as "longhaired men and shorthaired women." Another Princeton citizen observed: "The attendants at these conventions were among the most curious in dress that I had ever seen, or have ever seen since, although I have since then been around the world, and seen some queer people. Once there was the famous Dr. Mary Walker, and there were several women who affected masculine dress. There was one who wore a woman's bonnet, but a man's suit of clothes, and threw over her shoulders a feminine shawl. My grand-mother on seeing her pass would say 'There goes the Man-woman.' "[73]

The Heywoods were connected to their community in certain ways. Operating the Mountain Home was one link to others in town. Lucien V. Pinney noted that it was a "curious and significant fact that the wine which on communion days becomes the blood of Christ in the Methodist Church of Princeton is kept in Mrs. Heywood's cellar, and the bread which also becomes the body of Christ is regularly made of Mr. Heywood's flour and baked in Mrs. Heywood's oven." In 1873, Ezra Heywood was offered but turned down a post on the town school committee. He maintained that *The Word* enjoyed a decent circulation in Princeton. In 1877, Heywood lectured on "Exchange—Its Theory and Practice" before the Princeton Farmers Club, which according to Francis Blake's history of Princeton was extremely influential in social and agricultural circles in the town. At his second obscenity trial, a number of Heywood's neighbors testified to his good character. One neighbor wrote that one issue of *The Word* had been deposited in his father's barn in order to conceal it from vice-suppression authorities. Princeton had been a base for the Shays' Rebellion, and the spirit of resentment against intrusive federal action was still strong. Harris Hawthorne Wilder recalled that Ezra Heywood was a "very scholarly man." Wilder remembered listening to his father and Heywood converse while sitting on his father's piazza: "My father was very witty, and very sarcastic, and his talk tickled Mr. Heywood, but naturally they didn't agree, for my father in religious matters was well brought up and the two used to discuss endlessly without ever agreeing, but both liked to discuss."[74]

According to Stephen Pearl Andrews, Ezra Heywood was more popular than Angela Heywood among Princeton residents. Angela Heywood was a "riddle" to many of them. They acknowledged her "beautiful household, her children at the head of the schools and public exhibitions, their deportment, the chasteness and elegance of their dress & c. . . ." and yet she encountered suspicion and hostility. In contrast, Ezra Heywood, according to Andrews, was "fairly popular; the people, especially the women, strongly inclining to lay all the blame on Mrs. Heywood. . . ." Mrs. Houghton recalled it was the common belief that Ezra Heywood would never have been sentenced to prison were it not for Mrs. Heywood. Kenneth Davis writes: "The redoutable Angela was more radical than he, according to local belief, and less respectful of the opinions of others. For instance, she insisted on washing her clothes on mornings and hanging them out to dry just as people were gathering for church services across the Common." The strong feelings regarding Angela Heywood may have stemmed from her being a strong-tempered advocate of sexual reform. That she was "lively, jovial . . . ladylike . . . eminently domestic," would have pleased her neighbors; but, Andrews noted, she was "hard as flint when her rights, or the rights of those whom she represents, are invaded." That was not ladylike behavior. She was also uncommon in that she was a medium who communicated with spirits. Prejudice against Angela Heywood may have stemmed from the old notion that an evil woman can cause the downfall of a good man.[75]

By 1876, Ezra and Angela Heywood had established a modest degree of success and stability in their lives in Princeton. They were not making a lot of money, but the Mountain Home was producing some income and the publications of the Co-Operative Publishing Company were known among reformers. They were raising a family, pursuing their reform efforts, and had gained respect, or at least toleration, from a good many of their neighbors. Any stability they had would be shattered by the reaction against Ezra Heywood's publication of his pamphlet *Cupid's Yokes*, a denunciation of the marriage institution.

Ezra Heywood involved himself in a wide range of social activities including labor reform, free love, spiritualism, the psuedosciences and dress reform. His frenetic activity could be interpreted as an unpatterned, activist agenda, difficult to summarize and lacking coherence. If there was a reforming cause to join, Ezra Heywood always seemed to be there. Yet, there was an internal logic to Heywood's thinking. At the core of Ezra Heywood's activism was his belief that either the millennium or a total collapse of society was close at hand. He took to heart this evangelical concept as a young man and, despite leaving behind organized religion, the belief stayed with him. If the nation stood on the verge of perfection or disaster, no amount of activity could be too great. Heywood enthusiastically embraced any reform effort that he saw as moving in the direction of human progress.

Just as the religious conversion experience was a highly individual affair, so Heywood believed that social change resulted from an individual transforming his or her ideas. Repeatedly referring to his reform efforts as bringing light to darkness, truth to combat ignorance, spreading the good word, Heywood focused on changing the individual utilizing the language of conversion. In all of Heywood's social change efforts, transformation of the individual, rather than the development of a mass movement, was the critical goal. Heywood's anarchist philosophy and use of the natural rights arguments of the American Revolution were consistent with his insistence that the individual be the central focus of any reform effort.

NOTES

1. Hal D. Sears, *The Sex Radicals: Free Love in High Victorian America* (Lawrence: Regents Press of Kansas, 1977), pp. 6–7.

2. *The Word*, June 1883, p. 2; April 1877, p. 3.

3. *The Truth Seeker*, October 29, 1892, p. 697.

4. Autograph album of Josephine S. Tilton, Denton Family Papers, Labadie Collection, University of Michigan, Ann Arbor; *The Word*, October 1883, p. 1.

5. *Lucifer*, February 19, 1892, p. 3; November 7, 1890, p. 3; *The Word*, November 1888, p. 3. For an example of Lucy Tilton as an officer, see *The Word*, June 1873, p. 1.

6. *The Word*, November 1888, p. 3.

7. Ibid., October 1883, p. 1.

8. Ibid., February 1875, p. 2.

9. Ibid., October 1876, p. 1; March 1884, p. 3; *Liberty*, November 19, 1887, p. 4; *The Word*, October 1881, p. 2; May 1880, p. 2.

10. Ibid., July 1876, p. 1; *Daily Evening Voice*, October 12, 1866, p. 2.

11. In effect, Angela Heywood was criticizing a patriarchal society, although that expression was not in use at her time. Gerda Lerner defines patriarchal values as "the assumption that the fact of biological sex differences implies a God-given or at least a 'natural' separation of human activities by sex, and the further assumption that this leads to a 'natural' dominance of male over female." Gerda Lerner, *The Majority Finds Its Past: Placing Women in History* (New York: Oxford University Press: 1979), p. 169; *The Word*, July 1876, p. 1.

12. Ibid., July 1875, p. 4. For another example of such an incident, see *The Word*, December 1873, p. 4.

13. For Victoria Woodhull's life, see the following: Madeleine B. Stern, "Biographical Introduction," *The Victoria Woodhull Reader* (Weston, Mass.: M and S Press, 1974), pp. 1–11; Geoffrey Blodgett, "Victoria Woodhull," in *Notable American Women, 1670–1950: A Biographical Dictionary* vol. 3, ed. Edward T. James (Cambridge: Harvard University Press, 1971), pp. 652–55; Emanie Sachs, *"The Terrible Siren": Victoria Woodhull* (New York: Harper and Brothers, 1928); Marion Leighton, "Victoria Woodhull Meets Karl Marx," *Liberation Magazine* 20 (Fall 1977): 15–21; Elizabeth Stevens, "Victoria Woodhull," research paper, Brown University, Providence, R.I., 1981.

14. For biographical information on Andrews, see the following: Madeleine B. Stern, *The Pantarch: A Biography of Stephen Pearl Andrews* (Austin: University of Texas Press, 1968); James J. Martin, *Men Against the State: The Expositors of Individualist Anarchism, 1827–1908* (Colorado Springs: Ralph Myles, Publisher, 1970), pp. 153–66; Charles Shively, ed., *Love, Marriage and Divorce and the Sovereignty of the Individual: A Discussion Between Henry James, Horace Greeley, and Stephen Pearl Andrews* (Weston, Mass.: M and S Press, 1975); Stephen Pearl Andrews, *The Science of Society*, ed. Charles Shively (Weston, Mass.: M and S Press, 1970); for Heywood's recollection of learning about Andrews, see *Lucifer*, April 3, 1891, p. 3.

15. Stern, "Biographical Introduction," *Woodhull Reader*, pp. 6, 7; Shively, "Introduction," *Love, Marriage and Divorce*, p. 9; Sachs, "The Terrible Siren," pp. 136–37.

16. Paxton Hibben, *Henry Ward Beecher: An American Portrait* (New York: George H. Doran, 1927), p. 269; Robert Shaplen, *Free Love and Heavenly Sinners:*

The Great Henry Ward Beecher Scandal (New York: Alfred A. Knopf, 1954), pp. 140–52; Sachs, "The Terrible Siren," pp. 167–68; Shaplen, *Free Love*, p. 158; *Boston Globe*, November 19, 1872.

17. Sachs, "The Terrible Siren," pp. 166–68; Shaplen, *Free Love*, pp. 156–59; Hibben, *Beecher*, p. 278.

18. Sachs, "The Terrible Siren," pp. 169–71; Stern, "Biographical Introduction," *Woodhull Reader*, p. 7.

19. Ibid., pp. 7–8.

20. Ralph E. McCoy, "Banned in Boston: The Development of Literary Censorship in Massachusetts," Ph.D. diss., University of Illinois, Urbana, 1956, p. 54; Heywood Broun and Margaret Leech, *Anthony Comstock: Roundsman of the Lord* (New York: Albert and Charles Boni, 1927), pp. 80, 43; Anthony Comstock, *Traps for the Young* (New York: Funk and Wagnalls, 1883), pp. 240–41.

21. Broun and Leech, *Comstock*, pp. 45–67.

22. Ibid., pp. 69–78.

23. McCoy, "Banned in Boston, " p. 51.

24. David Pivar, *Purity Crusade: Sexual Morality and Social Control, 1868–1900* (Westport, Conn.: Greenwood Press, 1973), p. 7.

25. Sears, *The Sex Radicals*, p. 69; McCoy, "Banned in Boston," p. 55.

26. Sears, *The Sex Radicals*, p. 70.

27. Ibid., p. 71.

28. Ibid., p. 72.

29. Sears, *The Sex Radicals*, pp. 37, 69; Broun and Leech, *Comstock*, pp. 184–86.

30. Ibid., p. 188; D. M. Bennett, *The Champions of the Church: Their Crimes and Persecutions* (New York: Liberal and Scientific Publishing House, 1878), p. 1011; Ezra Heywood, *Cupid's Yokes* (Princeton, Mass.: Co-Operative Publishing, 1876), p. 11.

31. Sears, *The Sex Radicals*, p. 74; Broun and Leech, *Comstock*, p. 214.

32. *The Word*, December 1877, p. 3; January 1878, p. 2; Broun and Leech, *Comstock*, p. 274.

33. Sachs, "The Terrible Siren," pp.193–95.

34. Ibid., p. 243; *The Word*, September 1874, p. 3; August 1874, p. 2; January 1873, p. 3; July 1875, p. 1.

35. Ibid., January 1873, p. 3; March 1873, p. 2; *Woodhull and Claflin's Weekly*, December 28, 1872, p. 8; Sachs, "The Terrible Siren," pp. 244–45.

36. *Woodhull and Claflin's Weekly*, March 15, 1873, pp. 5–6.

37. See "Moral Cowardice and Modern Hypocrisy; or, Four Weeks in Ludlow Street Jail, the Suppressed Boston Speech of Victoria Woodhull," *Woodhull and Claflin's Weekly*, December 28, 1872, pp. 3–7.

38. Ibid., March 15, 1873, p. 3; *The Index*, March 15, 1873, pp. 129–30.

39. *The Word*, May 1874, p. 2; July 1874, p. 2; January 1876, p. 2; Blodgett, "Victoria Woodhull," p. 655; for Tucker, see *Liberty*, January 19, 1889, p. 4. Also, see the chapter he wrote in Sachs, "The Terrible Siren," pp. 236–66.

40. *Woodhull and Claflin's Weekly*, April 5, 1873, pp. 3–4.

41. Ibid., p. 4.

42. *The Word,* January 1876, p. 2; May 1876, p. 2.

43. Ibid., September 1873, p. 3; April 1877, p. 2; September 1876, p. 2.

44. *The Word,* May 1876, p. 1.

45. Ibid., p. 2; in an editorial denouncing marriage (*The Word,* April 1877, p. 3), Heywood sought to explain the apparent contradiction of his own marriage in 1865. He was compelled to pay interest, which he believed was robbery, and forced to pay taxes, in his view a form of tyranny. Sending his children to public schools, Heywood argued, was a choice of evils. "When married," Heywood writes that he "acquiesced in the form of marriage, while repudiating it theoretically. Were I placed back 12 years, I should tread underfoot the forms of repression."

46. R. Laurence Moore, *In Search of White Crows: Spiritualism, Parapsychology, and American Culture* (New York: Oxford University Press, 1977), pp. 117, 70–71; Sears, *The Sex Radicals.*

47. Taylor Stoehr, ed., "Introduction," *Free Love in America: A Documentary History* (New York: AMS Press, 1979), p. 35; Sears, *The Sex Radicals,* pp. 8–9; Moore, *In Search of White Crows,* pp. 105–6, 115, 117.

48. Moore, *In Search of White Crows,* pp. 76–77, 85.

49. See chapter on "Spiritualism and the Complaint of Orthodox Christianity," in ibid, pp. 40–69; *The Word,* June 1885, p. 2; Sears, *The Sex Radicals,* p. 15.

50. Moore, *In Search of White Crows,* pp. 117, 70–71.

51. *The Liberator,* October 2, 1863, p. 2; *The Word,* November 1874, p. 4.

52. Ibid., October 1883, p. 1; June 1890. p. 1; Angela Heywood to Elizabeth M. F. Denton, July 3, 1884, Denton Family Papers, Labadie Collection, University of Michigan, Ann Arbor; George E. Macdonald, *Fifty Years of Free Thought* (New York: Truth Seeker, 1929), p. 350.

53. *The Word,* March 1875, p. 2.

54. Ibid., May 1875, p. 2; September 1875, p. 2.

55. Ibid., December 1880, p. 3.

56. For discussion of the psudeosciences, see Taylor Stoehr, *Hawthorne's Mad Scientists: Psuedoscience and Social Science in Nineteenth-Century Life and Letters* (Hamden, Conn.: Shoe String Press, 1978); Stoehr, "Introduction," *Free Love in America.*

57. On dress reform, see *The Word,* April 1874, p. 3; *Woodhull and Claflin's Weekly,* August 8, 1874, p. 14; for more details on dress reform by two people who wrote regularly in *The Word,* see Mary E. Tillotson, *An Essay on the Sanitary and Social Influences of Woman's Dress* (Vineland, N.J.: Self-published, 1873) and J. H. Cook, "Sexual Science and Dress Reform," Parts 1 and 2, *Lucifer,* April 8 and 15, 1892, p. 1; on the abolition of taxes, see *The Word,* December 1875, pp. 1–2 and December 1877, p. 3; on the life insurance plans, see *The Word,* February 1877, p. 3 and November 1876, p. 2.

58. "Humanity—A Call to the Union Reform Convention," undated broadside, Labadie Collection, University of Michigan, Ann Arbor; Ezra Heywood, *The Evolutionists: Being a Condensed Report of the Principles, Purposes, and Methods of the Union Reform League* (Princeton, Mass.: Co-Operative Publishing, 1882),

pp. 3–4, 8; "First Metropolitan Congregation—A Scientific Sermon by Stephen Pearl Andrews" (New York: n.p., n.d.), Labadie Collection, University of Michigan, Ann Arbor; Stern, *The Pantarch*, pp. 105–6.

59. Ibid., pp. 95, 105; *The Word*, February 1881, p. 2; October 1881, p. 3.

60. George H. Bumgardner, *Princeton and the High Roads, 1775–1975* (Princeton, Mass.: Princeton Bicentennial Commission, 1975), pp. 36–37, 40–42; Francis E. Blake, *History of the Town of Princeton, 1759–1915*, vol. 1 (Princeton, Mass.: published by the town, 1915), p. 350; Marion F. Murphy, "The Princeton Story," n.p., n.d., p. 2; for a glowing description of Princeton as a resort in a national magazine, see Helen Hunt Jackson, "Hide and Seek Town," *Scribner's Monthly* 12 (August 1876):449–62; on Princeton's healthy atmosphere, see Atherton P. Mason, "Wachusett Mountain and Princeton," *Granite Monthly: A New Hampshire Magazine* (May-June 1886):152–57.

61. Kenneth S. Davis, "Talk on Ezra H. Heywood," Princeton Historical Society, November 7, 1967; Ceres Heywood Bradshaw to Agnes Inglis, April 10, 1948, Agnes Inglis Papers, Labadie Collection, University of Michigan, Ann Arbor; *The Word*, May 1872, p. 4.

62. Ibid., October 1888, p. 2.

63. Ibid., October 1883, pp. 3, 1; September 1880, p. 3.

64. Ibid., September 1874, p. 2; July 1873, p. 3; July 1877, p. 2.

65. Worcester District Registry of Deeds, Book 1051, pp. 294–96, January 18, 1872; "Old Age and Heart Trouble Bring End to Life of Samuel R. Heywood, Dean of Worcester Business," undated newspaper clipping, Worcester Historical Museum; Charles Henry Bouley, *Biographical Sketches of the Pioneer Settlers of New England and Their Descendants in Worcester, Massachusetts* (Barre, Mass.: Barre Publishers, 1964), pp. 284–86.

66. *The Word*, March 1888, p. 2.

67. Ibid., March 1876, p. 2; interview with Dee Heywood, Boston, October 2, 1981.

68. "Samuel R. Heywood," undated clipping; interview with Dee Heywood; for letters by Joseph H Heywood, see *The Word*, March 1877, p. 3; June 1877, p. 3; for his activities with Ezra and Angela Heywood, see *The Word*, January 1878, p. 2; October 1881, p. 3; for Dwight Heywood, see *The Word*, September 1888, p. 2.

69. Blake, *History of Princeton*, vol. 2, p. 146.

70. *The Word*, October 1883, p. 1; April 1890, p. 2; Ezra Heywood to A. G. Pope, April 4, 1893, bound in Volume 3 of the copy of *The Word*, Rare Book Collection, State Historical Society of Wisconsin, Madison; *The Word*, March 1887, p. 3.

71. Ceres Heywood Bradshaw to Agnes Inglis, April 10, 1948; *The Word*, October 1883, p. 1; May 1884, p. 2.

72. Ibid.; Davis, "Heywood," p. 15.

73. Harry C. Beaman to Zechariah Chafee, September 30, 1929, Hay Library, Brown University, Providence, R. I.; Heywood, *The Evolutionists*, p. 8; Harris Hawthorne Wilder, *The Early Years of a Zoologist: The Story of a New England*

Boyhood, ed. and arranged by Inez Whipple Wilder (Northampton, Mass.: Smith College, 1930), pp. 26–27.

74. *The Word*, June 1890, p. 1; March 1873, p. 3; March 1874, p. 3; January 1877, p. 3; Harry C. Beaman to Zechariah Chafee, May 23, 1929; Wilder, *Early Years of a Zoologist*, p. 26.

75. *The Word*, October 1883, p. 1; Davis, "Heywood," p. 11; *The Word*, October 1883, p. 1.

CHAPTER 5

Cupid's Yokes

I n 1870, Ezra Heywood wrote and published *Uncivil Liberty*, a pamphlet that supported suffrage for women, criticized the institution of marriage, and presented a general argument for women's rights. In 1891, he wrote that *Uncivil Liberty* was intended to be "introductory to *Cupid's Yokes*, showing that woman's suffrage means the abolition of marriage." Heywood saw *Cupid's Yokes* (1876) as his definitive critique of the marriage institution. The 1873 edition of *Uncivil Liberty* indicated sixty thousand copies in print, and, because it was available until the 1890s, its total circulation might have been higher. According to the historian James J. Martin, "It is not believed anything published in the individualistic circle ever exceeded the scope of diffusion of *Uncivil Liberty*."[1]

Heywood based his argument for suffrage on the inviolable sovereignty of each individual and the natural equality of individuals. He condemned "exclusive male sovereignty, which rules one-half of our adult citizens—the women against their consent." The cardinal principle of civil liberty, Heywood declared, "allows every one to do what she or he will, provided they invade not the equal rights of every other one to do the same." The women's declaration of independence drafted at Seneca Falls in 1848 "enumerated grievances equal in number & seriousness to those set down in the famous manifesto of '76, and is destined to work a more extended and beneficent revolution." Heywood condemned suffrage opponents as the moral equivalents of slavemasters or exploiters of labor: "To rule adult citizens against their will is tyranny; women are adult citizens, hence those who deny them the ballot are tyrants."[2] Ezra Heywood shared the Victorian belief that women were more moral than men. Because of this supposed advantage, women's entrance into politics would guarantee "increased order and cleanliness." Woman's suffrage, Heywood felt, would be "a renovating tendency, an entrance into new fields of ethics. . . ."[3]

In *Uncivil Liberty*, Heywood denounced the institution of marriage. He rejected the argument that women were naturally dependent upon men, a position that he maintained was just as false as arguing that slaves required the protection of their masters. He wrote that "Marriage is not a free civil contract, cognizant of mutually grave moral responsibilities as it should be, but a consolidated union, of which man as proposer and disposer, is supreme law. . . . The Negro was just whose cuffy he happened to be; the wife is just whose birdie or drudge she happens to be. As masters quoted law and gospel over their slaves, so husbands emphasize their claim to wedded chattels." Heywood branded marriage coerced consent, which "annihilates existing love and makes its revival impossible." Love would flourish only if men and women were free agents. Heywood argued that people did not make love by statute, but rather that natural affinities dictated social interactions. In attacking marriage, Heywood did not reject the nuclear family, which would retain its place while "enlightened liberty" would "eliminate its defects and universalize its merits."[4]

Heywood believed that when women were truly free, many would reach heights impossible to predict. "Doubtless many superiors to Elizabeth Browning, Margaret Fuller, Charlotte Bronte, and George Sand are buried under our household, sewing shop, fashionable and factory life. . . . Woman, 'as God made her,' we wait to see, having already too much of the man-made woman. . . . In requiring woman to be the shadow, or echo of man, we mar creative intention. . . ." For women to be free, Heywood argued, they must control their own bodies, especially their reproductive functions. Heywood contended that "the makers of men should have free choice of materials, methods and conditions wherewith to perfect her wondrous work."[5]

Heywood emphasized the plight of working-class women in his pamphlet: "We form societies to prevent cruelty to dumb animals, but horses and dogs are better fed and lodged, in our cities, than thousands of working women." Working girls, he maintained, were sucked into "whirlpools of vice" if they managed to escape the harshness of household and factory life. American social life was so dominated by men and so injurious to women's rights that "our laws and customs to-day actually destroy more girls and women than slave codes murdered Negroes!"[6]

By the time Ezra Heywood wrote *Uncivil Liberty* he had been connected with the women's suffrage movement for several years. His earliest radical mentors, Phebe Jackson and Ann Whitney, were dedicated suffragists. During his abolitionist years, his status as a leading Garrisonian meant that he met and worked with many key suffrage advocates. Heywood cooperated with Elizabeth Cady Stanton and other suffragists in the National Labor Union. In its earlier years, *The Word* often covered the suffrage movement. Heywood sided with the Stanton-Anthony faction against the more conservative Stone-Blackwell contingent. Stanton and Anthony, especially in the late 1860s and 1870s, were militant feminists who sought to extend their natural rights principles in an effort to connect the demand for political equality with changes in women's economic and sexual circumstances. As Heywood focused more on free love, he devoted less space in *The Word* to a discussion of suffrage issues, but he remained connected with suffragist organizations.[7]

Elizabeth Cady Stanton was a leading figure in the suffrage movement from the Seneca Falls convention through the 1890s. In the 1870s, she was concerned with the sexual exploitation of women, the nature of marriage, and the need for reform of divorce laws. Her close companion, Susan B. Anthony, focused on economic concerns such as low wages, lack of mobility, and the overall powerlessness of women. Stanton and the Heywoods shared a political sensibility that emphasized individual rights, natural equality, a special concern with the plight of women, and a commitment to radical social change. Thus, in the first year of *The Word*'s publication, Stanton wrote: "I like your little paper exceedingly. Am talking Labor and Suffrage on the 'Stump' and feel that I shall do much good." Stanton remained a loyal supporter of Ezra and Angela Heywood over the years. For example, in the 1870s she was listed as one of the vice presidents of the American Labor Reform League (ALRL).[8] In later years, Stanton's radicalism regarding marriage and the Bible isolated her from the mainstream of the suffrage movement but sustained her close links with the Heywoods.

The chief concern of the women's suffrage movement clearly was not a critique of marriage. Gaining the right to vote, many suffragists believed, would elevate the social status of women in many ways, including increased respect in marital relations. Many suffragists did not share Stanton's critical assessment of marriage; there was a willingness to discuss and criticize marriage in the early phase of the suffrage movement. For example, marriage and divorce were debated at the tenth National Women's Rights Convention in 1860 and in the pages of *The Revolution*, the paper of Stanton and Anthony, in the late l860s. Meeting with small groups of women, Stanton initiated discussions on marriage and maternity. Although she played a key role in initiating discussions on sex and marriage within the suffragist movement, her views were the minority position, and many feared that liberalized divorce would hurt women. Their solution was to try to make men live up to their marital obligations.[9]

Many nineteenth-century suffragists did criticize inequities within marriage. Even so, virtually no one was interested in identifying herself as a free-love advocate. Ernestine L. Rose, an advocate of reformed divorce laws, carefully enunciated her stance regarding free love in 1860: "The question of a Divorce law seems to me one of the greatest importance to all parties, but I presume that the very advocacy of divorce

will be called 'Free Love.' For my part (and I wish distinctly to define
my position), I do not know what others understand by the term; to
me, in its truest significance, love must be free, or it ceases to be love.
In its low and degrading sense, it is not love at all, and I have as little
to do with its name as its reality." Nine years later, in a debate of the
American Equal Rights Association, a resolution introduced by Mary
Livermore declared: "We abhorrently repudiate Free Loveism as horrible
and mischievous to society, and disown any sympathy with it." Also
seeking distance from identification with free love, Lucy Stone spoke
against the resolution: "I feel it is a mortal shame to give any foundation
for the implication that we favor Free Loveism." Ernestine Rose and
Susan B. Anthony, both critics of marriage, felt it was an insult to bother
denying that suffragists were connected with free love.[10]

Elizabeth Cady Stanton, however, declared herself a free-love partisan
in 1870 in an open declaration that was the exception rather than the
rule among suffragists. This was a "major step forward in her ideas,"
according to historian Ellen DuBois, "a move which she attributed to
changes in the 'social medium' and to her own growing 'boldness.'"
DuBois relates that the basic point of Stanton's speech, "On Marriage
and Divorce," was her "criticism of the external regulation of private
affection, either by law, 'dogmatic' public morality, or mutual consent."
Stanton declared: "Freedom, and on this subject! Why, that is nothing
short of unlimited freedom of divorce, freedom to institute at the option
of the parties new amatory relationships, love put above marriage, and
in a word the obnoxious doctrine of Free Love. Well, yes, that is what
I mean. . . . If I mistake not, the true free lovers are among the most
virtuous of men and women."[11]

In his controversial pamphlet *Cupid's Yokes*, Heywood argued that
marriage obliterated individual freedom and denied women the right of
self-government. Church and state interference with feelings of natural
affinity weakened love. Society's efforts to confirm love "by visible bonds
tends to destroy Magnetic Forces which induce unity." Marriage laws
and religious sanctions were ill-fated attempts at superimposing human
devices over "the essential principle of Nature, Love . . . a law unto
itself." Heywood believed that American traditions of liberty and natural
right demanded personal and sexual freedom. He declared that "The
belief that our Sexual Relations can be better governed by state, than
by Personal Choice, is a rude species of conventional impertinence, as
barbarous and shocking as it is senseless. Personal Liberty and the
Rights of Conscience in Love, now savagely invaded by Church, State
and 'wise' Freethinkers, should be unflinchingly asserted." The guar-

antees of personal liberty, derived from the "inspired energy of ancestral reformers," were sufficient weapons for the free-love battle. Asserting faith in human progress and the eventual triumph of superior moral values, Heywood stated: "Protestantism, Magna Charta, Habeas Corpus, Trial by Jury, Freedom of Speech and Press, the Declaration of Independence, Jeffersonian State Rights, Negro-Emancipation, were fore-ordained to help Love and Labor Reformers bury sexual slavery with profit-piracy in their already open graves."[12]

Relationships between men and women, Heywood asserted, should be the result of "mutual discretion—a free compact, dissolvable at will." This freedom of choice, requiring the abolition of marriage, would be of particular importance to women. Heywood wrote that "On account of her political, social, and pecuinary vassalage, woman is the chief martyr to the relentless license granted man." Women could either opt for celibacy, which Heywood viewed as unhealthy, or choose between two types of prostitution. "Social pleasure, being an object of common desire, becomes a marketable commodity, sold by her who receives a buyer for the night, and by her who, marrying for a home, becomes a 'prostitute' for life." Heywood argued that the chief sources of prostitution were marriage, usury, and the exceptionally low wages of women. Thus, the abolition of marriage, the transformation of the economic system, and the elevation of the social and economic status of women were the necessary steps to achieve the emancipation of women.[13]

Heywood believed that love would perish if restricted. He wrote that the "human heart can find its home only in social concord which does not invade the sanctity of Individual Liberty." Consequently, for love to be genuine, which meant voluntary and natural, it had to be free love. Otherwise, love became distorted in the coercive and invasive arrangement of marriage. For Heywood, sexual freedom meant that "every one's person is sacred from invasion." He saw love existing freely in nature and determined by magnetic attractions. Under conditions of freedom, men and women would find suitable mates. Heywood argued that in the absence of marriage, most people would opt for monogamy. The key for Heywood was that any human association be based on freedom, mutual respect, and reciprocal treatment. Free love, he claimed, was not "unrestrained licentiousness." Rather, it depended upon control not generated by the state or church, but from within each individual. Hence, with the triumph of free love, "the sexual instinct shall no longer be a savage, uncontrollable usurper, but be subject to Thought and Civilization."[14]

In the past, Heywood had proclaimed the abolition of slavery and, later, labor reform, as reforms that would change the face of the earth if embraced by the American people. He now spoke of free love in the same fashion: "The loud clamor of words will cease, the majesty of courts fade, churches vanish, Christianity itself pass away, but the still, small voice of Love will continue to be heeded by Earth's millions gathering at its shrine!" Heywood rhapsodized that love, sired by wisdom and born of truth, "stimulates enterprise, quickens industry, fosters self-respect, reverences the lowly and worships the Most High, and harmonizes personal impulse with the demands of morality, in a well-informed faith. . . ." Heywood transposed the millennial faith of his abolitionist years to free love, declaring that *Cupid's Yokes* was announcing the "New Heavens and the New Earth, the Natural Society, foreseen by sensitives, poets, and philosophers."[15]

Heywood believed that the study of human physiology was essential. Only with such knowledge could women and men exercise self-government. He urged young men and women "to give religiously serious attention to the momentous issues of Sexual Science." However, Anthony Comstock sought to prevent such discussion: "In families, schools, sermons, lectures, and newspapers . . . candid conversation is so studiously suppressed that children and adults know nothing of it, except what they learn from their own diseased lives and imaginations, and in the filthy by-ways of society." Heywood denounced Comstock for acting with the "spirit that lighted the fires of the Inquisition." He branded Comstock a "religious *mono-maniac*, whom the mistaken will of Congress and the lascivious fanaticism of the Young Men's Christian Association have empowered to use the Federal Courts to suppress Free Inquiry."[16]

Ezra Heywood's writing style in the twenty-three page *Cupid's Yokes* was scholarly and rather wordy; he attacked marriage, defended women's rights, and issued a challenge to Comstock and his supporters. Most of this was done employing logic and careful argumentation. Despite some dramatic rhetorical flourishes, the pamphlet's prose was much less racy than the lewd materials that obscenity opponents may have expected.

In contrast, Angela Heywood's prose was much more spontaneous, rapturous, and undisciplined. The reformer Lucien V. Pinney described how they differed: "She is volatile in expression and frets under the inexorable and necessary editorial condensation of Mr. Heywood, which she rightly feels is fatal to flexible and melodious expression. He is the sententious writer of resolutions butchering her beauties of song to expose the bare bones of an idea. . . ." Heywood did edit some of Angela Heywood's articles, but he allowed her a good deal of free expression in the pages of *The Word*. He had the highest praise for her writing, calling her a "priestess of purity" and "an oracle of what is right best natural and modest in human-body life."[17]

Angela Heywood wrote spirited attacks on male supremacy, focusing especially on men's sexual attitudes. She coined the phrase "invasive heism." She argued that heism—later to be termed sexism—had subjected women to men's desires in past history but now faced insurgent woman. She was delighted to see "woman's growing impulse to be *mistress of her own Person*." Angela Heywood understood that men would change their social and sexual attitudes only if confronted by strong, independent women. She argued that women were much more than household drudges or sexual objects. Man, she declared, "has not yet achieved himself to realize and meet a PERSON in woman, except as he needs her to cook, wash, sew, and give him prone flesh acceptance." Beginning in 1848 at Seneca Falls, women were actively asserting their natural rights, she argued, and men had better learn their natural responsibilities. Regarding sexuality, Angela Heywood believed that men needed to temper their violent natures and not reduce sex, as so often happened, to virtual rape. Angela Heywood declared that man "*should have solemn meeting with, and look seriously at his own penis until he is able to be lord and master of it, rather than it should longer rule, lord and master, of him, and of the victims he deflowers.*" Heywood declared that any woman had a right to use birth control devices or even procure an abortion in order to maintain control over her own body.[18] She believed that an active women's movement would force men to behave responsibly in sexual encounters and, further, lead to changes in society where men and women eventually would become equals.

Angela did not confine her discussion of sexual issues to criticism of men's behavior and attitudes. Rather, much of her writing constituted a joyous, celebratory ode to the human body and sexuality. The human body, she enthused, was the "sweetest exhalation of life." She urged women and men to wake up and "see that human bodies are naturally wholesome, and that the obscenity scare lies mainly in *diseased* mentality." Angela Heywood often referred to the beauty and charm of the penis and, as she termed the female genitals, the womb. For example, she wrote: "Verily how hath Natural Modesty forgotten herself if the Penis and Womb be not elegant organs of the Human Body, equal, in ability to entertain us, with the eye and tongue." Her pronouncements on sex were some of the boldest of any sex radical. She not only extolled the sensuality of the penis, but also praised it in spiritual terms for being the source of children. Her expression was simultaneously one of playfulness and physical delight coupled with a solemn, controlled role for the penis in sexual relations. She wrote: "What mother can look in the face of her welcome child and not religiously respect the rigid, erect, ready-for-service, persistent male-organ that sired it? . . . Built projective, carrying the seed of Life, ordained to propose what woman may accept. . . ."[19]

Angela and Ezra Heywood argued that the cross in Christianity represented the phallus. Despite their desire to do away with Christian phallic symbolism, the Heywoods argued that the penis should be a subject for frank conversation and treatment because it played such an important representational role in human history and such a key role in human sexuality. The cross, Angela Heywood maintained, denoted generation and regeneration. The penis as symbol in history had immense importance, she argued: "There is not a form, an idea, a grace, a sentiment, a felicity in art which is not owing, some way, to phallicism, and its means of indication which at one time in the monuments—statuesque, architectural—covered the whole earth. There is not a religion that does not spring from it. . . . The tower denoted the male power of the universe; the pyramid, triangle or cone, bespoke procreative female energy."[20]

One of the central contributions of free-lovers to sexual reform was their recognition of the existence, legitimacy, and positive value of women's sexual drive. Angela Heywood wrote clearly on this issue: "It is insipid falsehood for woman to pretend to man that the sex-fact is not as much to her, as it is to him; of the confluent contracting parties she is an equal unit, able to give, as to receive, good. . . . Esthetic approach, intelligent Touch, the art of sex-conminglement, their power for good is omnipresent in human being!" It was unnatural, she maintained, to assert that women's sexuality was any less potent than men's. The natural rights theory was extended here to the bedroom.[21]

Like other free-lovers, Ezra and Angela Heywood believed that separation of amative and propagative functions served to distinguish sexual feelings of attraction from a desire to bear children. Amative sex, which excluded male ejaculation, produced an exchange of electric or magnetic charges between a man and a woman, resulting in health and energy for both persons. Angela Heywood was poetic about the magnetic exchange, which she understood to be the physiological correlative of love. Genuine lovers, she asserted, should be "touched by the electric energy of Truth." This form of lovemaking was noble, pure, and invigorating. It would signal, she believed, the coming of a new man and a new woman and the dawning of an age of social justice: "the light beam of thought between two builds society, is transition from the old unto the new."[22]

Angela Heywood's tone of expression was open, bold, and liberating. She believed that sexuality was "a divine ordinance, elegantly natural from any eye-glance to the vital action of penis and womb, in personal exhilaration or for reproductive uses." Sexuality was a part of every person's being, "an ever-present irresistibly-potent fact; effort to outwit Actuality, to ignore, stultify or repress the very Soul of Nature befits immature times." Angela Heywood maintained that sexuality was an immense force, "fraught with immeasurable power for good or ill." Thus, it should be "inspired by the well-informed sense of moral obligation born on Love." In contrast to this emphasis on control, Angela Heywood was capable of extolling passion and sexual activity. For example, she wrote: "What is inexpressible in words the generative organs speak by feeling, so alive are they." Or, she declared: "In sex adjustment what have I to work with if not the glowing heats of man's body waiting for throbbing, answering heats in woman's person? To behave well both in thought and deed one must know that nothing in its proper time, place or use is 'common' or 'unclean.' "

Angela Heywood took a swipe at the critics of free love by berating them for posing lust in diametrical opposition to love. She observed that "the antithesis of Love is *hate*; while lust means full, glowing healthy animal heat. Passion is a fruitful source of beneficent power." The paradoxical attachment to both control and freedom was frequently expressed in her articles and, at times, in the very same sentence. Thus, she wrote: "Lust, passion is good and will be everywise serviceable when, receptive to intonations of right, we honestly speak of our body-selves in face-to-face thought."[23]

In frank language, Angela Heywood urged men and women to recognize that they were sexual beings and to express their sexual feelings. In this sense, her position was profoundly radical. Her writing reflected the overall tension among free-lovers between control and freedom. Her thinking was internally consistent in that, for her, self-control was a crucial aspect of human sexuality and a requirement for a free exchange based on mutual respect.

Taylor Stoehr has described the history of the free-love movement as the "history of a lunatic fringe." However, he quickly qualifies himself and writes that this description is not quite fair, "for few and eccentric as they were, the free lovers stood for a serious alternative to monogamy, which many observers in the middle of the nineteenth century recognized as in need of repair." No people, with the exception of chattel slaves, writes Ellen DuBois, had less proprietary rights over themselves than married women in the eighteenth and early nineteenth centuries.

The free-love movement was numerically strongest in the decades before the Civil War. It included the hydropathists Mary Gove and Thomas Nichols, part of the popular health movement, and several men and women in such utopian communities as Modern Times and Oneida. Stoehr argues that in the post-Civil War period, the free-love effort was "no longer evangelical or coherent enough to be considered a movement. Anthony Comstock was kicking a dead horse back into life, and the last gasps of free love were as a libertarian holding-action against censorship."[24]

The scale of the postwar, sexual reform movement was small, but its intensity was great. Newspapers like Ezra Heywood's *The Word*, Moses Harman's *Lucifer the Lightbearer*, *Foote's Health Monthly*, edited by Dr. Edward Bliss Foote, and D. M. Bennett's *The Truth Seeker* maintained a network of supporters and disseminated sex-reform ideas across the country. Heywood and Harman were self-avowed free-lovers; Foote emphasized health issues, while Bennett was a free-thought advocate. Still, Bennett and Foote published many free-love writers and offered support to the movement.

Free-lovers advocated freedom in personal relations and challenged the repressive ideology of Comstock and his supporters. They rejected conventional marriage and moral standards and demanded that women have the sexual autonomy customarily enjoyed only by men. Free-lovers asserted that sexual intercourse should occur only when both partners were willing. Free love focused on a restrictive definition of freedom: a woman had the right to deny her vagina to anybody, including her husband. An active choice and not coercion or a sense of duty should be the basis upon which a woman would decide to have sex. Ezra Heywood declared: "Free love simply appeals from collective despotism to Individual discretion; and state-marriage, like a state-church, denies the right of private judgment in morality, puts science under the censorship of ignorance, and assails the nature and tendency of things." Signers to the call for the national free-love convention in Ravenna, Ohio, on December 7, 1873, included Ezra and Angela Heywood, Josephine Tilton, and Benjamin Tucker. The resolutions of the convention declared that human rights inhered in human nature and were inalienable, and denounced the United States government as a fraud and conspiracy. Women's freedom and equality were emphasized. Freedom for women involved their right to vote; to choose their own vocation; to dress as they liked; to control their sexuality; and their right to birth control. The assembled free-lovers demanded that the slavery of women be abolished. For espousing these views, free-lovers were subjected to regular and vicious attacks. A representative but especially biting comment was Brick Pomeroy's characterization of free-lovers in the *Democrat*: "long-haired men, short-haired women, drowsy boozers who see visions, grass widows who go hell-pestling over the land for affinities, bleary-eyed old roues, who claim to be pillars of the new Jerusalem, luscious-lipped virgins in training for the new church, and discarded husbands."[25]

There were differences within the free-love camp. Exclusivists, who were the majority, argued that true love could only exist between two people. Varietists held that love, like lust, naturally sought variety in its arrangements. Ezra and Angela Heywood actually argued both positions at different times, but could be most clearly identified with the exclusivists. The leading exponents of the varietist view were Victoria Woodhull and Moses Hull, who edited a paper, *Hull's Crucible*. Still, all free-lovers believed a woman should be absolutely free to live as she pleased; she might have many sexual partners or none at all. No outside authority had the right to intervene.[26]

Comstock's attacks on free-lovers Victoria Woodhull, George Francis Train, John Lant, and Dr. Edward Bliss Foote prompted Ezra Heywood to write *Cupid's Yokes*. Woodhull's "crime," described in chapter 4, consisted of exposing the Beecher-Tilton affair in the pages of her paper, *Woodhull and Claflin's Weekly*. In 1872, the remarkable eccentric Train, acting in support of Woodhull, deliberately provoked Comstock by printing some arguably obscene portions of the Old Testament in his journal, *The Train Ligue*. Arrested by Comstock on an obscenity charge, Train spent five months in prison before the trial judge ducked the issue of obscenity by declaring Train insane. Train regularly contributed long, outlandish poems to *The Word*. Lant edited a free-thought journal called *The Toledo Sun*, first in Ohio and later in New York. D. M. Bennett observed that the most objectionable matter in this paper "was a letter from Dr. E. P. Miller on physiological matters and a prayer by G. F. Train called 'Beecher's Prayer.'" He found the paper "far from immoral." Nonetheless, Comstock arrested Lant and secured an obscenity conviction for which Lant served eighteen months in prison and was fined $200.[27]

Foote had built his career as a writer and reformer in part on public advocacy of prevention of conception and free speech about sexual matters. He was an ardent feminist in the tradition of the popular health movement, and his writing on birth control and sex emphasized women's rights. He sold hundreds of thousands of his medical publications, and his New York City establishment contained a small pharmaceutical factory where he manufactured patent medicines. Foote also contributed to the development of contraceptive technology with his invention of the rubber cervical cap that he termed the "Womb Veil." In 1876, he was arrested for mailing a letter of advice on contraception, along with his pamphlet *Words in Pearl*, which contained contraceptive information, in response to a decoy inquiry sent by one of Comstock's agents. He was convicted and fined $3,000, however he and his son, Edward Bond Foote, continued to be advocates of women's rights and contributed a great deal of time and large sums of money from the profits of their medical practice to the defense of those Comstock persecuted.[28]

Anthony Comstock was part of a larger social phenomenon, the movement to achieve social purity (chapter 4). Social purity advocates encompassed critics of prostitution, temperance advocates, dress reformers, censors of obscene literature, and others. Purity reform had no philosophical consistency other than a deep concern for the future if public morality continued to decline. Purity reformers sought social perfection, which depended upon the the remolding of social character.[29]

Social and sexual relations were changing as the economy changed. The nineteenth century brought rapid industrialization, with farmers and artisans increasingly disappearing into the urban workforce. This urbanized working class was swelled by foreign immigrants. In place of the relatively egalitarian division of labor in pre-industrial society came a type of social organization that placed women in the role of tending to the home while men worked in the outside world. Women's new role as the "true woman" called for piety, purity, submissiveness, and domesticity. The cult of the true woman conflicted with an alternative image of woman as a totally sexual creature.

Sexual standards for men were also changing. Although men's natural sexual appetite was perceived as enormous, in order to advance in the industrial capitalist order, they were expected to conserve their energies. Sexual energy, viewed as highly potent and forceful, could be reined in to a man's advantage in the commercial world. A sexual double standard emerged in which many men were virtuous and restrained with their wives and sought pleasure with prostitutes. Other men spoke of virtue, but in the privacy of their bedrooms either assaulted their wives or simply sought their own pleasure with little consideration for the pleasure or even comfort of their wives. Still other men behaved with the greatest restraint sexually, not wanting to injure the frail female. Charles Rosenberg has written that it was not so much repression that characterized male Victorian sexuality, "but rather a peculiar and in some ways irreconcilable conflict between the imperatives of the Masculine Achiever and the Christian Gentleman. Few males were completely immune from the emotional reality of both." Women's sexuality was generally perceived as passive, with the dangerous reverse image of a voracious libertine, and male sexuality had an active image of uncontrollable force and power.[30]

Victorian sexual prudery had a complexity that represented its complex social function. Linda Gordon writes that it was a result of "a norm set by the bourgeois itself, a discipline imposed on the labor force, and the working class's own adaptation to new conditions of production." Precisely because male authority among the working class was being weakened by changing industrial relations, the stability of the traditional family required the imposition of a repressive ideology. Self-denial and chastity were imposed on women, while men created the greatest prostitution industry in history.[31]

Ezra Heywood emphasized self-control for working men and women because he feared the anger and volatile sexuality that he believed lay just beneath the social fabric of the city. However, self-control should be voluntary, not imposed by church or state. Free love in fact may be seen as a version of social purity. Free-lovers sought social improvement by emphasizing reason and liberty rather than stressing a repressive morality that portrayed sexuality as evil and promoted strict regulation of people's lives. The differences between the two groups overshadowed the similarities. Advocates of purity saw conventional marriage, home, and the family as the moral and organizational bases of society. In contrast, free-lovers saw the individual, not the conventional family, as the natural basis of society. Still, both Comstockers and free-lovers saw sex as an awesome power that demanded control of one sort or another. Comstockers feared sex, were repelled by it, and could not accept liberty. The sex radicals argued that all societal restrictions should be abolished so that individual reason could control sexuality. The sex radicals believed that individual reason was the basis of society, the strongest civilizing force, and the real power that could curb the dangers inherent in unbridled sexuality.[32]

According to Benjamin Tucker, the first legal attack on *The Word* came in April 1875, when A. B. Westrup, agent of *The Word* and the American Labor Reform League, was arrested for selling obscene literature in New Martinsville, West Virginia. Westrup was able to get the case dismissed. Attacks on Ezra Heywood and his printed utterances were to become sharper and more frequent following the publication of *Cupid's Yokes*, which did not receive a warm reception from many commentators. Two examples from "The Opposition" column in *The Word* are indicative. The Reverend William Fishbough wrote in *Religio-Philosophical Journal*: "Thus away goes the family institution, and with it down go all the existing institutions of society—all ruthlessly knocked to pieces and annihilated! . . . Its direct tendency is to overthrow all forms of civilization, and to re-inaugurate savageism, animalism, and universal bestiality. . . ." *The Worcester Press* warned that Ezra Heywood was making Princeton a "hotbed of free love. . . . He has just published a piece of smut—*Cupid's Yokes* . . . and will perhaps forgive the impulse which made us burn it. He appears to be a gentleman of culture, acts well, talks well, but writes and prints fearful things. . . ." In the summer of 1877, Josephine Tilton was arrested in Newburyport, Massachusetts, for selling *Cupid's Yokes*, but was released for lack of a case against her.[33]

Only a few months later, in the fall of 1877, Anthony Comstock arrested Ezra Heywood for distributing *Cupid's Yokes* and forced him to face a trial. Comstock went after Heywood because he believed free love "crushes self-respect, moral purity, and holy living. Sure ruin and death are the end to the victims caught by this doctrine . . . it is the mantle for all kinds of license and uncleanliness. . . . It should be spelled l-u-s-t. . . ." Comstock characterized free-lovers as "a few indecent creatures calling themselves reformers—men and women of foul speech, shameless in their lives, and corrupting in their influences—we must go to a sewer that has been closed, where the accumulations of filth have for years collected, to find a striking resemblance" to the true character of the free-lovers. He continued: "I know of nothing more offensive to decency, or more revolting to good morals," than this class of publication. Comstock warned: "All restraints which keep boys and girls, young men and maidens pure and chaste, which prevent our homes from being turned into voluntary brothels are not to be tolerated by them. Nothing short of turning the whole human family loose to run wild like the beasts of the forest will satisfy the demands of leaders and publishers of this literature." Comstock termed Ezra Heywood "the chief creature of this vile creed," and the author of "a most obscene and loathsome book," *Cupid's Yokes*.[34]

Comstock's description of his arrest of Ezra Heywood at a Boston free-love convention is filled with melodrama and self-righteousness: "I looked over the audience of about 250 men and boys. I could see lust in every face. After a little the wife of the president (the person I was after) took the stand, and delivered the foulest address I ever heard. She seemed lost to all shame. The audience cheered and applauded. It was too vile; I had to go out, I wanted to arrest the leader and end the base performance. There my man sat on the platform, puffed up with egotism. I looked at him and at the 250 eager faces, anxious to catch every word that fell from his wife's lips. . . ." Comstock left the hall to regain his composure. Outside, he thought to himself: "It is infamous that such a thing as this is possible in any part of our land, much more in Boston. It must be stopped. But how?" Comstock found the "fresh air never was more refreshing." He resolved to "stop that exhibition of nastiness, if possible. I looked for a policeman. As usual, none was to be found when wanted. Then I sought light and help from above. I prayed for strength to do my duty, and that I might have success. I knew God was able to help me. Every manly instinct cried out against my cowardly turning my back on this horde of lusters. I determined to try. I resolved that one man in America at least should enter a protest."

Comstock climbed the two flights of stars and reentered the hall. He declared that the "stream of filth continued until it seemed to me I could not sit a moment longer." At that point, Ezra Heywood left the stage for an anteroom on the side and there Comstock arrested him. The vice hunter grabbed Heywood by the nape of the neck and rushed him down the stairs. To his rear, he heard the yell of the audience and the sounds of people scrambling out of the hall. He shoved Heywood into his waiting carriage and set off for Charles Street Jail. Thus, Comstock concluded, was the "devil's trapper trapped."[35]

The scene Comstock so melodramatically described took place at a New England Free Love League convention on Friday night, November 2, 1877, in Nassau Hall, Boston. Writing after his arrest, Ezra Heywood declared: "Today I am held as a criminal under United States law on the complaint, not of one who knows me or favors the beneficent object to which my life is devoted, but of a person from another state, a prominent exponent of prevailing unreason. . . ." He described his arrest: "While lawfully and peacefully at work . . . in Boston, as I had momentarily left the chair in which I was presiding over a public convention to transact business in an anteroom, a stranger sprang upon me, and refusing to read a warrant, or even give his name, hurried me into a hack, drove swiftly through the street, on a dark, rainy night, and lodged me in jail as a 'US prisoner.' " It was only the next morning that Heywood was permitted to read the arrest warrant and discover that the "rude stranger" was Comstock. Heywood reacted with some amazement that his personal integrity was being challenged: "Twenty years, before the intelligent eyes and pure minds of New England citizens, have I pursued my work unmolested, except by sporadic mobs from the streets which all reformers have to encounter; never before was my ability to use intelligent and chaste language questioned." He also felt fury and indignation: "Knowing the purity of my life and writings, the severely chaste objects and methods of my work, I *scorn* even to defend myself from 'obscenity' against the mercenary assassin of liberty!"[36]

A federal grand jury in Boston presented a two-count indictment against Ezra Heywood. He was charged with mailing two obscene publications in September 1877, R. T. Trall's *Sexual Physiology* and *Cupid's Yokes*, to E. Edgewell of Squam Village, New Jersey. Edgewell was one of the many bogus names Comstock employed. Severe restrictions were placed on Heywood's right to defend himself. The prosecutor had decided which passages were obscene, underlined them, and presented them to the grand jury. The returned indictment only mentioned the title of the book, without specifying the particular sections that were held obscene.[37]

Heywood went on trial before Judge Daniel Clark of the United States Circuit Court in Boston on January 22, 1878. The individualist anarchist Sidney Morse described the scene: "The court-room was crowded by a remarkably intelligent and intensely interested audience. . . . Large numbers of Mr. Heywood's personal friends and sympathizers were present, but much the larger portion of the audience was made up of the general public, brought together not by mere curiosity, but in all seriousness of purpose." The case, in the view of Morse and many others, would try the right of free expression of opinion. The assistant district attorney declared that there were only two questions for the jury—did Ezra Heywood mail the works as charged, and were they obscene? The prosecution called only two witnesses, Anthony Comstock and David H. Gregory, the Princeton postmaster. The impact of their testimony was to affirm that Ezra Heywood had indeed mailed the publications in question. Comstock, of course, testified that the works were obscene.[38]

Throughout the trial, Ezra Heywood was hampered by the limitations set by the court. The prosecutor was not required to read the allegedly obscene passages into the court records or to the jury. The prosecutor in the Heywood case, Charles Almy, Jr., chose not to read the passages, stating that they were too foul for the court records. Thus, the jury did not see or hear the allegedly obscene materials until they entered the jury room for their deliberations. In addition, Heywood was not able to present a defense that dealt with the issues of obscenity. Obscenity was a question for the jury to decide without being confused by the defendant's arguments. Heywood's lawyers had to restrict their case to a discussion of whether or not Heywood had mailed the materials in question. Heywood was not allowed to discuss the purpose of *Cupid's Yokes* or its overall philosophy; he was even prohibited from calling character witnesses.[39]

Heywood's lawyers, George F. Searle and J. W. Pickering, attempted to introduce certain medical books as evidence. They hoped that the jury would find that these books, which were not subject to censorship, were similar in nature to R. T. Trall's work. However, Judge Clark ruled that these texts were irrelevant to the case and that their obscenity could not be passed on by the jury.[40]

Trall was a significant figure in nineteenth-century health reform, and his book, *Sexual Physiology* (1864), was a popular work that went through several editions. A hydropathist, Trall edited the *Water-Cure Journal* and ran a hydropathic establishment in New York City. Trall was a moving spirit in the forming of the American Vegetarian Society, and the society held its 1855 annual meeting at his New York Center with Lucy Stone, Amelia Bloomer, Susan B. Anthony, and Horace Greeley in attendance. The fact that Comstock went after Trall's book in this instance and Foote in an earlier case was proof that Comstock made no fine distinctions in his war on sex education.

Trall was a sexual conservative whereas Foote, a clear advocate of contraception, suggested in *Plain Home Talk* that frequency of sexual intercourse "ought to be determined by pleasure," at least in part. Millions of copies of sexual and marriage manuals written by Trall, Foote, and others were sold. Through *The Word* and the Co-Operative Publishing Company, Ezra Heywood regularly offered for sale Trall's book, Foote's *Plain Home Talk* and *Medical Common Sense*, and Robert Dale Owen's *Moral Physiology*. It is unclear how greatly Americans profited from these books. Taylor Stoehr writes: "Perhaps people bought these books called *Home Treatment, Plain Home Talk, Plain Facts*, and so on because they were in need. Perhaps for them it was a form of pornography, as Anthony Comstock firmly believed."[41]

The defense called twenty witnesses to the stand, but only a handful— Elizur Wright, Sidney H. Morse, A. E. Giles, and Dr. J. M. Bruce—were permitted to testify. Their testimony was ineffective, however, because they were not allowed to speak about Ezra Heywood's character or to assess whether or not, in their views, *Sexual Physiology* and *Cupid's Yokes* were obscene publications. Attorney Pickering, in his closing argument, portrayed Ezra Heywood as a man of education and a reputable reformer. He defended the books in question, calling them moral and useful. Further, Pickering stressed that freedom of the press was a key question in the case.[42]

In closing for the government, District Attorney Cummings argued that the defense had raised a number of irrelevant issues: Ezra Heywood's character, his reform work, the danger to free speech and press, and criticism of Anthony Comstock. The facts of the case were that Ezra Heywood had mailed the two books and that they were obscene. Cummings spoke about the terrible effect such a pernicious doctrine as free love would be likely to have upon boys and girls in school and upon others who had not reached the age of mature judgment. He read extracts to illustrate his point, in a manner, according to Sidney H. Morse, "to say the least, not calculated to impress the jury with a fair idea of its author's spirit or the meaning of his words." From Morse's courtroom observations, he concluded: "The whole force of the Attorney's argument is directed to showing that such doctrines have an immoral tendency, and for that reason he pronounces them obscene. . . . In other words, the whole objection to the book is that it advocates ideas which the District Attorney does not conceive to be moral and sound."[43]

Judge Clark delivered an extremely biased charge to the jury. Sidney Morse observed: "The undisguised partisanship of the Court is commented on by nearly all present." For example, Clark told the jury that Heywood's free-love doctrines would turn Massachusetts into one great house of prostitution. Judge Clark declared that an obscene book was one that was offensive to decency by exciting impure or lewd thoughts or by inciting the practice of impure desires. An obscene book needed only to contain an immoral tendency, and only part of the book needed to be obscene for it to come within the meaning of the Comstock law. Many free-speech advocates were shocked and pointed out after the trial that works by Byron, Shakespeare, and Burns, as well as the Bible itself, could be proscribed under the prosecution's arguments and Clark's interpretations. For example, an editorial in *Foote's Health Monthly* argued that it was not possible to regard *Cupid's Yokes* as an obscene publication "calculated to pollute the minds of the youth, for the youthful mind, unless given to dry, philosophic, or scientific study, would not be likely to proceed for more than a page or two without throwing it down as devoid of interest." The editorial advised the Society for the Suppression of Vice "to go for the writing of Benjamin Franklin, Robert Owen, Herbert Spencer, John Stuart Mill, and a great variety of other literary productions from which Mr. Heywood makes quotations quite as startling to the conservative mind as much that he himself has written. We would like to have District Attorney Cummings look through some of our best libraries and proceed according to the standard he has erected for the arraignment of *Cupid's Yokes*. . . ."[44]

The jury found that *Sexual Physiology* was not obscene, but ruled that *Cupid's Yokes* was and pronounced Heywood guilty of mailing this objectionable publication. Sentencing was postponed pending an appeal by Heywood's attorneys. On June 25, 1878, before Nathan Clifford, the Honorable Associate Justice of the United States Supreme Court, and Judge Daniel Clark, Heywood's lawyers appealed on the grounds that the Comstock law was a violation of the First Amendment in that it denied free speech. The appeal was delayed until June because the court wanted to hear the outcome of a relevant case being heard before the

Supreme Court. That case, *Ex parte Jackson* (1877), challenged the con-
stitutionality of the Comstock law on the grounds that it denied free
speech. The Supreme Court ruled that the law was constitutional, and
Heywood's appeal was denied. The defense counsel then made a motion
for arrest of judgment based on a flaw in the indictment. This was denied
and, subsequently, Ezra Heywood was sentenced to two years in Dedham Jail in Norfolk County, Massachusetts, and fined $100; he could
have been fined up to $5,000 and received up to three years in jail. To
the anger and dismay of Angela Heywood and Heywood's many supporters, he was escorted from the Boston courtroom and to prison in
Dedham.[45]

   Shortly after Ezra Heywood entered prison, Josephine Tilton, W. S.
Bell, and D. M. Bennett were arrested in August 1878, in Watkins Glen,
New York, for selling *Cupid's Yokes*. The three were attending a meeting
of the New York State Freethinkers Association when they were appre-
hended by local officials, who acted under a state Comstock law. Repression often results in popularizing the suppressed item, and that occurred
in this case. *Foote's Health Monthly* reported that "we have information
which enables us to state that the book trade of these enthusiasts was
decidedly dull until the arrests were made." Flora Tilton wrote that
Josephine Tilton took six hundred copies of *Cupid's Yokes* to the meeting
"and sold all, and could have sold more if she had them; most of them
were sold after the arrest. . . . Sunday we could have got a dollar apiece
for them so I heard [regular price was fifteen cents per copy]." Josephine
Tilton decided to refuse bail, preferring, as *Foote's Health Monthly* put
it, "that the people of Watkins should be left with the white elephant
on their hands in view of their illiberal proceedings." Flora Tilton noted
that Josephine Tilton was happy and confident that everything would
work out for the best. A defense lawyer convinced Josephine Tilton that
her action so angered local citizens that if she remained in jail the
prosecution of the case would be much worse. She relented and decided
to accept bail, posted by the veteran abolitionist Lucy Colman. The
three went to court in December 1878, but the case was postponed and
never brought to trial.[46]
   D. M. Bennett was a leading proponent of free speech. In Cincinnati,
he had operated a lucrative business selling various cures based on his
knowledge of botanicals. Bennett read Thomas Paine's *The Age of Reason*
and became committed to free thought, eventually dedicating himself
full time to anti-clericalism. He published a successful free-thought paper, *The Truth Seeker*, in New York City. Bennett saw the Comstock law
as a threat to liberty and was instrumental in organizing repeal efforts.[47]

Unable and unwilling to distinguish between free-speech advocates and actual pornographers, Comstock pursued Bennett aggressively. Watkins Glen had been the second arrest for Bennett. Shortly after Ezra Heywood's arrest, Comstock raided Bennett's *Truth Seeker* office and arrested him on charges of blasphemy as well as obscenity for mailing a scientific pamphlet, *How Do Marsupials Propagate*, by H. B. Bradford, and a tract written by Bennett, *An Open Letter to Jesus Christ*. As usual, Comstock had used a decoy letter to set up the charges. Dr. Edward Bliss Foote paid the bail and used his influence to seek a dismissal. The noted free-speech fighter Robert Ingersoll's protest to the postmaster general and other Washington officials succeeded, and the charges against Bennett were dismissed.[48]

In the aftermath of Watkins Glen, D. M. Bennett decided to challenge Anthony Comstock directly. In *The Truth Seeker*, he pledged a crusade for his right to distribute *Cupid's Yokes* even though he did not endorse its views. In October 1878, Flora Tilton wrote from Boston to a friend that "Bennett has sold one thousand copies of *Cupid's Yokes*. They are more active in New York than they are here." Anthony Comstock was acutely aware of this activity and wrote another decoy letter, a semiliterate request from "G. Brackett, Granville, N.Y.," which ordered some pamphlets and "that Heywood book you advertise Cupid's something or other." Comstock again arrested Bennett, and this time won a conviction against the editor. Judge Samuel Blatchford, who wrote the landmark decision, fined Bennett $300 and sentenced him to thirteen months in prison.[49]

For more than half a century Blatchford's decision on *Cupid's Yokes* would be the basis of obscenity law in the United States. Even before this 1879 decision, lower courts had been aware of the English "*Hicklin* standard," a formula for determining obscenity advanced in *Queen v. Hicklin* (1868). This standard held that the test for obscenity was, in the words of Lord Chief Justice Cockburn, "whether the tendency of the matter charged as obscenity is to deprave and corrupt those whose minds are open to immoral influences, and into whose hands a publication of this sort may fall." The *Hicklin* case permitted a work to be judged according to certain isolated passages, not by its general import. Further, it provided that an indictment for obscenity did not have to spell out the alleged obscenity in the court records provided that its offensiveness was cited in the indictment and that the work was sufficiently identified so that the defendant knew the identity of the work. In Ezra Heywood's case, Judge Clark and District Attorney Cummings were familiar with and endorsed the *Hicklin* standard. Indeed, Blatchford's opinion drew substantially from the *Cupid's Yokes* trial a year earlier.[50]

The small New England town of Dedham was located south of Boston. In the twentieth century, the town jail held the Italian anarchists Sacco and Vanzetti while they stood trial for murder and robbery. Ezra Heywood was employed in the jail weaving cane bottoms for chairs. He recalled that prison officials were "very liberal," allowing him to receive mail regularly, to write letters freely, and to have all the newspapers he wanted. Heywood exercised his writing privileges fully; Flora Tilton wrote that she heard from Heywood nearly every day, and several of his letters appeared in various reform journals. The little evidence available suggests that Heywood got along well with his fellow prisoners. He thanked a friend for fruit recently received "which reached me in good time and was indeed welcome to me and the other prisoners who shared it with me." In another letter from prison, Ezra Heywood lamented his separation from family, the breaking up of his business, the exposing of his family to beggary, and the clouding of his name with odium. However, he wrote that he could suffer all of this "cheerfully that liberty and truth be upheld." Heywood had developed an image of himself during his abolitionist years as a martyr, suffering indignities for the greater good of humankind. With his arrest, such thinking intensified, as he identified himself with Socrates, Jesus, and John Brown.[51]

After his release from prison, Ezra Heywood lectured and wrote about his experience. He declared that prison life "implies social, financial, and physical death." In being given permission to choose his own location for internment, he observed sarcastically that it was "something to have choice of your own hell." Heywood asserted that a prisoner had no rights that the keepers were bound to respect. He likened prison life to "communism, relentless communism, where everyone is broken on the same wheel" and subjected daily to the deadening regimen of the same schedule. Jails were breeding grounds for criminals, Heywood claimed. He documented unhealthy conditions and poor food that led to sickness and suicides at Dedham Jail. Heywood presented a sophisticated analysis of prison industry, which paid inmates next to nothing while contributing to unemployment in the general population. The business of seating chairs was carried on in the jail, "while the boys of my county, who formerly earned their living by trade, are turned on the highways as tramps and the girls crowded toward the fearful vortex of the social evil in cities. Every chair I seated there helped make a pauper of a boy and a prostitute of a girl in my county!" Heywood appealed for love and intelligent charity in place of punishment and inhumanity. Expressing his anarchist spirit, he "looked forward to a new world—

churches without a hell, states without a sword, and society without a jail."[52]

While in prison, Heywood expanded his critique of Christianity. After his first week of incarceration, Heywood decided to discard the Christian calendar system. Instead of A.D., *anno domini*—in the year of the Lord—Heywood proposed a new notation, Y.L.—Year of Love—dating Y.L. 1 from the formation of the New England Free Love League in Boston on February 25, 1873. Accordingly, upon his release, all subsequent issues of *The Word* were dated with the new notation. Heywood explained that the A.D. notation "recognizes a mythical God in the calendar, puts Christian collars marked 'J.C.' on naturally free necks, and registers us subjects of the lascivio-religious despotism which the male-sexual origin and history of the cross impose." The cross, he argued, was a phallic symbol and with the removal of the A.D. system, he envisioned "crass penis tyranny in ruin." In addition, Christian time "breeds idiotic servility to usurped power and poisons youth with pernicious deference to false authority." In later years, he expanded the meaning of Y.L., claiming that it also denoted Year of Liberty and Year of Life.

Heywood was not the only social reformer to discard the A.D. notation in an effort to overcome the Christian domination of thought and language in society. The free-lover Moses Harman employed an alternative notation, adopted in 1882 by the National Liberal League, in his journal *The Kansas Liberal*, later renamed *Lucifer*. Harman reported that the league, at its sixth annual congress, devised for its journals "a universal freethought calendar commemorative of the rise of science and reason as a result of the teachings of the glorious martyr for science and man, Giordano Bruno, so inhumanly burned at the stake by Christians in 1600, for proclaiming scientific facts." Like Heywood's, the purpose of the new notation, E.M.—the Era of Man—was to abolish the Christian era.[53]

Heywood also decided while in prison that he favored the "abolition of God." Before his imprisonment, Josephine Tilton had written to him that looking through his essay *Yours or Mine*, "I see you still refer to a male God. Why not stop using pronouns, relative to Deity, until one is invented that includes both masculine and feminine genders?" He did not invent a new pronoun, but did realize the importance of trying to eliminate language and social concepts that reinforced hierarchical thinking and male domination. Doing away with the notion of God was "a greatly needed reform to which Atheists have devoted much beneficent service . . . the *idea* of an invisible, irresponsible MASTER of whom we are helpless slaves, ineffably demoralized thereby; and the *fact* that Deity, judged by his most learned human exponents, sanctions oppression, cruelty, fraud, war, murder, wherever popularly deemed 'necessary,' make it an imperative duty to depose God and allow him henceforth to serve as an extinct transgressor in historical museums with other relics of mythological savagery. We substituted for the word LIFE. . . ." Heywood believed that neither God nor any external master should impose authority. He declared: "Loyal to Truth as I understand it, calling no man or God master, I shall henceforth stand clear of this coercive superstition [Christianity], a free citizen in the banner state of life, Love." Love, Heywood believed, was the "primary and ultimate force in human affairs which existed before State, Church, Christs, Gods, and will survive them."[54]

Heywood escalated his attack on Christianity in response to the strong support many organized Christians gave to Anthony Comstock and the local vice-suppression societies. Organized religion's waffling or outright hostility to abolitionism and labor reform had profoundly disillusioned Heywood, for whom Christianity had become synonymous with ignorance, superstition, and the suppression of free expression. After his release from prison, he campaigned for the end of the compulsory use of the Bible in public schools. Heywood criticized the "false system of morals imposed by Christianity . . . [it] must give way to Essential Truth as interpreted by individual reason and conscience." Heywood totally denied any value to organized religion. He declared: "Favoring war, the robbery of Labor, the oppression of Woman, the persecution of Free Lovers, the church is the tomb of Faith, the charnel-house of Growth."[55]

Yet Ezra Heywood remained deeply religious in a basic sense and continued to proclaim a millennial faith in human progress. Lucien V. Pinney aptly described Heywood: "He must be regarded as a devout man, acting from profound religious conviction, i.e., in the firm belief that there is wise predestination of events by super-human, or at least super-terrestrial intelligence, to the end that purposeful unfoldment of good go on in the universe with certainty forever." While rejecting Christianity, Heywood broke with other free-thinkers who heaped criticism upon Jesus Christ. Heywood saw Christ as an exceptional human being, someone who did much good, from whose actions there was much to learn, and who suffered nobly for his high ideals. The theme of martyrdom, which runs deeply in Christianity, resonated in Heywood's soul. The veteran labor reformer John Orvis wrote, in a religious vein, that Heywood's many years of evangelizing "were bringing forth abundant fruit. The eyes of the multitude have been touched by the divine finger of truth. . . ."[56]

In addition to his deeply religious personal outlook, Heywood often utilized quotations from the Bible to support his social reform efforts.

Thus, even though he wished to see the Bible discontinued as compulsory reading, he still believed it was an important book with great value. Making good use of his religious training, he also knew that citing the Bible would help bolster his arguments with many people. In *Cupid's Yokes*, Heywood wrote that Christ was "theoretically a woman's emancipationist." He argued that if modern Christians would honestly follow Jesus, Jesus would take them into his "Free Love Kingdom of Heaven," where Jesus says, "They neither marry nor are given in marriage." At his trial, Heywood had wanted to employ the old free-thought tactic of comparing alleged obscenity with certain passages from the Bible, but was not permitted to present this argument. However, he did publish such an exposition by Parker Pillsbury, a veteran abolitionist and long-time friend.[57]

In addition to Anthony Comstock's attacks on liberty, the issue that most distressed Ezra Heywood while in prison was the loss of the Mountain Home resort to foreclosure. During the depression years of 1875 and 1876, Heywood had not been able to meet mortgage payments to his brother Samuel. Two weeks before sentencing, Ezra Heywood had a long talk with his older brother, who promised that if Ezra were imprisoned, his debt would not be an issue. However, two days after Ezra entered Dedham Jail, Samuel visited to inform him that he was taking legal action. Ezra Heywood wrote: "I appealed to and pleaded with him in letters from the Jail, to relent, but he persisted, foreclosed and the estate was sold under the hammer," with Samuel Heywood himself the purchaser. Ezra characterized his brother as "friendly, fair, in all respects, to me and also to my family until Comstock's assault upon me." However, after the arrest, his brother branded Ezra insane and charged that he was throwing his life away. Ezra wrote that his brother "seems to seek to hold me his vassal in order to convert me from what he deems my errors!" A. H. Simpson, Flora Tilton's companion, called Samuel Heywood "a smugly pious, respectable purist."[58]

The Mountain Home, home for the Heywoods since 1871, was sold at auction on July 26, 1878. Angela Heywood and the two children, Vesta and Hermes (then nine and four years old), were turned out of the house. Ezra Heywood credited his sisters, Mary and Delia Heywood, and his sisters-in-law, Josephine S. and Flora Tilton, with caring for his family. Meanwhile, he languished in prison, frustrated by his inability to help his family and enraged by his brother's actions against "our cherished home with all its precious and sacred associations." Heywood stated: "During the six months I lived in a brick vault, tomb 52 of

Dedham Jail, not the loathsome savagery of Anthony Comstock, or harsh treatment from pulpit and press, or vindictive persecution by a government I had given my earlier years and energies to relieve from the curse of chattel slaveholding—nothing caused me so much suffering as did this action of one who, after having been a financial backer 25 years, in *the* hour of my life when I had a natural right to expect him to be friendly, instead of being active to assist them, was an object of fear and terror to the loved ones I was forbidden to aid."[59]

With the generosity of his other creditors and the aid of contributions from sympathizers, Ezra Heywood was able to repurchase the Mountain Home on April 28, 1879, a few months after his release from prison. All of his Princeton creditors were willing to absorb losses in order that the Heywood family might have the opportunity to resume their normal lives in the Mountain Home. Heywood's two sisters, Mary and Delia, offered their "slender means." His older brother Joseph Heywood, "a manual laborer and comparatively poor," nonetheless loaned Ezra part of the $5,000 he needed. Joseph Heywood had put his bank book in Ezra's hands and told him to "draw every dollar if you need it." In addition, readers of *The Word* contributed varying amounts.[60]

In the winter of 1881–82, Samuel Heywood decided to press his old financial claims regarding the Mountain Home. Ezra Heywood was furious, convinced his brother was acting out of sympathy with Comstock's vendetta against him. While Samuel was pursuing his case, Ezra was fighting for his freedom in federal and then state courts. In March 1883, a jury ruled in favor of Samuel Heywood and assessed damages against Ezra and Angela Heywood totalling nearly $8,000. Ezra wrote that unless an appeal was granted, Samuel would have legal claim to two slaves for twenty years.[61]

In response to the constant threat of foreclosure, Ezra and Angela Heywood decided to sell the Mountain Home to a joint stock corporation that they organized in 1882. Stockholders of the Mountain Home Corporation consisted of relatives, Princeton friends, and other supporters. Ezra Heywood served as secretary and treasurer of the corporation, and the constitution and by-laws reflected his thinking. The stated purpose of the corporation was "to advance ethical culture, industrial, political, social and moral developments of life; in order that natural development, by evolution, may transcend disastrous revolution, misery be dissolved by mind power, opportunity and reciprocity prevail, Labor rejoice in the fruits of Enterprise, and that Society, manifesting the latent harmony of nature, may be realized by all in Liberty, Temperance, Growth, Love, Peace."[62]

The formation of the Mountain Home Corporation did not alter the fact that the Heywoods constantly lived with the threat of their assets being seized and assigned to their major creditor, Samuel Heywood. Ezra and Angela Heywood did not have the necessary income to pay either the judgment against them or back mortgage payments. This threat hung over their heads for several years. Samuel Heywood again threatened to bring Ezra Heywood to court in 1888, but then decided suddenly to surrender all legal claims against his brother. Ezra Heywood wrote his brother that his decision was the best news he had received since President Rutherford B. Hayes's pardon message had arrived in his Dedham jail cell. Perhaps Samuel Heywood thought his brother had suffered enough and wanted to demonstrate Christian charity and forgiveness. Ezra Heywood admitted that Samuel Heywood had "lost much, but never made any money out of me, and never intended to." Further, Ezra Heywood wrote that his brother had had "power to imprison us, without further legal process." He was wrong on this point: imprisonment for debt in Massachusetts had been abolished several decades earlier. However, he was correct that his brother "could have gone much further than he did in pressing us. . . . Thankful indeed am I for all the mercy he has shown, and for his heroic conclusion of the whole matter."[63]

Heywood's imprisonment in 1878 had a disastrous impact on the Mountain Home's value as a summer resort. No summer guests visited in 1878 because of the foreclosure, but the negative consequences of Ezra Heywood's notoriety hurt business for as long as the Heywoods operated the Mountain Home. Even before Anthony Comstock arrested Heywood, *The Worcester Press* warned that "Princeton will lose caste as a Summer resort unless town authorities exercise a more rigid censorship upon its local press." Stephen Pearl Andrews wrote that the resort owned by the Heywoods "was in prosperous operation under their management, until its success was much disturbed by the scare of Mr. Heywood's repeated arrests; since the first of these its fortunes have been varied." Heywood's friend A. E. Giles commented that Heywood "had intended and expected to make it a summer resort for Liberals, spiritualists, etc. I attended two or three of them—but the Comstock officers destroyed the place."[64]

Ezra and Angela Heywood lived on the edge of poverty. Sales of radical books and pamphlets published by the Co-Operative Publishing Company did not generate a substantial income. The summer resort business of the Mountain Home was damaged irreparably by Heywood's repeated obscenity arrests. Summer guests were a source of some income, but not enough for the Heywoods to meet all their expenses. They often had to rely on the financial generosity of friends and supporters in order to sustain themselves, prevent foreclosure on their home, do needed home repairs, provide for their children's education, purchase clothing or bedding, and occasionally to obtain food. For example, Ezra Heywood gratefully acknowledged the assistance of Isaac and Elmina Drake Slenker, who sent yarn and knit goods over the years from their manufacturing concern in Virginia. Their donations, Heywood wrote, warmed and delighted young and older "Wordocrats."[65]

There was no margin for illness in the Heywoods' reform efforts. In 1885, for the first time in the history of *The Word*, Ezra Heywood was forced to suspend publication for three months. He reported: "Mrs. Heywood's severe and protracted illness, followed by Hermes' and Psyche's sickness compelled cessation of printing. . . ." Angela Heywood had been very sick for more than seven weeks, and her recovery, which was problematic for awhile, took several more weeks. Heywood admitted that he was close to being destitute and, thus, *The Word* "would appear for a while, as it can, rather than as a monthly." Until it ceased publication in 1893, *The Word* suffered occasional lapses and was totally silenced during Heywood's second imprisonment during 1890–92.[66]

Life for the Heywoods was a constant, difficult struggle. Heywood readily admitted the tremendous price he had to pay for acting on his convictions. For example, in 1885 he wrote that "repeated raids have so crippled us that am forced to ask special aid to get on foot; financially, and go forward. . . . Incessant work, much of which brings little or no money, (averaging seventeen hours in twenty-four except when in Jail); constant frontier service with no leisure; family on the verge of want, due education of children impossible, growing years, failing health, impel me to speak." Yet the Heywoods did much more than merely struggle to survive. Inspired by their faith in the individual and the possibility of limitless improvement, they sustained their work and family. Heywood believed his own future was of "trivial account compared with Truth imperilled."[67]

The chief organized opposition to Anthony Comstock was the National Liberal League, founded in 1876 at a convention of free-thought advocates called together by the Free Religious Association. In February 1878, the league presented Congress with a petition bearing seventy thousand names protesting the provisions and enforcement of the Comstock Act of 1873. To league members, the word *liberal* had a simple meaning: belief in the complete separation of church and state. However *liberal* came to be used by Liberal Leaguers themselves as a synonym for free-thinker, especially one who questioned the supernatural aspects of Christianity. The term's meaning was further confused by the presence of denominational progressives or "religious liberals" in the league. To the devout Christian there was no confusion; all liberals were infidels. Over the course of its history, the league, writes Hal D. Sears, "which included capitalists and anarchists, unitarians and atheists, materialists and spiritualists, could agree on little else save secularism."[68]

Anthony Comstock lumped all liberals together even though there were significant differences within their ranks. In his book *Traps for the Young*, Comstock deplored the "alliance of the free-lust and liberal elements." Liberals of all ideologies generally rallied to the call for free speech and liberty of the press. By creating some martyrs and by attacking freethinkers directly, Comstock brought much attention to the federal postal legislation that he had drafted and helped to enact. Comstock embodied a censorious spirit of social purity, a significant motif in the American tradition. However, another vibrant part of the American heritage, which served as a partial brake on Comstock's designs, was the widely held conviction that the Constitution guaranteed freedom of speech and thought.[69]

Because liberals were an eclectic grouping, the issues of obscenity and legal restrictions led to divisions among them. At the 1878 convention of the National Liberal League in Syracuse, there was a split over whether the league's goal should be to repeal or modify federal and state Comstock laws. The president of the league, Francis E. Abbot of Boston, represented the minority group that favored modification. Abbot resigned as president and was succeeded by Elizur Wright, who favored repeal. Robert Ingersoll, although praised by Clarence Darrow as one of the world's greatest champions of human liberty, was not able to bring himself to defend Ezra Heywood's right to free speech. Despite Ingersoll's commitment to free expression, his social conservatism regarding marriage and sexuality led him to compromise his principles regarding Heywood. Ingersoll's aversion to free-lovers and his position for modification of the Comstock laws caused him to resign as a vice president of the National Liberal League at the 1880 convention.[70]

Ezra Heywood and his circle called for repeal of the Comstock laws. Benjamin Tucker presented the anarchist assessment that unless the state was abolished, the roots of repression would survive. He wrote: "Comstock is a true child of the State, of which nearly everybody is mortally afraid. The State is, by necessity, a breeder of sneaks and spies. It cannot live without them. Therefore, all liberals who oppose the work of Comstock from any platform other than that of the abolition of the State are wasting good ammunition. By some fortunate chance they may succeed in displacing the man himself, but Comstock*ism* will live after him, and will fall only with the State, its creator and sustainer."[71]

In 1878, the younger Dr. Foote and eight others began the National Defense Association. Foote served as its first secretary, and the executive committee in 1879 included Ezra Heywood, Flora Tilton, and Benjamin Tucker. The association proposed to investigate all questionable cases of prosecution under both federal and state Comstock laws and to defend those who were "unjustly assailed by the enemies of free speech and free press." The organization provided valuable assistance to Ezra Heywood and D. M. Bennett in their legal battles. In addition to soliciting defense funds and circulating protest petitions, the association challenged vice-suppression groups at their meetings, handing out anti-Comstock propaganda. Also, with some success, the group mounted lobbying campaigns in Washington and in state capitals against attempts to strengthen existing Comstock legislation. The core of the organization, which was composed of "friends of liberty, justice, and equality, of freedom of thought, speech, and press," consisted of such veteran reformers as Elizur Wright, Stephen Pearl Andrews, Theron C. Leland, and Thaddeus B. Wakeman.[72]

The National Defense Association had an uncompromising motto: "Eternal Vigilance is the Price of Liberty." The group sought repeal of the Comstock laws, vowing "to employ all peaceful and honorable means to roll back the wave of intolerance, bigotry, and ignorance which threatens to submerge our cherished liberties." An 1879 *Foote's Health Monthly* editorial provides a good sense of the spirit of the organization:

> The association is not doing battle for indecent people, nor has there been so much as a single contribution to the fund from a dealer in, or manufacturer of, what can be called obscene matter. Both members and contributors are the cleanest people in the land. . . . There is one advantage which the National Defense Association has over the Society for the Suppression of Vice (so-called). It is this: The former is an inexpensive concern comparatively. All of its officers are unsalaried. It has no secretary or agent to which it pays the handsome sum of $4,000 per year [referring to Comstock]. If the $7,000 or $8,000 required to carry on the Vice Society for one year were to be put into the treasury of the Defense Association for just once those phases of Comstockism which interfere with popularizing physiology and discussing the live social and theological questions of the day would die a natural death. It is only necessary that the people be enlightened. Gradually but steadily the National Defense Association is enlightening the people. Important documents of various kinds are constantly being printed and circulated far and wide. Let all those who would assist in carrying on this work make some contribution however small.[73]

Benjamin Tucker, an activist in the National Defense Association, had been introduced to radical politics by Ezra Heywood and went to Heywood's assistance when he was attacked by Comstock. Declaring that Heywood had been thrown in jail by a "band of jesuitical conspirators," whose aim was to halt abruptly his "career of reformatory usefulness," Tucker stepped in and assumed the position of editor pro tem of *The Word*. He also played a leading role in efforts to secure Heywood's release from prison. Ambitiously, Tucker announced his desire to transform *The Word* into a weekly—a goal that failed—and to increase its circulation. The editorial and publication offices were moved temporarily from Princeton to Cambridge, Massachusetts.[74]

The campaign to free Ezra Heywood was extensive. In a letter from prison in November 1878, the forty-nine-year-old Heywood listed some of the efforts on his behalf. He had strong support from *The Index*, *Banner of Light*, *The Truth Seeker*, *The Evolution*, and other reform papers. The large convention of freethought activists at Watkins Glen, New York, in August (where Josephine Tilton and D. M. Bennett had been arrested) denounced Heywood's persecution. Both wings of the Liberal League, Heywood wrote, although differing over whether the obscenity law should be modified or repealed, "condemn its present sectarian use and virulent enforcement." Several daily newspapers, including *The New York Graphic*, *The Springfield Republican*, *The Boston Herald*, and *The Boston Globe*, had "deprecated the persecution of opinions which the Comstock movement instigates." In addition, Heywood noted, petitions for modification or repeal of the Comstock laws, bearing seventy thousand names, were sent to Congress during the previous winter.[75]

The major event in the defense efforts, spearheaded by the National Defense Association, was a meeting at Faneuil Hall on August 1, 1878, to protest the injury done to freedom of the press by Ezra Heywood's conviction, sentence, and imprisonment. This date, the anniversary of the freeing of the slaves in the British West Indies in 1834, had been celebrated annually by the abolitionists at large open-air rallies. The meeting, which lasted nearly four hours, attracted from four to six thousand people, an impressive figure. Benjamin Tucker, instrumental in organizing the gathering and secretary of the event, presented a series of resolutions that were passed with a roar of approval. The resolutions declared: 1) that the right to free expression was inviolable; 2) that no vague law be permitted that allows "designing knaves or narrow-minded bigots" the right to deny the exercise of free speech; 3) that because Heywood's case was clearly one of persecution under the law, he should be released by the president of the United States; and 4) that because Anthony Comstock had repeatedly attempted to suppress free thought, speech, and press, and had employed despicable, immoral methods, he should be dismissed immediately from government service. Tucker printed the entire evening's proceedings as a pamphlet.[76]

The tone of the meeting was decisively civil libertarian. Most speakers focused on the violation of free speech without addressing the social issues Ezra Heywood raised in *Cupid's Yokes*. In fact, the chairman of the meeting, Elizur Wright, who had posted Heywood's bail after his arrest, held no personal liking for Heywood's free-love doctrine but still staunchly defended his right to free expression. A. L. Rawson, president of the National Defense Association, went so far as to say that much of Comstock's work in attacking obscene publications was necessary. What Rawson deplored above all else was the manner in which Comstock did his work and that he went after Heywood, who was clearly not a purveyor of pornography. Thaddeus Wakeman, the attorney who wrote the petition to Congress requesting total repeal of the Comstock law, delivered a long keynote speech that focused on what Wakeman saw as the legitimate powers of Congress and the courts and how the Constitution was violated by the obscenity laws. He declared that the central question in the Heywood case was "the liberty that is the heart of the living social organism." Unless the Comstock law was repealed, Wakeman warned that "the birthright secured to us all in the Bill of Rights, by Massachusetts and Patrick Henry and Jefferson, as the very condition of accepting the written Constitution, at all" would be destroyed.[77]

Besides a defense of imperiled liberty, other major themes included attacks on Anthony Comstock and the church and testimony about Ezra Heywood's upstanding moral character. Comstock was characterized as a lying rogue and a hypocrite. Theron Leland argued that Heywood's punishment was the work of the Christian church, "in spiteful revenge for outspoken dissent from her works and ways. . . . The Church is responsible for Comstock. He is her agent." Alfred Giles saw Heywood as a compassionate man who "has almost wept over the seas of troubles which toss the sexes, both in marriage and out of it." He deplored the fact that Heywood, "a scholar, a thinker, a conscientious reformer, one of the most honest and upright men in Massachusetts" was consigned to a felon's cell. J. H. W. Toohey summarized his view of Heywood: "Enough to know we are in the presence of an American citizen; a gentleman and a scholar; a man who has earned a right to particular opinions by special studies and painstaking methods; a thinker of marked and acknowledged ability, alike unimpeachable in his private character and public ministrations; a liberal among liberalists, and a reformer of the old anti-slavery type and school." The free-lover Moses Hull was the only speaker to present a clearly anarchist position. He thundered: "In heaven's name, give us anarchy, give us bedlam, pandemonium, or the Commune—any thing that will deliver honest people out of the hands of the mob called a government, which spends its strength persecuting an individual for the expression of an honest opinion."[78]

The Faneuil Hall meeting provided great impetus for efforts to free Heywood. In November 1878, the National Defense Association gathered together the numerous petitions for Heywood's release and sent the eloquent Laura Kendrick to Washington with them. Benjamin Tucker wrote about the spiritualist: "Hers was a life, hers is a character, fit to be treated by the combined genius of the foremost of biographers and the foremost of novelists." Angela Heywood was not very happy about Kendrick's role, however. In a letter to her friend Elizabeth Denton, she expressed her belief that Kendrick was focusing on obscenity while the great issue before the American people was the question of gender. Angela Heywood objected most strongly to being left out of the forming of defense strategy. "Mr. Heywood['s] 'friends' can do whatever they please for & with him & *his* claims but . . . *they* have *so far* left me *entirely scrupulously,* unspoken to *in any & all ways.*" She strenuously objected to Kendrick's portraying her as a poor wife in need of her husband and protested she was not "a *poor little imbesile* [sic] *woman unfit* to live without a man." Angela Heywood asked Denton to intercede discreetly with Kendrick, but despite her objections, Kendrick carried on in Washington, meeting with members of Congress and aides to President Rutherford B. Hayes.[79]

Laura Kendrick was successful in her efforts to convince President Hayes to release Heywood. She was able to convince Attorney General Charles Devlin that the arguments posed against marriage in *Cupid's Yokes* were not obscene. Benjamin Tucker wrote that "by her infinite tact and persuasive tongue she procured his pardon from the president." After Devlin made his recommendation to the president, Ezra Heywood submitted a carefully worded application for pardon to President Hayes. Tucker speculated that the president had insisted that Heywood himself ask for pardon as a result of incessant efforts by Samuel Heywood to humiliate his brother. In his statement, Heywood made it clear his goal was not clemency, which might imply an admission of guilt. Rather, he asked that the president exercise his pardoning power. He made six points: 1) he never committed a crime; 2) he had no criminal intent in mailing *Cupid's Yokes*; 3) *Cupid's Yokes* was a sincere expression of seriously held ideas; 4) his health was being impaired daily because of his imprisonment; 5) his jailing was an outrage upon the rights of free speech and a free press; and 6) his family was suffering bitterly from his imprisonment.[80]

President Hayes's pardon, dated December 16, 1878, was unconditional; the specific reasons cited for his action were the great number
of Massachusetts citizens seeking Heywood's release and that Heywood's health was suffering. In his diary, Hayes listed two other reasons:
Heywood had not intended to violate the law and in fact the law had
not been violated because *Cupid's Yokes* was not obscene. President Hayes
wrote: "I entertain as little doubt as those who assail me" that Heywood
maintained the wrong side of the marriage question. However, "It is no
crime by the laws of the United States to advocate the abolition of
marriage." Pamphlets critical of marriage could be obscene, Hayes asserted. However, in this case, although *Cupid's Yokes* was objectionable,
it was "not obscene, lascivious, lewd, or corrupting in the criminal
sense."[81]

Ezra Heywood became a free man upon his release from Dedham
Jail on December 19, 1878. He had entered Dedham on June 25, 1878;
his imprisonment had lasted about six months. Heywood noted sarcastically, "As a graduate from Brown University we became AM, Master
of Arts; reigning superstition conferred upon us the further degree of
USC—United States Convict." Heywood's supporters organized a rous-
ing reception for him on January 3, 1879, in a filled Paine Hall in Boston.
Above the speaker's platform hung an inscription made from evergreen
that read: "Free Speech and a Free Press Forever." Suspended from this
sign was a white dove, representing purity, with poised pinions, and
bearing in its beak an olive branch representing peace. Speakers included Laura Kendrick, D. M. Bennett, Moses Hull, A. L. Rawson, Ezra
Heywood, and others. Looking pale and emaciated, Heywood received
a great ovation when he declared: "Liberty is as dear to me as to any
other; home, family, and the dear form of friends present are as precious
to me as to any other individual. But there is something dearer even
than those; it is the right to think, the right to speak, the right to acquire
and impart knowledge. I therefore thought it better to be an exile from
my home and from society for years even, rather than surrender the
right of a citizen to acquire and impart knowledge."[82]

Heywood and his fellow reformers tempered their celebration with
the knowledge that the movement to suppress ideas was still a grave
threat to American society. Thus, Benjamin Tucker, in an editorial in the
last issue of *The Word* he edited, celebrated Heywood's release as another
victory in the great struggle for freedom of the press but warned, "let
us not forget that though Mr. Heywood is free, the law under which he
was convicted still exists, and the same infamous instrumentalities are
at work to enforce it. The battle is not over, and our work is but begun."[83]

It did not take long for the vice-hunters to register a harsh blow to freedom. In March 1879, only a few months after Ezra Heywood's release, Judge Blatchford announced his important decision in the *Cupid's Yokes* case of D. M. Bennett. Elderly and in ill health, Bennett faced a thirteen-month prison term. Indignation meetings were held across the country while a petition for Bennett's release with more than two hundred thousand signatures was delivered to President Hayes. Robert Ingersoll, who had refused to defend Ezra Heywood, took up the case of the more moderate D. M. Bennett. According to freethought veteran George E. Macdonald, "The secular press almost unanimously condemned the conduct of the trial, the conviction, and the sentence that followed."[84]

Despite much public outcry, President Hayes decided against pardoning Bennett, who served his entire sentence. In part, the president was motivated by the adverse reaction against his Heywood decision. He had been accused then of giving in to liberals, infidels, free-lovers, and smut dealers. The religious community and the powerful Society for the Suppression of Vice of New York applied much pressure to keep Bennett in jail. Samuel Colgate, president of the society, Anthony Comstock, and nine other members wrote President Hayes that *Cupid's Yokes* was a free-love book, "advocating indiscriminate intercourse between the sexes, indecent and unfit for the youth to read; and destructive alike to the sacredness of the House, the sanctity of marriage, and the moral, physical and spiritual life of the youth. Its whole tendency is to create vice and licentiousness, where they do not exist." In his own letter to the president, Comstock wrote that Bennett had for more than two years "been active in defense of the worst criminals engaging in the manufacture, sale, and dissemination of the most obscene books, pictures, and articles of obscene and immoral use and nature." Hayes's wife, a devout Methodist, also sought to influence her husband against Bennett. Hayes wrote subsequently that he did not want to interfere with the courts or intrude on the province of the legislature. However, he had overruled the courts in his Heywood decision. Clearly, he had succumbed to the intense pressures brought to bear upon him and inconsistently refused to do for Bennett what he had done for Ezra Heywood. Hayes was more easily able to drop the whole affair from public discussion after Anthony Comstock secured and released some indiscreet letters which Bennett, long married, had written to a young woman.[85]

The Hayes decision on D. M. Bennett provided new impetus for Heywood's attacks on the Republican party. After the Republican Hayes had upheld Comstock, Heywood's condemnation of the party and his parallel, seemingly naive, backing of the Democrats became more pronounced. He editorialized in the fall of 1879 that the Democratic party of Jefferson had been a party of personal rights except for its "incidental" siding with slavery. This was a remarkable observation for the former abolitionist, but Heywood could be quite narrow and obtuse when he had decided to adopt a position. He argued that the Democrats stood for the people against the invasion of citizen rights by the Republican-controlled government. He apparently believed that a Democratic presidential administration would not sanction Comstock's attacks on free speech. However, in his two terms in office, the Democrat Grover Cleveland allowed Comstock to remain active. Heywood also saw the Republicans as the party of the great monopolies, which oppressed the common person. Thus, since black emancipation, Heywood maintained, the Republicans had favored steadily increasing restrictions on natural rights. Commenting on the 1880 presidential election, Heywood wrote that a vote for the Republican candidate James A. Garfield was a vote for Anthony Comstock and God in the Constitution. A vote for the Democrat Winfield S. Hancock was a vote in favor of religious freedom, free speech, and mails.[86]

Fiercely committed, both Ezra Heywood and Anthony Comstock sought a moral transformation of society. Of course, their means and goals were completely different. Comstock was furious that Heywood had received a presidential pardon. Heywood's imprisonment only strengthened his commitment to advancing the free-love doctrine. The threat to free expression posed by Comstock fueled Heywood's passionate fire for activism. Comstock believed that God had chosen him to silence Satanic free-lovers such as Ezra Heywood. Heywood saw his own efforts as the struggle for truth, natural rights, and liberty against the backward forces of repression. Each possessed combative, uncompromising spirits and indomitable wills; future conflicts were bound to develop.

Many labor reform and suffrage advocates distanced themselves from Ezra Heywood as he became a more outspoken free-love advocate. Taylor Stoehr is accurate in his assessment that the "essence of the free-love movement was that it proposed itself as a single solution to multiple problems. . . ."[87] Reformers who did not share Ezra Heywood's enthusiasm for free love viewed matters differently. Many viewed free love as an impediment, an embarrassing issue that alienated people from making a commitment to social reform.

Heywood supported women's suffrage because it represented "wholesome revolt against male usurpation." Heywood believed that the social movement for suffrage would necessarily have to move beyond the particular struggle for the ballot and confront male supremacy in all of its manifestations. In that regard, the historian Ellen DuBois declares that in the mid-nineteenth century, "enfranchisement offered women a route to social power, as well as the clearest possible vision of equality with men." Yet, Heywood's anarchism led him to criticize the limitations of gaining the vote. Suffrage, Heywood warned, was "but the initiative, the beginning of wisdom." For Heywood, "being equal tyrants in, and equal victims of, majority despotisms will not rescue the sexes from internecine conflict." The ballot, Heywood asserted, was not nearly sufficient if women were to achieve social, sexual, and political equality with men. Women would be assured "prosperous destiny," Heywood believed, only if they gained "freedom from all authority outside of her own choice, elective affinity in spiritual, industrial, and Social Enterprise. . . ."[88]

Heywood's involvement in free-love efforts took a dramatic turn with his advocacy of Victoria Woodhull's right to free speech. The historian William O'Neill argues that the Woodhull-Beecher scandal had the opposite impact among suffragists, "effectively stifling all further discussion of the marriage question. Mrs. Stanton continued to defend free divorce, but otherwise the outburst of public feeling drove radical feminists back from their advanced position and forced them to concentrate more narrowly than before on law and politics."[89] No doubt the Woodhull episode had a major impact, but O'Neill may have overemphasized its consequences.

Nonetheless, the suffrage movement did become more conservative. Ellen DuBois presents a more compelling analysis. The failure to achieve women's suffrage in the 1870s, she argues, may have been "an aspect of the defeat of Reconstruction radicalism. . . ." With the demise of radicalism, for example, it was easier for suffragists to turn to playing on white women's racism in enlisting support for the suffrage cause.[90]

Large-scale organizing for the single issue of woman's suffrage acted as a brake on the radicalism of Elizabeth Cady Stanton and Susan B. Anthony. The feminism of many women joining the suffragist movement was not nearly as broad or as radical. As the complexion of the suffrage effort became more conservative, Stanton continued periodically to assert the logical conclusions to her ideas by sharply criticizing marriage and sexual relations. Anthony, more comfortable with the obligations and limitations imposed by choosing to narrow their focus, would rein Stanton back in.[91]

Heywood and Stanton had much in common regarding their free-love views, but Ellen DuBois points out a critical distinction: "unlike most other free-love advocates, Stanton was anchored to a social movement. She limited her exposition of free love to a few select audiences and continued to speak in public only on the reform of marriage and divorce law and the struggle of individual women for dignity within their marriages."[92] Constrained by her commitment to the suffrage movement, Stanton could not regularly address free-love issues. Heywood, on the contrary, thrived on those social issues that were most scorned. As the label *free love* became more and more opprobrious, Heywood became prouder of the label and of his free-love advocacy. Thus, it was left to Heywood and his small cohort of free-lovers to provide a sustained and thorough critique of the sexual, social, and economic inequality between men and women.

NOTES

1. Heywood published *Uncivil Liberty: An Essay to Show the Injustice and Impolicy of Ruling Woman without Her Consent* at his Co-Operative Publishing Company in Princeton; James J. Martin, ed., Introduction to Heywood, *Uncivil Liberty* (Colorado Springs: Ralph Myles Publisher, 1978), p. 5. All subsequent references in this chapter refer to the pagination of this edition; *The Truth Seeker*, September 26, 1891, p. 613.

2. Heywood, *Uncivil Liberty*, pp. 7–8, 11–12.

3. Ibid., pp. 25, 26.

4. Ibid., pp. 17, 21, 20.

5. Ibid., pp. 23, 22.

6. Ibid., pp. 13, 28.

7. Ellen Carol DuBois, ed., *Elizabeth Cady Stanton/Susan B. Anthony: Correspondence, Writings, Speeches* (New York: Schocken Books, 1981), pp. 89, 94; for Stanton and the National Labor Union, see David Montgomery, *Beyond Equality: Labor and the Radical Republicans, 1862–1872* (Urbana: University of Illinois Press, 1981), pp. 395–98; for an example of Heywood's ongoing association with suffragists, see *The Word*, November 1877, p. 2.

8. DuBois, *Stanton/Anthony*, p. 94; *The Word*, October 1872, p. 3; June 1877, p. 3. Stanton often contributed to *The Word* in its early years. For example, see "Woman's Rights Beyond Jordan," *The Word*, May 1872, p. 1, in which she argues that most wives are simply upper servants without wages; in "Beecher's Brutality," *The Word*, November 1874, p. 3, she calls into question the institution of marriage; in "The Laboring Classes," *The Word*, March 1875, p. 3, she declares that the laboring classes, waking from a lethargy of ages, had nothing to lose but their chains, echoing the words of Karl Marx in *The Communist Manifesto*. According to Ellen DuBois, Stanton was "trying to construct for the woman suffrage movement" an extremely broad theory "which she hoped would link the enfranchisement of women with other reforms into a single movement for human liberation." See "On Labor and Free Love: Two Unpublished Speeches of Elizabeth Cady Stanton," *Signs* 1 (Autumn 1975):258. In that sense, her aims and those of Heywood overlapped substantially.

9. For the debate on marriage and divorce, see "Document 18 (I: 716–35): Debates on Marriage and Divorce, Tenth National Women's Rights Convention, New York City, May 10–11, 1860," in *The Concise History of Woman Suffrage: Selections from the Classic Works of Stanton, Anthony, Gage, and Harper*, ed. Mari Jo Buhle and Paul Buhle (Urbana: University of Illinois Press, 1978), pp. 107–89; DuBois, *Stanton/Anthony*, pp. 95, 97, 175.

10. Buhle and Buhle, eds., "Debates on Marriage and Divorce," p. 183; "Document 30 (II: 381–98): Debates at the American Equal Rights Association Meeting, New York City, May 12–14, 1869," ibid., p. 265

11. DuBois, "On Labor and Free Love," pp. 263–68.

12. Ezra Heywood, *Cupid's Yokes, or, The Binding Forces of Conjugal Life: An Essay to Consider Some Moral and Physiological Phases of Love and Marriage, Wherein Is Asserted the Natural Right and Necessity of Sexual Self-Government* (Princeton, Mass.: Co-Operative Publishing, 1876), pp. 4, 6, 22.

13. Heywood, *Cupid's Yokes*, pp. 3, 8, 21.

14. Ibid., pp. 16, 19.

15. Ibid., p. 23.

16. Ibid., pp. 10–11.

17. *The Word*, June 1890, p. 1; October 1887, p. 2.

18. The modern analogue for *invasive heism* is the term *sexism*. For a discussion of sexism, see Gerda Lerner, *The Majority Finds Its Past: Placing Women in History* (New York: Oxford University Press, 1979), pp. 40–42; *The Word*, January 1883, p. 2; February 1893, p. 3; March 1893, pp. 2–3.

19. Ibid., January 1880, p. 1; October 1889, p. 2; January 1883, p. 3; April 1887, p. 2.

20. Ibid., January 1884, p. 2; January 1889, p. 3.

21. Linda Gordon, *Woman's Body, Woman's Right: Birth Control in America* (New York: Penguin Books, 1977), p. 98; *The Word*, October 1889, p. 2.

22. Gordon, *Woman's Body, Woman's Right*, pp. 85–86; *The Word*, June 1889, p. 3.

23. Ibid., April 1881, p. 3; March 1883, p. 3; June 1889, pp. 2–3.

24. Taylor Stoehr, "Introduction," *Free Love in America: A Documentary History* (New York: AMS Press, 1979), pp. 3–45, esp. pp. 3, 45; Ellen C. DuBois, *Feminism and Suffrage: The Emergence of an Independent Woman's Movement in America 1848–1869* (Ithaca: Cornell University Press, 1978), p. 45.

25. Hal D. Sears, *The Sex Radicals: Free Love in High Victorian America* (Lawrence: Regents Press of Kansas, 1977), p. 22. This book is the only full-length treatment of Ezra Heywood's free-love circle; *The Word*, April 1878, p. 3; December 1873, pp. 2, 3; January 1874, p. 3; Pomeroy quoted in Sidney Ditzion, *Marriage, Morals, and Sex in America* (New York: W. W. Norton, 1978), p. 188.

26. Sears, *The Sex Radicals*, p. 22.

27. *The Word*, February 1889, p. 2; Sears, *The Sex Radicals*, p. 107; D. M. Bennett, *The Champions of the Church: Their Crimes and Persecutions* (New York: Liberal and Scientific Publishing House, 1878), pp. 1023–24.

28. Gordon, *Woman's Body, Woman's Right*, pp. 167–70; see also the chapter on "The Doctors Foote" in Sears, *The Sex Radicals*, pp. 183–203.

29. David Pivar, *Purity Crusade: Sexual Morality and Social Control, 1868–1900* (Westport, Conn.: Greenwood Press, 1973), pp. 10, 160.

30. Ann D. Gordon, Mari Jo Buhle, and Nancy Schrom Dye, *Women in American Society* (Somerville, Mass.: New England Free Press, 1972), pp. 23–26; on the true woman, see Nancy F. Cott, *The Bonds of Womanhood: "Woman's Sphere" in New England, 1780–1835* (New Haven: Yale University Press, 1977); on male sexuality, see G. J. Barker-Benfield, *The Horrors of the Half-Known Life: Male Attitudes Toward Women and Sexuality in Nineteenth-Century America* (New York: Harper and Row, 1976); Charles E. Rosenberg, "Sexuality, Class and Role in Nineteenth-Century America," in *The American Man*, ed. Joseph H. Pleck and Elizabeth H. Pleck (Englewood Cliffs, N.J.: Prentice-Hall, 1980), pp. 219–54, esp. p. 242.

31. Gordon, *Woman's Body, Woman's Right*, pp. 16–25.

32. Sears, *The Sex Radicals*, pp. 26–27, 272.

33. *The Word*, June 1875, p. 3; September 1879, p. 2; April 1876, p. 2; July 1877, p. 3.

34. Anthony Comstock, *Traps for the Young* (New York: Funk and Wagnalls, 1883), pp. 158–59, 163.

35. Comstock, *Traps for the Young*, pp. 163–66.

36. *The Word*, December 1877, pp. 3, 2. The item in *The Word* entitled "The Impolicy of Repression" also appeared in the *Boston Commonwealth*, November 24, 1877, p. 2, and in *The Index*, November 29, 1877, p. 573.

37. *United States v. Heywood, Circuit Court Federal Records*, vol. 78, 1877–78, District Court of United States of America, for District of Massachusetts at Boston (handwritten volume, n.p.), pp. 539–41, 692–96; Mordechai E. Liebling, "Ezra Heywood: Intransigent Individualist," research paper, Brandeis University, Waltham, Mass., 1970, p. 29.

38. Sidney H. Morse, "Chips from My Studio," *The Radical Review* 1 (1877–88):821; *The Index*, January 31, 1878, p. 52.

39. Liebling, "Heywood," pp. 29–30.

40. *The Index*, January 31, 1878, p. 52.

41. Stephen Nissenbaum, *Sex, Diet, and Debility in Jacksonian America: Sylvester Graham and Health Reform* (Westport, Conn.: Greenwood Press, 1980), pp. 149–51; Stoehr, "Introduction," *Free Love in America*, pp. 48–53; Heywood, *Cupid's Yokes*, pp. 24–25.

42. *The Index*, January 31, 1878, p. 52.

43. Ibid.; Morse, "Chips from My Studio," p. 822.

44. Ibid., p. 823; *The Index*, January 31, 1878, p. 52; *Foote's Health Monthly*, August 1878, p. 10.

45. Liebling, "Heywood," pp. 27, 30, 64; *The Index*, July 4, 1878, p. 318.

46. Sears, *The Sex Radicals*, p. 168; *Foote's Health Monthly*, October 1878, pp. 9–10; Joan Flora Tilton to Mrs. Elizabeth M. F. Denton, August 31, 1878, Denton Family Papers, Labadie Collection, University of Michigan, Ann Arbor; George E. Macdonald, *Fifty Years of Free Thought: Being the Story of "The Truth Seeker" with the Natural History of Its Editor*, vol. 1, parts 1 and 2 (New York: Truth Seeker, 1929), pp. 227–30.

47. Sears, *The Sex Radicals*, pp. 166–67; for details on Bennett, see Macdonald, *Fifty Years of Free Thought*.

48. Sears, *The Sex Radicals*, pp. 168–70.

49. Ibid., p. 168; Joan Flora Tilton to Mrs. Denton, October 16, 1878, Denton Family Papers, Labadie Collection, University of Michigan, Ann Arbor.

50. Sears, *The Sex Radicals*, pp. 168–70.

51. *Boston Commonwealth*, July 13, 1878, p. 2; *Lucifer*, November 7, 1890, p. 3; Joan Flora Tilton to Mrs. Denton, August 31, 1878; Ezra Heywood to Mrs. Elizabeth M. F. Denton, December 14, 1878, Denton Family Papers, Labadie Collection, University of Michigan, Ann Arbor; *The Word*, August 1878, p. 3.

52. Ibid., March 1879, p. 3.

53. Heywood, *Cupid's Yokes*, p. 23; Ezra Heywood to Mrs. Elizabeth M. F. Denton, July 26, 1878, Denton Family Papers, Labadie Collection, University of Michigan, Ann Arbor; *The Word*, April 1880, p. 3; *Kansas Liberal*, October 10, 1882, p. 3.

54. *The Word*, February 1880, p. 3; April 1875, p. 3; January 1879, p. 2; March 1885, p. 2.

55. Ibid., November 1878, p. 3; December 1878, p. 3; May 1882, p. 1.

56. Ibid., June 1890, p. 1; October 1879, p. 3.

57. Martin, *Men Against the State*, p. 112; Heywood, *Cupid's Yokes*, p. 13; Sears, *The Sex Radicals*, pp. 169–70; Parker Pillsbury, *"Cupid's Yokes" and the Holy Scriptures Contrasted in a Letter from Parker Pillsbury to Ezra H. Heywood* (Princeton, Mass.: Co-Operative Publishing, 1878).

58. Joan Flora Tilton to Mrs. Elizabeth M. F. Denton, August 31, 1878, Denton Family Papers, Labadie Collection, University of Michigan, Ann Arbor; *The Word*, March 1888, p. 2; February 1882, p. 2; A. H. Simpson to Mr. Koopman, not dated, Hay Library, Brown University, Providence, R.I.

59. *The Word*, September 1878, p. 3; March 1888, p. 2; Ezra Heywood to Mrs. Denton, July 26, 1878; *The Word*, February 1882, p. 2.

60. Ibid., June 1879, p. 2; February 1882, p. 2.

61. Ibid., March 1888, p. 2; March 1883, p. 2; May 1883, p. 2.

62. Ibid., June 1882, p. 2; Ezra Heywood, *Constitution and By-Laws of the Mountain Home Corporation* (Princeton, Mass.: Co-Operative Publishing, 1882), pp. 3–4.

63. *The Word*, March 1888, pp. 2–3; Redmond J. Barnett, "The Movement Against Imprisonment for Debt in Massachusetts, 1811–1834," senior honor's thesis, Harvard University, Cambridge, Mass., 1965, pp. 78–79.

64. *The Word*, April 1876, p. 2; October 1883, p. 1; A. E. Giles to Mr. Koopman, January 19, 1898, Hay Library, Brown University, Providence, R.I.

65. *The Word*, March 1882, p. 2; December 1883, p. 2; *The Word Extra*, November 1886, Hay Library, Brown University, Providence, R.I.

66. Ibid., December 1885, p. 2; *Lucifer*, October 9, 1885, p. 2.

67. *The Word*, March 1885, p. 2.

68. Sears, *The Sex Radicals*, pp. 34–41.

69. Comstock, *Traps for the Young*, p. 160; Broun and Leech, *Comstock*, p. 188.

70. Ralph E. McCoy, "Banned in Boston: The Development of Literary Censorship in Massachusetts," Ph.D. diss., University of Illinois, Urbana, 1956, pp. 84–85; Orvin Larson, *American Infidel: Robert G. Ingersoll* (New York: Citadel Press, 1962), pp. 279, 146.

71. *Liberty*, February 4, 1882, p. 1.

72. Sears, *The Sex Radicals*, pp. 199–200; *Constitution of the National Defense Association*, Labadie Collection, University of Michigan, Ann Arbor, p. 1.

73. Certificate of Membership of the National Defense Association, Denton Family Papers, Labadie Collection, University of Michigan, Ann Arbor; *Constitution of the National Defense Association*, pp. 1–2; *Foote's Health Monthly*, March 1879, p. 11.

74. *The Word*, August 1878, p. 2.

75. Ezra Heywood, "Persecution of Opinions," *Boston Commonwealth*, November 16, 1878, p. 2.

76. *The Liberator*, July 27, 1860, p. 3; *Proceedings of the Indignation Meeting Held in Faneuil Hall, Thursday Evening, August 1, 1878, to Protest Against the Injury Done to the Freedom of the Press by the Conviction and Imprisonment of Ezra H. Heywood* (Boston: Benjamin R. Tucker, Publisher, 1878), pp. 3, 4, 50–51.

77. *Proceedings*, pp. 4–9, 14–37, 48.

78. Ibid., pp. 7, 53, 62, 56, 60, 12, 52–53.

79. *Liberty*, January 21, 1882, p. 3; for an example of a petition for Heywood's release, see *Foote's Health Monthly*, August 1878, p. 14; Angela T. Heywood to Elizabeth M. F. Denton, undated letter, Denton Family Papers, Labadie Collection, University of Michigan, Ann Arbor.

80. *The Word*, December 1878, pp. 1, 2; *Liberty*, January 21, 1882, p. 3.

81. *The Word*, January 1879, p. 2; Charles Richard Williams, ed., *Diary and Letters of Rutherford B. Hayes*, vol. 3 (Columbus: Ohio State Archeological and Historical Society, 1924), p. 518.

82. *The Word*, January 1879, p. 2; February 1879, p. 2; *Foote's Health Monthly*, February 1879, p. 2; Providence, Rhode Island *Daily Journal*, January 6, 1879, p. 5.

83. *The Word*, December 1878, p. 2.

84. Sears, *The Sex Radicals*, p. 171; Larson, *American Infidel*, pp. 146–48; Macdonald, *Fifty Years of Free Thought*, p. 247.

85. Larson, *American Infidel*, pp. 148–49; Samuel Colgate et al. to President Rutherford B. Hayes, July 7, 1879, Rutherford B. Hayes Papers, Rutherford B. Hayes Presidential Center, Fremont, Ohio; Anthony Comstock to President Rutherford B. Hayes, August 18, 1879, Hayes Presidential Center; Macdonald, *Fifty Years of Free Thought*, p. 269; *Diary and Letters of Rutherford B. Hayes*, vol. 3, p. 567.

86. *The Word*, September, 1879, p. 2; September 1880, p. 1.

87. Stoehr, "Introduction," *Free Love in America*, p. 7.

88. *The Word*, November 1884, p. 3; DuBois, *Feminism and Suffrage*, p. 17; Heywood, *Uncivil Liberty*, p. 18; *The Word*, November 1884, p. 3.

89. William L. O'Neill, *Everyone Was Brave: A History of Feminism in America* (New York: Quadrangle Books, 1969), p. 29.

90. DuBois, *Feminism and Suffrage*, pp. 200, 95–96, 174–78.

91. Ibid., pp. 184, 192.

92. DuBois, "On Labor and Free Love," pp. 263–68.

Chapter 6

Free Love and Further Arrests

A n attempt to suppress the poet Walt Whitman's *Leaves of Grass* led to Ezra Heywood's second major confrontation with Anthony Comstock. In the fall of 1881, the Boston publishing house of James R. Osgood and Company issued an edition of Whitman's book. In the spring of 1882, at Comstock's urging, Oliver Stevens, Suffolk County district attorney in Boston, advised Osgood and Company that portions of the book were obscene. The publishers, before printing a second edition, invited Whitman to omit the offending verses. When he refused, they broke their contract with him and returned the printing plates to Whitman, who entrusted them to David McKay, a Philadelphia publisher. Meanwhile, the postmaster of Boston, L. S. Tobey, had declared the book unmailable.[1]

Ezra Heywood's fellow reformer Benjamin Tucker decided to challenge this assault on free expression engineered by the New England Society for the Suppression of Vice. Tucker obtained a quantity of copies of *Leaves of Grass* from Philadelphia and advertised the book for sale in his journal *Liberty* and in the daily Boston papers. He then challenged the Boston authorities, Anthony Comstock, and "all other enemies of liberty" to arrest him for committing an illegal act. Tucker reported that Comstock begged the United States district attorney for an indictment, but the request was refused. In August 1882, Tucker declared that his offer to meet the enemy had been declined. On October 14, he made a second announcement: "*Leaves of Grass* is now sold openly by nearly all the Boston booksellers. I have won my victory, and the guardians of Massachusetts morality have ignominiously retreated." A significant portion of public opinion had swung against the attempted suppression as several leading Boston papers, including *The Herald*, *The Globe*, and *The Commonwealth*, as well as *The Springfield Republican* opposed the action of Boston officials. Indeed, by attempting to suppress *Leaves of Grass*, the district attorney in Boston had managed to accomplish what Walt Whitman and his associates had failed to do in six earlier editions—make the book a financial success.[2]

Ezra Heywood took it upon himself to fight Whitman's battles because of the importance he attached to freedom of expression. He had a more difficult time than Tucker, whose strategy had been to make available the entire *Leaves of Grass*. Heywood's approach was to print two of the "objectionable poems," "A Woman Waits for Me," and "To a Common Prostitute," in a single sheet called *The Word Extra* and in the August 1882 issue of *The Word*. Comstock did not move against Tucker, the New York booksellers who reported a brisk sale of the Philadelphia edition, or the Boston book dealers. Instead, on October 26, 1882, acting in his capacity as a United States postal inspector, Comstock arrested Heywood at his home in Princeton on charges of sending obscene matter through the mail. Heywood faced a four-count indictment—mailing *Cupid's Yokes*, *The Word Extra* with the Whitman poems, and two counts pertaining to an advertisement giving information on how a contraceptive device that Heywood facetiously dubbed the "Comstock Syringe" could be obtained from *The Word* offices. The veteran abolitionist Elizur Wright once again posted Heywood's bail.[3]

Both Tucker and Heywood wrote letters to Walt Whitman expressing their commitment to free expression and opposition to the attempted suppression of *Leaves of Grass*. Tucker offered to reprint the book as a test of "how far [Americans] can safely indulge in the expression of their opinions." The offer was favorably received, but plans were already underway to have the book reprinted in Philadelphia. Heywood printed his letter, a lengthy indictment of Comstock, in *The Word*. With the letter, Heywood enclosed copies of *The Word Extra* for Whitman, along with resolutions of the New England Free Love League. Heywood praised Tucker for his courageous stand and declared that the "dark Spirit of persecution which hanged Quakers, mobbed Abolitionists and Free Lovers now revisits Massachusetts to hunt down and exterminate unpopular reformers who assert Personal Liberty, freedom of the press and the mails and the right of private judgment in morals. In this tragic struggle for liberty and life we are sustained by the 'Wit and Wisdom' of your inspirations and shall be glad of any suggestions from you or your immediate comrades, relative to the defense."[4]

Whitman responded to Tucker and Heywood very differently. In a letter to his friend William O'Connor in which he enclosed Heywood's letter, Whitman wrote: "As to the vehement action of the Free Religious and lover folk, in their conventions, papers, &c in my favor—and even proceedings like these of Heywood—I see nothing better for myself or friends to do than quietly stand aside and let it go on. . . . I shall certainly not do any thing to identify myself specially with free love." O'Connor replied: "You and McKay [Whitman's publisher] *did perfectly right* in keeping aloof and not contributing to the defense. Your connection could not help him and might hurt you. 'Against stupidity the gods themselves are powerless,' says Euripides, and Heywood is certainly a champion jackass. I am sorry for him, but his bed is his own making, and he should have known what Comstock could do to him if he advertised war on the ovaries. I only hope we shall escape the consequences of his folly."[5] Whitman and O'Connor were glad when Heywood was finally acquitted, but Heywood's outspoken advocacy of free love did not endear him to Whitman.

In contrast, Whitman had great respect for Tucker, who had moderated his public pronouncements on free love quite a bit since his earlier days with the New England Free Love League. "I often feel," wrote Whitman, "as though I would like to see Tucker and have a long, long, long confab with him, just for the sake of squaring up some old scores (gratitude on my part, gratitude to him): he is remarkable for outright pluck—grit of the real sort: for loyalty, steadfastness." He felt that the "literary class had been cowardly in their advice concerning the *Leaves of Grass* controversy, but Tucker's immediate rally to its support, his persistent advocacy in thick and thin, excites me to supreme admiration." Whitman did not "bank much on his anarchism . . . but on Tucker— well, he is a safe risk."[6]

Ezra Heywood was fortunate that the trial judge in his case, T. L. Nelson of Worcester, allowed him to discuss a broad range of issues including freedom of speech, the higher morality of free love, and women's rights. Many freethinkers commended Nelson after the trial for his openness and fairness. After an initial hearing in November 1882, and a postponement in January 1883, Heywood's trial took place in the spring of 1883. Heywood chose to represent himself in court. That the tone of this trial would be radically different from Heywood's earlier case was established immediately after the opening remarks by District Attorney Charles Almy, Jr. Judge Nelson threw out *The Word Extra* charge, ruling untrue the allegation in the indictment that it "was too grossly obscene and lewd to be placed on the records of the court." In addition, he threw out the *Cupid's Yokes* charge for the same reason, declaring: "The Court is robust enough to stand anything in that book."[7] After the opening minutes in court, two of the four counts in the indictment against Heywood had been dismissed. The remaining counts dealt with the issue of the vaginal syringe.

In the nineteenth century, the douche or syringe was used more widely than condoms as a birth control device. Douching equipment could be used for multiple purposes, many of them medically respectable. This was an advantage in terms of advertising because explicit notices offering contraceptives were subject to censorship and prosecution. Vaginal syringe advertisements appeared in a number of publications, including magazines of the popular health movement, as well as women's and general magazines and newspapers. After the Comstock law of 1873 explicitly defined all contraceptive devices as obscene, many advertisers and vendors of syringes had been arrested and brought to trial.[8]

Welcoming the challenge, Ezra Heywood courted arrest for selling the device with his advertisement for the Comstock syringe. Heywood knew that his gibe at Comstock would send the vice-hunter into a rage. His rhetoric regarding contraception was atypical. Advertisements for syringes, a popular form of birth-control, were everywhere, but only sex radicals like Heywood attacked the taboos against contraception openly and directly. The advertisement in *The Word*, offering the syringe for $10, declared: "Woman's Natural Right to *Prevent* Conception is *unquestionable*; to enable her to protect herself against invasive male use of her person the celebrated Comstock syringe, designed to prevent disease, promote personal purity and health, is coming into general use. . . ." Elsewhere in *The Word* Heywood offered the view that "if Anthony Comstock's mother had had a syringe and known how to use it, what a world of woe it would have saved us. . . ." Heywood eventually decided not to call the device the Comstock syringe and so he referred to it, more conventionally, as the vaginal syringe.[9]

After Comstock and the postmaster of Princeton David H. Gregory testified for the government, Judge Nelson permitted Heywood to present a broadly conceived defense. Comstock had established the charges against Heywood in his usual fashion of writing to his potential victim under various pseudonyms. In his first trial, Heywood had been unable to prevent a serious defense because of restrictions imposed by the court. In this trial Heywood called more than three dozen witnesses to the stand to testify that the charges were groundless, that his work and ideas were honorable, that free expression and the right of individual conscience were under assault, and that his character was unimpeachable. In an attempt to demonstrate a conspiracy against civil rights, Heywood called to the witness stand Henry Chase, agent of the New England Society for the Suppression of Vice, questioning his role in the attempted suppression of *Leaves of Grass*. Throughout the trial, Heywood found Judge Nelson's rulings to be "intelligent, impartial and firm for fair-play."[10]

Heywood's summation to the jury was an address that lasted nearly five hours. He emphasized that freedom of speech was an inalienable right, part of the natural heritage of humanity and the most glorious theme in American history. He dwelt at length on the government's case, pointing out many weaknesses. His central contention was that Comstock was a professional liar. He presented a critique of male domination and a forceful assertion of women's absolute right to control their bodies. He argued: "Since Comstockism makes male will, passion and power absolute to *impose* conception, I stand with women to resent it." Angela Heywood wrote in *The Word*: "Shall we submit to the loathsome impertinence which makes Anthony Comstock inspector and supervisor of American women's wombs?" She believed Ezra Heywood's position was of momentous significance: "This womb-syringe question is to the North what the Negro question was to the South; as Mr. Heywood stood beside the slave demanding his liberation, so now he voices the emancipation of woman from sensual thraldom."[11]

Heywood maintained in his summation that the sexes were naturally equal in social relations but that the "obscenists insist on male supremacy." He made it clear to the jury that he and other free-lovers did not prescribe or recommend vaginal syringes, but that women should have an unquestioned right to choose any type of birth control. Heywood likened the syringe to a toothbrush or towel and declared that it was used for cleanliness and health, not for vicious or criminal purposes. He told the court that he would not have advertised the vaginal syringe if Anthony Comstock had not made it illegal, severely curtailing women's liberty and available options. He told the jurors that if women's "ineffably sacred right . . . to do what seems wisely best" had not been "invasively, impudently, murderously denied, by Anthony Comstock and his backers, the publishers of *The Word* never would have thought of advertising the syringe."[12]

Calling his struggle spiritual warfare, Heywood stated: "Seeking truth rather than pleasant things; following Right, lead where it will and cost what it may, I live in the hope of a new Moral Order, of revived Intelligence which, not resisting Social Evolution, will rejoice in its beneficent tendencies." Freedom and liberty constituted a higher truth, along with labor reform and free love, and the eventual triumph of this new order, Heywood still firmly believed, would lead to the reign of heaven on earth. In concluding his summation, Heywood restated his frequently asserted conviction that he was destined to be a martyr in the great cause of human liberty, joining the ranks of Jesus Christ and John Brown. He declared that there were occasional moments in history "when one man, alone in Truth, strong in what he knows to be right, voicing the Higher Law of morals, scores a mark for Progress which is a beacon light of inspiration to all weaker mortals!" Heywood was willing to suffer any punishment in his battle to assert the right of all to freedom to "acquire and impart knowledge on all subjects of human interest."[13]

After deliberating for only two hours, on April 12, 1883, the jury found Ezra Heywood not guilty of the remaining charges against him.

Having determined Heywood's innocence at the outset of their deliberations, the only question for the jurors was how long they ought to remain out for the sake of propriety. They decided they should deliberate long enough to go through the midday dinner hour, and thus get one more meal out of the government before the case ended, a story that Heywood enjoyed retelling. Judge Nelson's charge to the jury helped Heywood secure his freedom; he reminded the jurors that the government case depended almost entirely on Anthony Comstock. Nelson directed the jurors to find Heywood innocent if they had any substantial doubts about Comstock's truthfulness and reliability as a witness. The judge declared that the burden was on the government, because of the indictment, to demonstrate that the object advertised was manufactured expressly for the purpose of preventing conception. Heywood's supporters in the courtroom burst into spontaneous applause when the verdict was announced, prompting Comstock to observe that the "court was turned into a free-love meeting." He accused Judge Nelson of having practically endorsed Heywood's livelihood of circulating vicious literature.[14]

A little more than a month after his acquittal, Heywood was once again arrested for mailing obscene material. Although indicted this time under Massachusetts and not federal law, Anthony Comstock had prompted the arrest through his contacts in the state. The allegedly obscene article, one of the "Leaflet Literature" series edited by Angela Heywood, argued forthrightly for women's right to birth control and spoke of the sexual organs in very direct language. Comstock arranged for the arrest of Ezra Heywood and not Angela Heywood because he did not see women as significant actors in the world. Although he had arrested women previously, he revealed his prejudice when given a choice between arresting a man and a woman. The trial was postponed four times, in part because of the fact that Angela Heywood was pregnant with her son Angelo, who was born in the fall of 1883. Heywood was fortunate because, in the course of the delays, the district attorney who had been extremely hostile died and was replaced by a somewhat more moderate prosecutor. While the charges were hanging over Heywood's head, Stephen Pearl Andrews organized a defense committee and petition drive in Princeton. The petition called for the dismissal of the charges against Heywood; more than half the many signatories were women, and several leading citizens were involved, including P. A. Beaman and George L. Bliss, two successful owners of summer resorts.[15]

When the case finally came to trial in May 1884, the charges against Heywood were dismissed. The initial judge in the case had been quite hostile, but the presiding justice at the trial, Robert Pitman, had a rep-

utation as a veteran reformer and a fair-minded judge. Heywood had
expected to conduct his own defense as he had in Boston one year
earlier before Judge Nelson. However, attorney H. L. Nelson, son of
Judge Nelson, volunteered to argue a motion in his behalf, and the
argument persuaded Pitman to dismiss the indictment. Judge Pitman's
ruling declared that prosecutors must charge and prove a willful intent
to corrupt the morals of youth, and that he did not believe that Ezra
Heywood had any such intention.[16]

Already having been arrested twice on federal charges and once on
a violation of state law, Heywood was arrested a fourth time in 1887.
However, the United States District Attorney George M. Stevens "vetoed
the obscenist plot."[17] In 1890, Heywood was arrested a fifth time, again
on federal charges. That arrest would exact a heavy toll.

In the Victorian era the rate of marital fertility declined dramatically.
Despite mounting restrictions on birth control, the use of birth control
devices or methods increased. Major practices involved not only the
control of male sexuality—withdrawal and abstinence—but also men and
women using sponges, pessaries, condoms, and the rhythm method.
With the conscious limitation of offspring, women were beginning to
more forcefully assert their rights as individuals.[18]

The intelligent dissemination of birth control information required an
openness about sexuality and how the human genitals functioned that
was totally lacking in the Victorian milieu. In 1873, Congress enacted
the Comstock law, a portion of which legally defined birth control devices as obscene. In the second half of the nineteenth century, more and
more religious and political leaders denounced sexual immorality. Regular physicians, whose power and authority greatly increased in this
period, confused contraception with abortion and condemned both. They
also disapproved of birth control for moral and health reasons and contributed to a developing fear and misunderstanding about women's reproductive systems.[19]

Ezra Heywood believed that any form of birth control except male
continence was unnatural. Still, his belief in personal freedom and commitment to liberty was so resolute that he strongly supported women's
right to use birth control devices or even to choose to have an abortion.
In addition to continence, Heywood advocated a form of the rhythm
method as another natural birth control method. However, like the majority of contemporary physicians, his conception of the fertility cycle
was entirely wrong, and his belief that a careful use of the calendar
could determine the sex of the child was unfounded.[20] In addition to
Heywood's unequivocal belief in women's right to control their bodies,

he supported the use of birth control because he understood that many men would be unable or unwilling to practice continence. He also believed in a form of eugenics and hoped that a restriction of the number of pregnancies and careful breeding habits would further human development.

A woman's right to control her own body was axiomatic to Heywood: "of course it is woman's right to protect herself, as best she can; if she chooses to use preventatives, I will defend her in that right. . . ." Women's right to limit the number of children they bear "is as unquestionable as their right to eat, breathe, walk or be still. This is the social side of woman's suffrage." The federal and state Comstock laws, charged Heywood, sought to regulate conception by "putting an officer in every bedchamber to supervise coition." In a New England Free Love League resolution, he declared that "one of the most impudent and revolting phases of reigning heism is the effort of Christian obscenists to rape women by denying them discretion in maternity . . . the Comstock statute . . . moves women to advertise and sell means to prevent conception, and *impels mothers to provide every girl with a [vaginal] syringe as a part of her wedding outfit*." He argued that if liberty were not a sham, then women were entitled, as a birthright, to control their own physical as well as social, political, and economic destinies.[21]

For most of history, abortion had been a primary method of birth control. It became a technique of last resort in the nineteenth century because of the increased use of contraceptive devices. Still a widespread phenomenon, by the end of the century abortion had become legally proscribed. A key group in the anti-abortion movement was the regular physicians. Ezra Heywood agreed with physicians that abortion was morally wrong because, in his view, it destroyed a life in the making. He termed abortion a "murderous practice" in *Cupid's Yokes*, but both he and Angela Heywood qualified this position in the pages of *The Word*. Angela Heywood asserted: "To cut up a child in woman, procure abortion, is a most fearful, tragic deed; but even that does not call for man's arbitrary jurisdiction over woman's womb." The Heywoods' dedication to freedom and women's autonomy transcended their moral revulsion against abortion, however; Heywood defended women's right to choose to have an abortion and attacked the laws that punished physicians for performing abortions.[22]

In addition to his commitment to liberty, Heywood supported the availability of birth control because he acknowledged that many men would not practice continence in their sexual relations. He wrote: "To those physically and mentally endowed with strong sexual feeling . . . a restraint like that which continence imposes would lead to harmful results as it would be a constant restraint. With those more spiritually organized it would not be productive of the same injurious results." In his view, continent lovemaking featured an exchange of magnetic impulses on a transcendent spiritual plane. In contrast, sexual intercourse with ejaculation permitted what Heywood thought of as disastrous indulgence. Heywood believed that those whose spiritual endowment was less fully matured should still be able to regulate fertility. The sex radical Elmina Drake Slenker argued the advantage of providing every woman, free of charge, with the best and most harmless contraceptive devices. She felt that the struggle to institute the continence system as a popular form would be long and difficult: "Born in lust, to many, continence is torture, and ages of civilization must ensue before we can even reach the border land of true sexual morality."[23]

Until the 1880s, most sexual reformers believed that contraception was morally wrong. However, Edward Bliss Foote advocated for the easy availability of contraceptive devices. Although he approved of the use of continence, he argued that only the most intelligent and conscientious people would be able to maintain it. He also claimed that the sexual organs would lose their power through inaction and believed that sexual intercourse was a healthy and good act in itself and did not require reproduction for its justification. Foote, Moses Harman, and Heywood were the most outspoken advocates for contraception among Victorian sex reformers, who, with the notable exception of Foote, promoted male continence as their preferred method of birth control.[24] Conventional marriage manuals stressed the necessity for male self-control. Marital excess, defined as too frequent coition, was the most recurrent theme. Many experts believed that man's sexual appetite was uncontrollable, and a man could ennoble himself by controlling his natural inclinations. Withdrawal, probably the most widely used means of contraception, was often rejected by doctors because it allowed for ejaculation and a wasteful spilling of male seed.

The conservation of sperm and the energy and vitality sperm held was the major, underlying rationale for continence. The Reverend John Todd's *Student Manual* (1835), which sold hundreds of thousands of copies, maintained that mental powers depended on strict conservation of physical and sexual energies. It was widely assumed that if a man carefully retained his sperm, he would have a physical, intellectual and competitive edge over other men. As Elizabeth and Joseph Pleck write: "Control over sexuality nicely fitted the business ethic of this age. An entire economy of the body emerged. A man needed to save his limited amount of sperm, to practice frugality, or he would bankrupt himself."[25]

Ezra and Angela Heywood's ideas on male continence reflected prevailing Victorian assumptions. Ezra Heywood believed that "the fearful loss of vigor through involuntary emissions, celibate abstinence and solitary vice probably engender more disease and death than all other causes combined." He argued that men have no vitality to waste and believed that one ounce of semen equalled, in life force, forty ounces of blood, although he never indicated exactly how he arrived at this ratio. Angela Heywood wrote that the "quintessence of life, Semen, need not be wasted, but . . . the potential seed should bear fruit in Nature's human planting ground, woman's womb; or be retained to invigor and exhilarate physical, mental and spiritual being."[26]

The Heywoods based their philosophy of male continence on the thinking of John Humphrey Noyes, who set high standards for members of the Oneida Community, challenging each individual to strive for perfection in body and mind. Noyes prohibited possessiveness of any kind; he felt that monogamy made a man or a woman unfit to practice the two central principles of Christianity, loving God and loving one's neighbors. In place of monogamy, Noyes instituted a system of complex marriage, where sexual relations could occur between any man or woman under conditions Noyes and the community elders defined.[27]

Noyes instituted male continence as a means of birth control among Oneidans. His wife had borne five children in succession, and all but one was stillborn. In response to her pain, and burdened by his own sense of responsibility, he had learned to practice continence in 1845. Employing phrenological categories, Noyes divided sexual intercourse into two distinct parts, the amative or social, which did not include male ejaculation, and the propagative. He believed that man should content himself with the "social act" unless he intended to produce a child.

Noyes gave four arguments for his system of continence. First, it was natural for "God cannot have designed that men should sow seed by the way-side. . . ." Noyes argued that his method simply proposed "the subordination of the flesh to the spirit" that would certainly be "natural and easy to spiritual men, however difficult it may be to the sensual." Second, it was healthy for men and women; continence stopped the drain on life caused by loss of semen and safeguarded women from "the curses of involuntary and undesirable procreation." Third, male continence greatly enhanced the pleasure of sexual intercourse. Noyes wrote that lovers who use "their sexual organs simply as the servants of their spiritual natures, abstaining from the propagative act, except when procreation is intended, may enjoy the highest bliss of sexual fellowship for any length of time," while ordinary sexual intercourse "is a momentary affair, terminating in exhaustion and disgust." Fourth,

male continence, which transformed sexual intercourse into a calm activity, in Noyes's terminology, was an effective means of birth control.
Noyes believed that the spread of the male continence system would
lead to a new order and hasten the coming of the millennium. He
asserted that it would "give new speed to the advance of civilization
and refinement. The self-control, retention of life, and ascent out of
sensualism . . . will raise the race to new vigor and beauty, moral and
physical."[28]

Although they viewed the Oneida Community as a significant social
experiment, Ezra and Angela Heywood strenuously objected to the patriarchal and collectivist aspects of Oneida. Continence, more than a
system of contraception, focused on men, treating male love as noble
and unselfish and female love as base, physical, and selfish. The men
of Oneida assured their own perfection by having women regularly
commit the very sin they most dreaded to commit themselves—having
orgasms. Oneidan women were encouraged to have orgasms because
they could physiologically do so without risking pregnancy. Still, wom-
en's autonomy was circumscribed. Men controlled the frequency and
duration of the sex act, the orgasms of both partners, and assigned the
sexual pairings.

However, the focus on female pleasure and the fact that many Oneidan women indeed experienced orgasm was a great advance over the
wider culture. Men at Oneida prided themselves on bringing women to
climax. The male continence method, which allowed a man to penetrate
a woman and remain erect inside her for minutes or even hours until
his erection subsided, was clearly conducive to female pleasure. Oneidans believed that the practice of sexual intercourse beyond their community was a selfish, brutal act of rape by men. They sought an alternative sexuality that safeguarded women from unwanted pregnancies
and provided greater equality for women.[29]

Sex radicals accepted the Victorian notion that the critical function
for women in society was bearing children. Thus, Heywood argued that
the sooner woman teaches man that "the highest pleasure they themselves can experience, and the greatest service they can render her, are
in continent attentions, rather than in disastrous indulgence, the more
quickly she will become what Nature intended her to be,—the Queen
of Social Order and of Creative Ecstasy." The "Queen" ruled by virtue
of her role as potential mother.[30]

Male continence allowed a man to ejaculate on those occasions when
reproduction was desired. Otherwise, an exchange of electric magnetic
energy, without wasteful ejaculation, defined sexual intercourse. *Magnetic exchange* was the term that the nineteenth-century pseudosciences

employed for making love. Male continence did not mean abstinence from lovemaking. Rather, sex reformers believed continent practice should include a joyous celebration of the human body and open sexual exploration. Elmina Drake Slenker explained Dianaism, her term for continence, in *The Word*: "Many think Dianaism is a cold, apathetic, distant unnatural Love, one that is designed to crush all sexfeeling and reduce the race to Neuters." Nothing could be further from the truth, she protested: "We oppose no form or act of love between any man and woman, save the one creative act. . . . Fill the world as full of genuine sex love as you can; make dear old Mother Earth one great universal courting field if you can, but forbear to rush in where generations yet unborn may suffer for your unthinking, uncaring, unheeding actions."[31]

Ezra Heywood believed that intimate sex association was possible "without waste or exhaustion," and Angela Heywood declared that "there are orgasms of thought as well as orgasms of feeling." The Heywoods held a highly romanticized view of relationships and sexuality. Male continence was considered a more exalted form of sex, and sex was considered the highest expression of love. Love, the Heywoods believed, was the transcendent force that would alter the world. Angela Heywood wrote that in lovemaking the penis should not be "entirely cooled off in impotency, for heat has proper use in continent exchange as in procreation: where love rules disaster ceases; plus mind, *temperance*, forbids physical excess, and the sexes become magnetic, electric providences to each other." Lovemaking for the Heywoods encompassed free eroticism and strict self-control.[32]

Male continence could include male orgasm, remarkable as that might seem. Noyes and his followers believed that the technique itself, constriction of the seminal ducts and the ability to think "higher" thoughts than merely passion while lying naked with a woman, was easy once learned. The sex researcher Alfred Kinsey also reports that orgasms may occur without the emission of semen. Sex researchers Alex and Ilene Gross contend that there is much to be learned from Taoist practices of lovemaking that emphasize sensuality to achieve physical and psychological self-knowledge. The Chinese method stresses that pleasure is open-ended; there is no clear goal and no guilt if a particular end is not achieved. The only goal is prolongation of pleasure and a mutual redefinition of ecstasy. Alex Gross maintains that "ultra-orgasmic sex" certainly can encompass orgasmic experiences. In a comment that echoes the Heywoods' rapturous praise for the charged, magnetic exchange between a man and a woman, Ilene Gross observed, "There's a real exchange of energy that's unlike even the closeness of coming simultaneously." Alex Gross writes that "it would be a mistake to suppose that all ultraorgasmic methods involve renunciation—some, like . . . Dianaism certainly would seem to—but others go in a quite different direction—one which the nineteenth-century sexual vocabulary made it all but impossible to articulate."[33]

Edward Bliss Foote reopened the issue of male continence in 1881, and a lively debate ensued over the most desirable form of birth control. One of the more advanced arguments against continence was posed by Edwin Walker, sex radical, anarchist, and free-thought advocate, in a debate with Elmina Drake Slenker in the pages of *Lucifer*. Walker termed Slenker an ascetic and argued that in the past it had been a deadly sin to be happy in any fashion. He declared that "The last stronghold of this baleful superstition is our sexual nature. . . . Sexual passion is as natural as the desire for food, and women are as strongly sexed as men. . . ." Walker argued that for men and women to be healthy, truly free, and independent of old, repressive dogma, they should exercise their sexual passions with no restraint except mutual respect.[34]

Free-lovers shared with the larger social purity movement a belief in eugenics, the uplifting of humanity through control of heredity. Continence proponents believed reproduction should occur only under optimal circumstances because they were committed to perfecting the human race. Nearly every piece of writing on voluntary motherhood between 1890 and 1910 asserted that unwanted children were likely to be either morally or physically defective. After the Civil War and into the twentieth century, there was an upsurge of interest in scientific breeding. Many leaders of society—doctors, clergymen, writers, and politicians—saw America as a white, Anglo-Saxon, Protestant nation threatened by the external danger of immigrants. Scientific breeding, advocates believed, would serve to ensure the preservation of a superior human stock and the proper place for women, which was to bear and raise children.[35]

As with male continence, Ezra and Angela Heywood derived their thinking about scientific breeding from John Humphrey Noyes, who used the expression *stirpiculture*, deriving it from the Latin *stirps*, meaning stock, stem, or root. The perfectionist Noyes believed that the human race could be refined, purified, and elevated if proper attention was given to breeding. He declared: "We believe the time will come when involuntary and random propagation will cease, and when scientific combination will be applied to human generation as freely and successfully as it is to that of other animals." He called for inbreeding of superior types among Oneidans, which would serve as an example to the rest of society. Noyes believed that society was in the midst of a tremendous crisis but that a perfected, harmonious order could emerge from the wreckage. He felt that the "powers above are summoning us to the great enterprise of peopling the planet with a new race." Marriage must be abolished and stirpiculture adopted, Noyes argued, before "the will of God can be done on earth as it is in heaven." Scientific propagation would be the means to move society from dissolution to the institution of the kingdom of heaven on earth.[36]

Ezra and Angela Heywood were ardent advocates of stirpiculture. In fact, almost all American birth control proponents put forward perfectionist eugenic ideas. Ezra Heywood wrote in *Cupid's Yokes* that "the sex and character of the child are predetermined by its makers, the parents." Heywood looked forward to a "wider future, which will *demand* that the reproductive instinct will be inspired by intelligence and placed under the dominion of the will." Many sex reformers argued that children born outside of marriage were usually superior because they were the products of love, not coercion. The Heywoods and other stirpiculture proponents believed that the independence of women from servility to men would automatically produce a eugenic effect. Angela Heywood posed the question: "Shall maternity be compulsive, accidental, or an act of royal choice?" Marriage, which denied woman's liberty, could not contribute to the perfection of the race.[37]

Free-love proponents believed that scientific breeding would elevate the spiritual level of humanity. Linking religion and science, F. H. Marsh, a long-time supporter of Heywood, wrote in *Lucifer* that the millennium would never come until men and women learned "how to bring human beings into life well made, instead of half-made or less as is the rule now; to bring into life organisms harmoniously developed, physically, mentally, and emotionally." Professor J. H. Cook, a regular contributor to *The Word*, hailed the living truth, stirpiculture, that "sex salvationists" like Ezra Heywood and Elmina Drake Slenker were advancing. Like "sacred heralds," they denounced "the greatest sin man does or can commit . . . to bring into being sensual, loveless, inhuman children. . . ."[38]

Stirpiculture lacked a sound basis in science. The influence of heredity versus environment on the development of a child has yet to be conclusively resolved. Eugenic thinkers were wrong in believing in the absolute heritability of characteristics influenced by both environment and heredity. By stressing that independent, healthy women would produce healthy offspring, eugenicists actually acknowledged the role of the environment in child development. These sex reformers believed that the future of the human race hinged on scientific breeding without adequately addressing the enormous influence that environment exercises on a child's character development.[39]

Stirpiculture easily became a philosophy of racism. Ezra Heywood argued that the "foreign element (mostly Irish and French Catholic) is gaining rapidly on all grades of native Protestant stock. . . . Remedy put forth by Stephen Pearl Andrews—seconded by the New England Free Love League—let 'old maids' have children—married or not." Heywood feared the influx of foreign laborers into the United States, believing that white Protestants were a superior genetic stock. Given his opposition to the state, Heywood never went along with some scientific breeding advocates' call for the state to bar unacceptable couples from having children. Stirpiculturists also developed an unfortunate pattern of blaming the victims of poverty for their own misery. For example, J. H. Cook stated: "The world is full of vice, crime, woe, want, disease and premature death, through reckless, thoughtless procreation." Cook, Heywood, and others placed their hopes for the future on breeding the best genetic stock. They overlooked the fact that most crimes and many diseases were socially rather than genetically determined. In American history, eugenic ideas have been used by conservative elites to talk about social problems without discussing actual social conditions. One logical outcome of stirpiculture was the development by Theodore Roosevelt and others of the race suicide theory. This theory supported nativism and racism, Yankee chauvinism at home and abroad, and women's domesticity.[40]

There were tensions in the free-love philosophy of Ezra and Angela Heywood. The Heywoods argued for freedom in social and sexual relations; freedom, though, meant rational self-control. The triumph of free love, the Heywoods believed, would extend the domain of reason and a new, higher spiritual order over the human system. They saw free love as both a scientific, rational approach to social change and and an article of faith. Their free-love ideas contained both liberatory and conservative aspects.

The Heywoods believed that an individual's right to personal freedom was sacrosanct. They sought the elimination of chattel slavery, wage slavery, and the sexual slavery of women. They derived these beliefs from the emphasis on the inviolability of individual rights articulated in the American Revolution. The theme of individual freedom—the natural endowment of each individual with natural rights and responsibilities—was central to the abolition, labor reform, and women's rights movements. The Heywoods translated this thesis into militant support for women's rights to birth control and a willingness to separate women's sexual drives from their maternal instincts.

Ezra and Angela Heywood, like many nineteenth-century social reformers, argued that society would move inexorably toward limitless improvement if only people had the necessary freedom to act on their own natural impulses. They passionately believed in the positive impact that rational discourse would have in an unfettered environment. A key factor in social change for the Heywoods was to bring down the barriers blocking men and women from achieving the natural harmony of human existence. In the nineteenth century, for many radicals there was no limit to progress if only reason and individual free will could be ascendent. According to Linda Gordon, Ezra Heywood assumed that "people's 'natural' instincts, left untrammeled, would automatically create a harmonious, peaceful, ecological society—an optimism certainly deriving directly from liberal philosophical faith in the innate goodness of man. . . ."

Ezra Heywood applied this thinking to sexuality, arguing that sexual instinct was naturally moderated and self-regulating. Essentially the same as Wilhelm Reich's theory of "sex-economy," the Heywood theory of self-regulation went beyond Reich's, according to Linda Gordon, in "providing a weapon against one of the ideological defenses of male supremacy. Self-regulation as a goal was directed against the prevalent attitude that male lust was an uncontrollable urge, an attitude that functioned as a justification for rape specifically and for male sexual irresponsibility generally. Since sexual repression had had the boomerang effect of intensifying human sexual drives far beyond 'natural' levels, effecting birth control now would require the development of the inner self-control to contain and repress sexual urges." Heywood expected, though, that in time sexual moderation would come naturally in a free, self-regulated society.[41]

No clearer example exists of the tension between liberatory and conservative aspects in the Heywoods' free-love philosophy than their simultaneous discourses on sexual freedom and the male continence system of control. In his description of free-love advocates Thomas Low Nichols and Mary Gove Nichols, the historian Stephen Nissenbaum could have been describing Ezra and Angela Heywood: "On the same page they were capable of rhapsodizing about sexual life and castigating it, of condemning marriage in the name of sexual freedom and condemning the exercise of sexual freedom in the name of health." This paradoxical stance constituted the central contradiction in nineteenth-century sexual radicalism in the United States.[42]

The free-love amalgam of license and conscience, writes Taylor Stoehr, led to doctrines that had pleasure built into self-denial, or that justified impulse. The polarity that existed at the heart of the free-love and continence crusades, Stoehr asserts, was the "impulse toward sensual indulgence on the one hand, and the need for justification in the eyes of conscience on the other." All of the continence theories were based on ambivalence toward sexual pleasure. Of course, Stoehr writes, these ambivalences did not come from nowhere; they were "somewhat eccentric manifestations of a much wider gulf in the culture itself—the classic dualism of Victorian sexuality, its prudery and its prurience, its chastity and its license, pornography and prostitution side by side with saintly virgins and wives of alabaster."[43]

NOTES

1. Ralph E. McCoy, "Banned in Boston: The Development of Literary Censorship in Massachusetts," Ph.D. diss., University of Illinois, Urbana, 1956, pp. 88–106.

2. Benjamin R. Tucker, "Walt Whitman and Anthony Comstock," *New York Herald*, Paris edition, November 23, 1930.

3. McCoy, "Banned in Boston," pp. 113–4, 107–18; *United States vs. Ezra Heywood*, United States District Court of Massachusetts, March term, 1883, pp. 368–80, criminal case 899.

4. McCoy, "Banned in Boston," p. 107; "An Open Letter to Walt Whitman," *The Word*, December 1882, pp. 2–3. Heywood's original letter to Whitman, dated November 5, 1882, is in the Henry W. and Albert A. Berg Collection, New York Public Library, Astor, Lenox and Tilden Foundations.

5. Walt Whitman to William D. O'Connor, November 12, 1882, in *Walt Whitman: The Correspondence*, vol. 3: *1876–1885*, ed. Edwin H. Miller (New York: New York University Press, 1964), pp. 314–15; William D. O'Connor to Walt Whitman, April 1, 1883, in Horace Traubel, *With Walt Whitman in Camden*, vol. 2 (New York: Mitchell Kennedy, 1915), p. 260.

6. Traubel, *With Walt Whitman in Camden*, vol. 2, pp. 241, 255; Horace Traubel, *With Walt Whitman in Camden*, vol. 1 (Boston: Small, Maynard, 1906), p. 350.

7. Ezra Heywood, ed., *Free Speech: Report of Ezra Hervey Heywood's Defense Before the United States Court, in Boston, April 10, 11, and 12, 1883* (Princeton, Mass.: Co-Operative Publishing, n.d.), pp. 5–7.

8. Linda Gordon, *Woman's Body, Woman's Right: A Social History of Birth Control in America* (New York: Penguin Books, 1977), pp. 64–65.

9. *The Word*, August 1881, p. 4; July 1881, p. 3; December 1882, p. 2.

10. Heywood, *Free Speech*, pp. 7–11.

11. *The Truth Seeker*, April 21, 1883, p. 252; Heywood, *Free Speech*, pp. 33, 37, 17–18; *The Word*, January 1883, p. 2.

12. Heywood, *Free Speech*, pp. 17–8, 20–21.

13. Ibid., pp. 37, 40–42.

14. Ibid., pp. 43–45; *Liberty*, May 12, 1883, p. 4.

15. *The Word*, July 1883, p. 2; January 1883, p. 2; September 1883, p. 2; November 1883, p. 2; Heywood, *Free Speech*, pp. 47–48; *Foote's Health Monthly*, January 1885, p. 11.

16. Ibid.; *The Word*, October 1884, p. 1; Heywood, *Free Speech*, p. 48.

17. *Lucifer*, October 10, 1890, p. 3.

18. Daniel Scott Smith, "Family Limitation, Sexual Control, and Domestic Feminism in Victorian America," in *A Heritage of Her Own*, ed. Nancy F. Cott and Elizabeth H. Pleck (New York: Simon and Schuster, 1979), pp. 223, 227; Carl N. Degler, *At Odds: Women and the Family in America from the Revolution to the Present* (New York: Oxford University Press, 1980), pp. 178–209, especially p. 189.

19. Gordon, *Woman's Body, Woman's Right*, pp. 23–24, 170.

20. Ibid., p. 101.

21. *Lucifer*, September 25, 1891, pp. 2–3; *The Word*, January 1883, p. 2; April 1878, p. 3; July 1883, p. 3.

22. Gordon, *Woman's Body, Woman's Right*, p. 60; James C. Mohr, *Abortion in America* (New York: Oxford University Press, 1978), pp. 160–70; Ezra Heywood, *Cupid's Yokes, or, The Binding Forces of Conjugal Life: An Essay to Consider Some Moral and Physiological Phases of Love and Marriage, Wherein Is Asserted the Natural Right and Necessity of Sexual Self-Government* (Princeton, Mass.: Co-Operative Publishing, 1876), p. 20; *The Word*, March 1893, pp. 2–3; August 1877, p. 2.

23. *Foote's Health Monthly*, June 1884, p. 12; *Lucifer*, May 29, 1886, p. 3; for details on Slenker, see Sears, *The Sex Radicals*, pp. 204–9, 215–28.

24. Gordon, *Woman's Body, Woman's Right*, pp. 174–75, 116.

25. Ibid., p. 174; Smith, "Family Limitation," pp. 233–34; Elizabeth H. Pleck and Joseph H. Pleck, "Introduction," *The American Man* (Englewood Cliffs, N.J.: Prentice-Hall, 1980), pp. 15–16; see also G. J. Barker-Benfield, *The Horrors of the Half-Known Life: Male Attitudes Toward Women and Sexuality in Nineteenth-Century America* (New York: Harper and Row, 1976).

26. Heywood, *Cupid's Yokes*, pp. 17–18; *The Word*, August 1892, p. 2; *Lucifer*, September 25, 1891, p. 3.

27. For details on Noyes, see Robert David Thomas, *The Man Who Would Be Perfect: John Humphrey Noyes and the Utopian Impulse* (Philadelphia: University of Pennsylvania Press, 1977), especially pp. 147–52 for ties with William Lloyd Garrison; Maren Lockwood Carden, *Oneida: Utopian Community to Modern Corporation* (New York: Harper and Row, 1969), see p. 14 for a discussion of his pefectionism; Lawrence Foster, "Free Love and Feminism: John Humphrey Noyes and the Oneida Community," *Journal of the Early Republic* 1 (Summer 1981):170; Carden, *Oneida*, pp. 24–25, 16–17.

28. Ibid., pp. 49–50; John Humphrey Noyes, *Male Continence* (Oneida, N.Y.: Oneida Community, 1872), pp. 7–8, 13–14, 16.

29. Louis J. Kern, *An Ordered Love: Sex Roles and Sexuality in Victorian Utopias—the Shakers, the Mormons, and the Oneida Community* (Chapel Hill: University of North Carolina Press, 1981), pp. 224–45; Stephen Nissenbaum, *Sex, Diet, and Debility in Jacksonian America: Sylvester Graham and Health Reform* (Westport, Conn.: Greenwood Press, 1980).

30. *Lucifer*, September 25, 1891, p. 3.

31. *The Word*, December 1889, p. 3. Slenker's choice of terminology was interesting. The Roman goddess Diana (Artemis for the Greeks) was a com-

plicated figure; she and her sister, Athena, were considered virgins because they had never married. However, they had enjoyed many lovers. Their failure to marry had been misinterpreted as virginity by succeeding generations of men. Diana had a dual identity as mother goddess and virgin; her lack of permanent connection to a male figure in a monogamous relationship was the basis for her independence. See Sara B. Pomeroy, *Goddesses, Whores, Wives, and Slaves: Women in Classical Antiquity* (New York: Schocken Books, 1976), pp. 5–6.

32. *The Word*, November 1889, p. 2; August 1882, p. 2.

33. Alfred Kinsey, Wendell Pomeroy, and Clyde Martin, *Sexual Behavior in the Human Male* (Philadelphia: W.B. Saunders, 1948), pp. 158–59; Howard Smith and Lin Harris, "The New Sex: Come Again Some Other Day," *Village Voice*, December 31-January 6, 1981, p. 18; Alex and Ilene Gross, letter to the author, undated.

34. Edward Bliss Foote, *Reply to the Alphites* (New York: Murray Hill, 1882); *Lucifer*, August 13, 1886, p. 1.

35. Gordon, *Woman's Body, Woman's Right*, pp. 121–23; Barker-Benfield, *Horrors of the Half-Known Life*. pp. 121–22.

36. Carden, *Oneida*, p. 61; Noyes, *Male Continence*, p. 15; John Humphrey Noyes, *Essay on Scientific Propagation* (Oneida, N.Y.: Oneida Community, 1875), pp. 15, 17, 24.

37. Gordon, *Woman's Body, Woman's Right*, pp. 87, 122, 128; Heywood, *Cupid's Yokes*, pp. 16–17; *The Word*, November 1888, p. 3.

38. *Foote's Health Monthly*, June 1884, p. 12; *Lucifer*, October 24, 1890, p. 3; *The Word*, July 1889, p. 3.

39. Gordon, *Woman's Body, Woman's Right*, p. 112.

40. *The Word*, October 1877, p. 2; *Foote's Health Monthly*, November 1889, p. 12; Sears, *The Sex Radicals*, p. 125; Gordon, *Woman's Body, Woman's Right*, pp. 136–41.

41. Gordon, *Woman's Body, Woman's Right*, pp. 101–3.

42. Nissenbaum, *Sex, Diet, and Debility*, pp. 165–66.

43. Stoehr, "Introduction," *Free Love in America*, pp. 58, 66, 62.

CHAPTER 7

THE FINAL BATTLE: FREE SPEECH

E zra Heywood and Moses Harman both aggressively campaigned for free speech and the right to use "offensive" words in their journals in the 1880s and 1890s. Heywood never met the beleaguered editor of *Lucifer*, but there was a political, spiritual, and temperamental affinity between the two men.

Frank discussion of sexuality, they argued, required the use of simple, graphically descriptive language. In the spring of 1886, Harman published a letter from the anarchist W. G. Markland in *Lucifer*. The letter, quoting from correspondence Markland had received, discussed the brutishness many husbands displayed during sexual intercourse. Heywood called the letter a "protest against rape in marriage." Markland was a longtime supporter of *The Word*, which occasionally published his letters and articles. For ten years Harman was in and out of court and prison for printing the Markland letter and other allegedly obscene letters. Harman's free-language policy alienated many reformers as well as conventional society. Although the editors of *The Truth Seeker* and *Liberty* supported Harman's right of free press, both were offended by his language tactics. Among contemporary reformers, Ezra Heywood was Harman's most vociferous supporter.[1]

Heywood observed that the phrase "generative sexual intercourse" was cumbersome, encompassing "three words, twenty-seven letters to define a given action commonly spoken of in one word of four letters that everybody knows the meaning of." Ezra and Angela Heywood argued for the use of three simple, clear words, "cock, cunt, and fuck," which merely described two human organs and their "associative use." Knowing that spelling out these words would mean immediate arrest and likely imprisonment, Heywood prudently referred to them in *The Word* as "c——, c——, and f——." Angela Heywood wrote that penis, womb, vagina, and semen were established terms, "well-revered in usage; other words, of equal dignity and trenchant familiarity form the clear-cut vocabulary in common use." She upheld the use of the word "fuck": "Such graceful terms as hearing, seeing, smelling, tasting, fucking, throbbing, kissing, and kin words are telephone expressions, lighthouses of intercourse centrally immutable to the situation; their aptness, euphony and serviceable persistence make it as impossible and undesirable to put them out of pure use as it would be take oxygen out of air."

Anyone was entitled, the Heywoods argued, to the free expression granted physicians and editors of medical journals. For Ezra Heywood, the issue of obscenity was not a matter of words, which were only "letters in line, associated in sentences." Rather, obscenity had its origins in "dirty thought, unclean habit, dishonest action relative to body forces." Heywood argued that the sex organs and sexual intercourse had "fit, proper, explicit, expressive *English* names."[2] The Heywoods' treatment of sex as a legitimate area of discourse was an attempt to undercut the morality that labelled sex a taboo, unclean subject.

In May 1890, Ezra Heywood was arrested on state and federal charges of sending obscene materials through the mail. The New England Watch and Ward Society (formerly the New England Society for the Suppression of Vice) was responsible for initiating the state charges; Anthony Comstock and his allies in the Republican Harrison administration were the forces behind the federal indictment.[3]

Because Comstock was a Republican, and the federal obscenity statute was passed by a Republican majority in Congress with the approval of a Republican president, most freethinkers adopted an anti-Republican stance. For years, Heywood had sharply denounced the Republicans for their support of censorship and for denying him and others freedom of speech. Until his arrest in May, Princeton postmasters had consistently refused to interfere in Heywood's work, despite repeated requests from Comstock. Princeton's postmaster before Heywood's federal arrest was a Democrat who identified himself as an infidel. Heywood believed that Comstock had directly influenced Postmaster General John Wanamaker in the selection of the new postmaster, who helped engineer Heywood's arrest by interfering with the mailing of *The Word*. Heywood's penchant for the Democrats earned him a sharp rebuke from fellow free-lover Francis Barry, who deeply admired Heywood but felt that "his support for the Democratic Party shows a want of perception that will forever unfit him as an exponent of Freedom."[4]

Heywood stood trial on the federal charges, which included three counts of printing obscene material in *The Word*: "A Physician's Testimony," by the pro-anarchist, New York physician Richard O'Neill; an anonymous letter from a mother; and an article by Angela Heywood.[5] Although none of the articles employed the three proscribed words, each piece dealt with sexuality frankly and directly.

Heywood's printing of the O'Neill letter in the April 1890, issue of *The Word* was probably the spark that led to his arrest. Heywood acted in solidarity with Moses Harman. While facing trial for the Markland letter, the Kansas editor had printed the O'Neill correspondence. Harman eventually served prison sentences for each letter. O'Neill, who had been a physician for nineteen years, detailed in his letter how he believed "thousands of women are killed every year by sexual excesses forced on them" and explicitly discussed oro-genital sex. Although he did not approve of this sexual practice, the letter is significant because it was one of the few instances in nineteenth-century published writing that took up the subject. Heywood warmly praised Moses Harman for printing O'Neill's letter and, after Harman was arrested for this action, felt compelled to take up the challenge. He called the letter "true, timely, chaste, vigorous"; O'Neill, Heywood maintained, had cogently presented the crucial argument against the "legalized outrage on women by men." Men, Heywood charged, claim their right to use "women's persons for murderous indulgence, because forsooth, these women are their wives!"[6]

The second count involved an anonymous letter from a mother that was printed in the March 1890, issue of *The Word*. Attorney Edward W. Chamberlain, who defended several sex radicals in court, had received the letter anonymously and sent it along to Heywood because he assumed Heywood would find it of great interest. Upon learning of Heywood's plans to publish the letter, Chamberlain visited him and made a vain attempt to persuade him to refrain from doing so. He argued that people were not educated enought to understand and appreciate the letter's value, and that Heywood would be risking prosecution. However, Chamberlain noted, Heywood was "resolute, and nothing could turn him from his purpose." In the letter, the mother described how her little girl had been approached in school by a boy who had used the word "fuck." In response to her daughter's inquiry about the word's meaning, the mother replied with a full description of the sexual organs and sexual intercourse. In her explanation, she wrote, she used plain English words. Further, by comparing her breasts and genitals with those of her daughter, she demonstrated their physical differences. She described how she and her daughter examined together a photograph of an erect penis and argued that when girls and boys are ready for their first sexual experiences, they should have sex with an older companion. The mother explained that when her little girl was prepared for her first sexual encounter, she would much rather "give her to a man double her age, provided there be . . . a mutual attraction between the two . . . than to one of her own. An inexperienced boy and girl would be apt to do each other much harm." The letter was a simple yet eloquent argument for sex education, total frankness, and the acknowledgment that adults and children are sexual beings.[7]

The third count concerned an article by Angela Heywood that had originally appeared in *The Word* in 1883 and was reprinted in 1889 wherein she defended women's right to use birth control devices. The vaginal syringe issue, for Angela Heywood, was as momentous as the question of slavery had once been. Woman, she insisted, would be "mistress of her own person." She called the penis and womb, "elegant organs of the Human Body, equal, in ability to entertain us, with the eye and tongue." The thrust of the article was a direct attack on Comstock for denying women the right to control their bodies. Ezra Heywood had been charged with obscenity for printing this article in 1883, but was acquitted. He described both this essay by Angela Heywood and the letter from the mother as articles "written by intelligent, honest, earnest women, mothers of children, who feel the imperative necessity of intelligence relative to physiology, morals, and language."[8]

When arrested on May 17, 1890, officials told Heywood that he would be granted ample time to prepare for trial. However, District Attorney Frank D. Allen subsequently told him "orders from Washington" were "to push Heywood," and the trial began in federal court in Boston on June 10. Unfortunately for Heywood, Judge Nelson, the trial judge who had presided at his acquittal in 1883 and who was slated to hear this case, was ill. In his place sat Judge George M. Carpenter of Rhode Island, a conservative supporter of the Comstock law, who was openly hostile to Heywood. This trial was reminiscent of the 1878 case when Heywood was given virtually no opportunity to present a defense. According to one of Ezra Heywood's supporters, attorney Edward W. Chamberlain, "the judge exhibited no disposition to be honest nor any willingness to be fair." Indeed, he argued, the entire conduct of the trial gave the impression of an orchestrated agreement on the part of the prosecutors and the judge "to get Mr. Heywood into prison, by any means, fair or foul."[9]

The prosecutor's case rested solely on proving that Ezra Heywood had sought to mail the issues of *The Word* named in the indictment, which was never read aloud in open court to the jury. Indeed, the jurors only heard the specific charges in the indictment after they had retired to their deliberations. The prosecution called the postmaster of Princeton and a postal inspector as witnesses and introduced the articles as evidence but did not present them in court to the jury or spectators. Defense attorneys George Searle and J. F. Pickering moved successfully to have the first charge, the O'Neill letter, dismissed because the person named on the wrapper as having received the item did not have the same name contained in the indictment. Comstock had misplaced or mistaken the particular alias he had used for the O'Neill letter.[10]

The defense wanted to call character witnesses, but the court rejected this approach. Angela Heywood was called to the stand and stated that she had written the article cited in the indictment, but the court refused to allow her to answer any questions about her husband's moral character or her motives for writing the article. The court ruled that "any evidence tending to show . . . the motive, purpose, or object" of the indicted material was irrelevant and thus inadmissible in court. The jury was to decide on the articles' obscenity without any discussion in open court of their value or purpose. The 1879 Bennett ruling had declared that the object of a publication was not a subject for consideration, and Judge Carpenter's rulings were in accordance with that earlier decision.[11]

Ezra Heywood followed Angela Heywood to the witness stand. The judge allowed him to testify that he had been convicted previously, but prevented the jury from learning that he had been pardoned or acquitted on other occasions. Because the indicted materials were never presented in the courtroom, Heywood could not discuss the nature of the articles and how he saw them contributing not to lewdness, but rather to the promotion of sexual health and purity. Defense attorneys questioned Heywood's motives for printing the indicted articles, but prosecution objections were sustained by the trial judge. Although the court prohibited discussion of what constituted obscenity, most of Heywood's testimony focused on whether or not he intended to mail obscene materials. The Bennett precedent again was relevant; a defendant could be found guilty even if he or she did not know the material was considered objectionable when mailed.[12] Judge Carpenter only considered as pertinent events related to the mailing of newspapers.[13]

Judge Carpenter's charge to the jury essentially sealed Ezra Heywood's fate. Writing in *Lucifer*, Clarence Swartz remarked it was difficult to discover one sentence in the charge that was "not a travesty of justice, a mockery of the liberty or right of citizenship." Edward W. Chamberlain found the charge to be vindictive and brutal. During the course of the trial, Carpenter had not allowed the issue of obscenity to be discussed, but he addressed it at length in his statement: "It is right for us to hold that no person should think that purity, manliness, and virtue could be promoted by sending through the mail a lewd, lascivious and obscene paper. We have before us an example of a person who apparently, with the education of a respectable man, yet believes it." With these words, Carpenter had virtually instructed the jurors that Heywood was guilty as charged in the indictment.[14]

Judge Carpenter stated that "the offense, so far as my imagination goes, is monstrous." It might fairly be designated, he claimed, "the foulest, meanest, lowest offense of which a human being can be guilty."

Carpenter called the obscenity statute plain and clear even though judicial opinion was seriously divided. In a series of articles analyzing the charge in *Lucifer*, Elmina Drake Slenker scoffed at the notion that the law was clear. She calculated that "by the rules of grammatical construction there are eighteen thousand different classes of matter declared by the Comstock law to be unmailable." Judge Carpenter instructed the jurors to determine whether or not the indicted materials were obscene without the hindrance of anyone else's opinions or arguments. However, he himself offered this judgment: "There is no freedom in this country for a man to do anything except to do right. The name of freedom is prostituted when it is employed to signify a privilege to do an evil thing." Many observers, Carpenter conceded, believed that if Heywood had "used obscene words and thus obscene thoughts, he had done so under a sense of duty." Carpenter conceded that Heywood claimed to be using certain expressions in the interest of promoting public morals and for the good of society. However, he cautioned, "it is familiar history that the greatest crimes have been committed by persons who believed that they were doing God service." He argued that however much Ezra Heywood's state of mind should be pitied, "we ought to punish him for any wrong and indecent acts which he may be guilty of or has done."[15]

With Judge Carpenter instructing the jurors that Heywood had committed a heinous crime, the decision of the jury—a finding of guilty on the two remaining counts—probably came as no surprise to Heywood and his supporters. Heywood's attorneys filed a lengthy petition for an arrest of judgment, but Carpenter overruled their motions. The sentencing was on July 24, 1890. When the district attorney began to ask Ezra Heywood if he had anything to say about the amount of punishment, Josephine Tilton sprang to her feet, walked over to stand by Heywood, and exclaimed: "Men of Massachusetts, in the name of the rights of man, I protest against these proceedings. I ask if you countenance a Court that does not weigh equity?" Judge Carpenter ordered that she be removed. While the judge continued to call for her ejection, she shouted out that the court did not countenance liberty. After order had been restored with Tilton's removal, Angela Heywood stood up, asked permission to speak, and was denied. Finally, Ezra Heywood sought to make a statement and was interrupted by Judge Carpenter's declaration: "I can hear you only on the amount of punishment." Heywood replied with calm and dignity: "I certainly am not here to ask for mercy." Judge Carpenter then proceeded to sentence the sixty-one-year-old Heywood to two years at hard labor at Charlestown State Prison, and Heywood was immediately taken to prison.[16]

Heywood's daily life at Charlestown Prison was difficult. No longer a young man, Heywood had worn himself down over the years with his many hours of work for social reform. However, confined within harsh prison walls, Heywood still had an indomitable spirit. Of the various prisons he had visited, Charlestown was most to his liking; the food was better, the work easier, and association with the inmate population of more than six hundred men was easily available. Heywood worked in the clothes-mending department of the prison during part of his incarceration. His reading and writing were seriously restricted. Although in Dedham Jail during his first prison term Heywood was permitted to receive all the newspapers he wanted and to write letters freely, he complained that in Charlestown Prison he knew little of what went on outside because prison authorities allowed no daily or reform papers. Further, Charlestown Prison rules permitted Heywood to write only sixteen letters per year, although he could receive an unlimited number. He could include four sheets per letter addressed to four different persons, but all had to go into one envelope addressed to one person, a restriction that forced Heywood to use very small writing and squeeze as many words as possible on a page. While in prison, at the suggestion of Angela Heywood, he began drafting his autobiography. Many of his letters, mailed to Moses Harman and printed in *Lucifer*, contained bits and pieces of his autobiographical history as Heywood used the time under confinement to reflect upon his life as a radical.

The prison environment weakened Heywood, especially during the winters of 1890–91 and 1891–92. He wrote in November 1891: "The chills, fever and racking cough that made it so hard for me last year have come on three months earlier than last year. Have lately been very ill, but am easier now. The outlook is not encouraging. Whether I can, physically, stand another winter here is uncertain." One of his supporters wrote that Heywood was suffering from tuberculosis. Just after his release from prison in the summer of 1892, Heywood stated: "From the seriously damaging physical effects of my imprisonment, especially from blood-poison caused by malaria in that tomb where 680 men are buried alive, I may never recover."[17]

One of Ezra Heywood's major preoccupations, as it had been during his 1878 confinement, was his family's impoverishment. He was frustrated by his total inability to be of any use to them. Taxes and interest on the Mountain Home mortgage were piling up unpaid. Angela Heywood was forced to appeal to readers of *Lucifer* for money to help pay for basic needs such as food and fuel and to cover the costs of emergency repairs to the Mountain Home so that she could house summer boarders. One appeal in *Lucifer* by Moses Harman informed concerned readers that any contribution to Angela Heywood, even a few postage stamps, would be greatly welcomed. Heywood wrote in a letter from prison in February 1891: "Mrs. Heywood and our two youngest, Psyche and Angelo, nine and seven years old, were here January 13, and it was a treat to set eyes on them once more. Had not seen them for six months. It took all but $1.00 of their money to come, 50 miles, and they must beg their way back. . . . While I am held here our publishing business is utterly suppressed, their means of existence destroyed and the mortgage (now held by a different and more friendly person) is liable to be again foreclosed."[18]

Ezra Heywood vented bitter feelings in prison. He was disgusted with Samuel Heywood and George Hoar, his two prestigious relatives. If they had lobbied for his release, Heywood was convinced, he would have been set free. He was also unhappy with Benjamin Tucker, whom Heywood viewed as having become conservative and afraid to take risks. Tucker had printed a series of articles in *Liberty* that criticized Harman and Heywood; he believed that they suffered martyrdom in vain. He declared: "We may admit their bravery, but their judgment was lamentably weak. Comstockism was not weakened but strengthened by their course." Tucker argued that Harman and Heywood had chosen the wrong issue with which to challenge Comstock. The persecution of *The Word* and *Lucifer*, Tucker feared, could carry over to such journals as his own *Liberty* with nothing gained for freedom of the press. Still Heywood hoped that "faith in the essential and that absolute of life" had not died out of Tucker. George E. Macdonald of *The Truth Seeker* took a different position from Tucker's. He claimed that "these venturesome men who drew the attention of the sadists to themselves were buffers for the rest of us. Anyhow their persecution marked the limits of safety for us."[19]

Heywood chafed at the silence of *The Word* and lamented that efforts to publicize his case were not as extensive as in 1878. The reformer Lucien Pinney, editor of *The Winsted Press* in Connecticut, had made a commitment to serve as temporary editor of *The Word* while Heywood was incarcerated. Heywood had prepared copy for two issues, but Pinney delayed the printing and never did publish an issue. Heywood speculated that Pinney may have been alarmed by the two-year term, which convinced him to withdraw. Heywood wrote in a letter to George Schumm: "Never was a newspaper more needed than it is needed and the delay disturbs me." He told Schumm that Angela Heywood and the children, overwhelmed with trying to sustain the summer boarding business, were totally preoccupied with survival issues. He believed that Angela Heywood would "do all a woman can do to carry the heavy work devolved upon her, but she needs editorial and typographical help such as you, Mr. Pinney, or some other man of faith and work can give her." Heywood proposed that supporters organize a series of public meetings on his case in Massachusetts, New York, Michigan, and Kansas and declared impatiently: "The people were never so ready to hear and read as now. Who will lead off in starting meetings?"[20]

Heywood's supporters did mount a campaign to free the imprisoned editor. These efforts were limited by scant resources and the fact that some free-speech advocates were wary of backing Heywood and thus being identified with his free-love doctrines. The National Defense Association in New York and Moses Harman and his *Lucifer* circle circulated two petitions. One, addressed to President William Henry Harrison, called for the immediate, unconditional pardon of Heywood, arguing that "social purity is not to be attained by a sacrifice of any of the constitutional guarantees whereby the rights of Free Speech and Free Press are assured to the citizen." Another petition condemned federal and state Comstock laws as violations of the United States Constitution and vowed to reverse this unjust censorship of the press and mails. Many individuals sent letters to the president, and several thousand people signed the petitions. *Foote's Health Monthly* reported that the signatories encompassed "the most prominent intellectual men and women of this and foreign countries." Signatories included the novelist Julian Hawthorne, Elizabeth Cady Stanton, Rabbi Solomon Schindler, Matilda Joslyn Gage, and Frederick Douglass, as well as such expected names as Benjamin R. Tucker, Alfred H. Love, Parker Pillsbury, and Edward Bond Foote, Jr. Petitions were also circulated in Scotland and England. Those petitions from Princeton, Massachusetts, included the signatures of the chairmen of the Republican and Democratic town committees, as well as the librarian, the dentist, the physician, several ex-postmasters, and the town's leading taxpayer. The National Defense Association circulated pamphlets explaining the facts and critical issues raised in the Harman and Heywood cases.[21]

Despite the efforts on Heywood's behalf, on August 7, 1891, President Harrison refused to grant a pardon to Heywood. Harrison, an article in *Lucifer* speculated, judged that public opinion favored keeping Heywood in prison. In response to continuing efforts on Heywood's behalf, Harrison issued a second denial in the fall. He declared: "I see no reason for interfering with this sentence. That there was a violation of law is clear, and the sentence is not extreme. The prisoner maintains his right to do what the law denominates a crime, and none of his reasons suggesting a pardon are present. His health is referred to, but no sufficient evidence that it is in a failing condition is offered. Denied."[22]

Despite Harrison's claim, Heywood's deteriorating health was apparent to all who visited him. Heywood himself had openly wondered whether he would survive a second winter in Charlestown Prison. Still, maintaining his fighting spirit he denounced his enemies as clearly as always: "I am caged two years in Mass[achuse]tts granite & iron for discussing physiology! But it is logical; the capitalists & church savages know that they must go, if our ideas prevail; we have struck at the root of their power to enslave women & rob Labor; hence 'these binds'. . . . The ultimate results, in human liberation, will be worth to the world all they cost us." Heywood noted the irony that Charlestown Prison stood under the shadow of the Bunker Hill monument: "as I go from my cell to the shop I see, over the prison wall, the top of Bunker Hill monument, a reminder of faith in freedom once actively insurgent here, yet now, in these opulent states, newspapers are suppressed, editors imprisoned. . . ." Heywood's willingness to be a martyr for his ideas helped him endure prison. He declared: "Life to one's family, self, and cause is precious; but I shall not commit moral suicide in order to live physically." In a letter to *Foote's Health Monthly*, Heywood likened himself to Jesus Christ. He wrote: "While *The Word* is suppressed by legalized savagery, its silence speaks effectively. Am sorry the case cannot have the benefit of its open advocacy, but *The Word* sleeping, is not dead, and bides its time to reappear. Jesus said his word would not pass away; there is quite as much never say die in ours."[23]

Josephine Tilton organized a banquet and reception for Heywood upon his release from prison on May 13, 1892, after he had languished for almost two years in Charlestown Prison. Many reformers from varied backgrounds attended the gathering. Freethought activist Robert C. Adams, who chaired the evening, called Heywood "probably the most advanced reformer of the day," who "rightly considers woman's emancipation the chief factor in world's progress." Dr. A. E. Gilbert, a woman physician and secretary of the New England Institute of Heredity, discussed her unsuccessful conveyance of the petitions favoring Heywood's release to President Harrison. She then introduced Heywood, who was quite ill at the time of his release and appeared very pale. However, the veteran reformer climbed the steps to the podium and delivered a brief but forceful speech. He said that he and other fighters for free speech were "the advance guard of progress, whom Republican tyrannists imprison or strangle." This whole obscenity craze, Heywood concluded, was a "dirty-minded delusion, libels Intellect and blasphemes Human Nature."[24]

Heywood resumed much of his heavy schedule of reform activities. He once again published *The Word*, answered his voluminous correspondence, gave speeches, and organized reform conventions. In a typical editorial from this period, Heywood upheld freedom of the press and denounced censorship: "Fortressed on the vantage ground of Truth Freedom never surrenders. . . . Type are stronger than bayonets; Ideas, Conscience, Speech, Press,—ever insurgent IMPULSE gives foul censors 'leave to withdraw' from Congress, courts, bed-chamber, and Nursery." The Heywood family, which in normal times flirted with poverty, was truly impoverished upon Heywood's release. They were heavily in debt from taxes and mortgage interest that had accumulated. Ezra and Angela Heywood had encountered great difficulty in paying for the necessities of life. The National Defense Association responded to their privation by organizing a Heywood Benefit Fund and hoped to raise $658, or $1 for every day Heywood spent in prison. In a few weeks the fund collected more than $100.[25]

In early May 1893, just one year after his release from prison, Heywood travelled from Princeton to New York to conduct the twenty-second annual convention of the American Labor Reform League. While in New York, he caught a cold that lingered because of his weakened physical condition. In Boston after the convention, his cold became more serious, and he tried to fight off what was probably a recurrence of the tuberculosis contracted while in prison. After a few days Heywood was forced into bed under the care of his friend and fellow reformer, Andrew Jackson Davis, a spiritualist physician. He struggled with his illness for several days at the home of his sisters-in-law, Josephine and Flora Tilton. However, despite the tender care of Angela Heywood, his daughter Psyche Ceres, and the Tilton sisters, on Monday, May 22, 1893, at 5:30 in the afternoon, Ezra Heywood died at the age of sixty-four. His mind had been lucid and his spirit hopeful to the last, and his death was peaceful and painless.[26]

In life, wrote *The Truth Seeker*, Ezra Heywood had been "tall and slender of frame, of sharp and rather delicate features, of a nervous and flexible temperament, animated in style . . . a pleasant voice and manner . . . fluent in speech and ready in debate." According to his friend A. E. Giles, Heywood died serene and calm in the knowledge that he had fought the good fight for his beliefs. Josephine and Flora Tilton had shown him a plaster cast of Heywood's head and face taken three days after his death. Giles found it to be a reasonable likeness, but was especially struck by the "loving joyful smile that lightens up the whole countenance." He offered a spiratualist explanation: "I am aware of the ordinary physiological explanation attempted by diplomatic MD's of such phenomena: but I find a more satisfactory revealment in my belief that the smile is caused by the joy of the dying person in his perception (through his spiritual vision) of the forms and countenances of loving relatives and friends, who have preceded him into the spirit world and are then and there welcoming him into the purer and higher life."[27]

Funeral services for Heywood were held in Boston and Princeton, the first in the home of Josephine and Flora Tilton on Wednesday, May 24, and the second at his home in Princeton the following day. Josephine Tilton wrote that Heywood was buried in the family burial ground "as fitting his life of poverty and his thought—in such matters—in a plain unpainted pine box." Heywood was as unconventional in death as in life; the Boston services were conducted on a totally informal basis in that anyone who wished might speak. *The Boston Globe* reported: "Reclining on a couch, as if in sleep, lay the body of the deceased, wrapped in a white robe. The finely chiseled and handsome features were as natural as in life. The hands were folded over the body, and in his left was a copy of *The Word*." There were no outward signs of mourning except the tear-stained faces of relatives and friends. The Tilton home was resplendent with baskets of laurels, similax, wisteria, violets, roses, and ferns. A large assembly of reformers came to commemorate Heywood. In addition to Angela Heywood and their children, relatives present were Angela Heywood's mother, Lucy Tilton; her two sisters, Josephine and Flora Tilton, and Samuel Heywood, who paid the costs of the funeral.[28]

The Boston funeral service lasted several hours and took on the appearance of a meeting of the New England Labor Reform or Free Love League. One speaker after another rose and spoke as he or she felt. The Beethoven Quartet performed "Still, Still with Thee," "He Is Risen," and other songs during the course of the ceremony. Several letters were read from friends and supporters of Heywood who were not able to attend the service. The funeral arrangements in Princeton involved a much smaller group of people, local and visiting friends and the few neighbors whose sympathy or curiosity was stronger than their prejudice and fear. Josephine Tilton angrily declared: "I must, before I part with my brother, rebuke Princeton folks for permitting Mr. Heywood to starve to death." Dr. C. H. Sims, one of the last speakers at the Princeton ceremony, concluded his eulogy: "He preached eight hours a day, and worked sixteen. He believed in peace and plenty, but toiled in the cause of liberty through difficulties and poverty for himself and family. He was the disciple of love and liberty, the victim of hate and oppression. Some one said he is beyond our prayers, and I join his little daughter Psyche in the reply: 'He is beyond our prisons, don't need our prayers, nor even those of his pious persecutors.' "[29]

Many present at the Boston services for Heywood delivered heartfelt and stirring eulogies. Archibald H. Simpson, longtime companion of Flora Tilton, declared that Heywood "stood for self-sovereignty. He saw that it must be carried through all phases of life. The right of the black was the right of woman. The burden upon him was due to those Comstock moralists who violated the principles for which he had always stood. They are trying to enforce morality. *This* is the essence of immorality. . . . So devoted was he to the principles he advocated that to say he could *not* outraged his sense of justice and made him immovably determined to do what was forbidden. . . . He was actually done to death by the society at the head of which is Comstock, the society of organized moralism."[30]

The veteran labor reformer John Orvis extolled Heywood for fearlessly pursuing truth and justice, placing him on a level with William Lloyd Garrison and Jesus Christ: "We are not here to pray—he is beyond our prayers, he is beyond the world's censure. Ezra H. Heywood seemed to me, among all the men I ever knew, to be a man, and with loftier conceptions of duty. . . . With him the perception of a truth was a conviction of duty. He never knew fear, never could know fear, with that conscience behind him. His eye was to the sun, and that eye, like the sun, penetrated to the evil recesses of society. He was devoted to what he held to be right. . . . He saw and denounced the evils of rent, interest, and profits. He was almost the first man since Jesus who said they were robbery. For his position on all these questions he has been cursed and persecuted—these truths have been crucified in the person of E. H. Heywood."[31]

The Heywoods had developed a special bond described by Lucien Pinney: "She has the same infatuation for the human race that leads her husband through the fires of persecution to ideal Liberty, but she has a more attractive and vivacious way of expression, and is as sunny and winsome in her various notions as he is solid and sedate. . . . The 'situation' without Mrs. Heywood would be no situation at all or worse. She is the light, the life, and I am tempted to say the motive power of the establishment." Although a strong woman, Angela Heywood without Ezra was unable to sustain *The Word* or substantial reform efforts. She confronted the difficult challenge of supporting herself and her four children because Heywood had left virtually nothing in terms of tangible assets, and his older brother Samuel provided no support for her and the children. When he died in 1913, he left a sizable estate of just under $1,000,000; most went to his wife and children, but he also left money in trusts for his two sisters, Mary C. and Fidelia Heywood. He left nothing for Ezra Heywood's family.[32]

The historical record is extremely fragmentary about the lives of Angela Heywood and her four children after Ezra Heywood's death. Recalling what her mother and grandmother, both Princeton residents, told her, Marguerite Davis related that Angela Heywood "in her last years, was last heard of as doing day work in office buildings," but the accuracy of her recollections, not firsthand accounts, is impossible to verify. Psyche Ceres Heywood wrote that her mother was a very strong person who thought clearly up to her death at the age of ninety-five, outliving Ezra by many years. Marguerite Davis wrote that the "youngest boy, Angelo, studied for an engineer's degree at Leland Stanford, I think, but became interested in Christian Science—lost his mental balance completely and died in an insane asylum." She thought that Vesta Heywood lived in California, but she provided no details of her life.[33]

A longtime Princeton resident, Mrs. Houghton, recalled that in the early 1900s, Hermes Heywood operated a summer business in the family home. He sold ice cream and soft drinks and, she recalled, had a successful business. Dee Heywood, Samuel Heywood's granddaughter, remembered that Hermes, whom she believed was unmarried, used to come to the Heywood shoe factory in Worcester operated by her father, Albert Samuel Heywood. Hermes would ask her father for money and consistently be turned away. Dee Heywood felt that Samuel Heywood was ashamed of Ezra Heywood and did not like to speak of him with his children. Whatever the level of Hermes' business success, his enterprise was destroyed in November 1908, when one of the largest fires Princeton ever experienced burned the old Mountain Home and an adjoining structure to the ground.[34]

As a mature woman, Psyche Ceres Heywood was an enthusiast of her father's ideas and activities. In 1947 and 1948, Ceres Heywood Bradshaw corresponded with Agnes Inglis, the curator of the Labadie Collection at University of Michigan. Like her parents, Bradshaw had worked in the summer resort business, owning and operating a camp in Maine for several decades. She wrote to Inglis that her "parents were unusual and very far in advance of the time in which they lived. . . . I am so thankful for your interest." She wrote proudly that two of her children sought, in their work and activities, to help solve the world's problems, just as her father had. Her daughter, Editha Hadcock, taught economics at DePauw University in Greencastle, Indiana from 1947 until 1963. Born in Wakefield, Massachusetts, Hadcock earned her B.A. degree in 1927 from Mt. Holyoke College and her M.A. and Ph.D. degrees

from Brown University in 1931 and 1946, respectively. Active in the
League of Women Voters, she was a member of the board of directors
of the Christian Science Church in Greencastle.[35]

Angela Heywood's sisters, Josephine and Flora Tilton, continued to
work for social reform. In 1917, Flora Tilton wrote in her sister's autograph book:

> Whence comes life? Life is love. Life is Beauty. Without Love, life is barren.
> Life is a great symphony—*Justice* is one of its chords,
> We should always keep in tune with that chord Justice.
> To commercialize sex is degradation. To be *free* women, we must first be
> *economically* free. *Love* to *work* for freedom—this too, is part of Life's
> Symphony.
> Love Life!

Josephine Tilton died in 1922, and Flora Tilton in 1918. At Flora
Tilton's funeral service in Boston, Archibald Simpson, her companion
for thirty-two years, eulogized his beloved Flora as a "pioneer in her
radical notions of woman's rights. . . . She was indeed a free woman . . .
ever master of herself." Simpson described her as a "Rationalist and
Freethinker," who discarded all superstition and "abhorred the mockery
of a Christian ritual over the remains of a Freethinker. So this simple
ceremony is in accordance with her wish. Those who loved her and wish
to commune with her will find her at any time in the 'green haunts of
man,'—in the parks and gardens, in the Arboretum, her special joy,
which she frequented regularly as the seasons came. She knew all the
flowers and plants and trees." After the recitation of a few poems, Flora
Tilton's body, according to her instructions, was cremated.[36]

An individualist anarchist, Ezra Heywood was an active participant
in the abolitionist, labor reform, and free-love movements in nineteenth-
century America. Heywood, and many of his contemporary reformers
schooled in Christian perfectionism, believed that society could be im-
proved without limit. They envisioned a decentralized social order regulated only by the rational self-control and voluntary cooperation of
individuals. The Jeffersonian model of a largely agricultural society, vol-
untarist, pluralist, and oriented toward the self-reliant individual's "pursuit of happiness," appealed greatly to Heywood, who espoused the
natural rights theory of the American Revolution. In an age of increasing
centralization of power, Heywood stood for individual freedom and res-
ponsbility. The guarantee of liberty for all, not social control by the state,
would be the path to a just society.

Radical individualism was a significant feature of nineteenth-century American social reform. According to the historian Eric Foner, the Civil War represented "in part the greatest triumph, in part the death-knell, of the antebellum tradition of radical individualism." The abolition of slavery represented a vindication of the ideals of personal freedom and autonomy. On the other hand, the war promoted a tendency on the part of many reformers to view government, rather than voluntary associations or individual efforts, as the source of future reforms.[37] It was left to Ezra Heywood and his fellow individualist anarchists to sustain the tradition of radical individualism in the post-Civil War period.

Lewis Perry's characterization of the nineteenth-century social reformer Henry Clarke Wright could apply to Ezra Heywood: "He lived with a keen sense that his world was shifting, that new arrangements were still being created. We may regard him as the citizen of a transitional world, no longer traditional, but not yet modern, a world characterized by unsettling change, one in which nostrums and slogans conveyed the hope that society was headed in the direction of liberation and progress. In this world Wright traveled with a classless, raceless dream of rewarding individual freedom and tidy social order."[38]

Ezra Heywood's commitment to individual freedom was a historical antecedent to the anarchism of the immigrant working people of the late nineteenth and early twentieth centuries. The Russian-born Emma Goldman, the leading exponent of anarchism among the immigrant radicals, defined anarchism as "the philosophy of a new social order based on liberty unrestricted by man-made law; the theory that all forms of government rest on violence, and are therefore wrong and harmful, as well as unnecessary." Anarchism, often maligned as a violent philosophy imported from Europe, was, in the words of Paul Avrich, "not an alien doctrine, but an integral part of the American past, deeply rooted in native soil." The libertarian tradition has been a powerful current in American political activism, including the religious and political dissenters of the colonial era, the abolitionists, the communitarian enthusiasts, Emerson and Thoreau, and many others to the present.[39]

Ezra Heywood's social reform was based in a rural, Protestant, New England Yankee tradition. In contrast, Emma Goldman was a Russian-born Jew who lived in the densely packed immigrant neighborhoods of New York City. Although they differed on questions of violence and organization, they were united, according to Paul Avrich, in their "rejection of the state, their opposition to coercion, and their faith that people could live in harmony once the restraints imposed by government had been removed." Notwithstanding their small popular following, Avrich asserts, anarchists have played a significant part in American history and had a deep and abiding impact on American life.[40]

Goldman was directly influenced by Heywood, hailing him as a trail-blazer in the fight for women's right to birth control in the United States. Goldman, like Heywood, denounced marriage, criticized the limits of women's suffrage, upheld women's right to birth control, and in general promoted the social, political, and economic equality of women as a central component of her radical message. Goldman's faith in freedom and the limitless potentiality of a society based on individual freedom was very similar to Heywood's.

In her important essay "Marriage and Love," Goldman's writing echoed Heywood's: "Free love? As if love is anything but free! Love, the strongest and deepest element in all life, the harbinger of hope, of joy, of ecstasy; love, the defier of all laws, of all conventions; love, the freest, the most powerful moulder of human destiny; how can such an all-compelling force be synonymous with that poor little State- and Church-begotten weed, marriage?" Like Heywood, Goldman frequently invoked the spirit of the American Revolution and the libertarian message of the abolitionists and Thoreau. Further, Goldman shared with Heywood the belief that the triumph of anarchism would bring the millennium. The spiritual light of anarchism, Goldman wrote, is the philosophy of the sovereignty of the individual, the theory of social harmony, and the "great, surging living truth that is reconstructing the world, and that will usher in the new Dawn."[41]

Ezra Heywood's ideas concerning freedom, the centrality of the individual, and hostility to powerful social institutions certainly have much relevance in contemporary society. Nowhere is this more true than in the area of women's rights. In concluding her history of birth control in America, Linda Gordon offers a program that echoes the agenda that Angela and Ezra Heywood elaborated in the nineteenth century. Gordon declares that her entire book has been "in a sense, a documented plea for the importance of a total program of female liberation, for a never-ending vigilance to view birth control and sexuality in the context of the overall power relations of the society, especially sex and class relations."[42]

The struggles that Ezra and Angela Heywood waged for women's social, economic, and sexual rights, as well as their advocacy for the rights of blacks, peace, and the efforts of working people for social justice were determined efforts. Their determination was fueled by their belief in the utter righteousness of their undertaking. Celia Morris Eckhardt, biographer of the nineteenth-century radical Fanny Wright, observes that "Idiosyncracy is hard to measure almost 150 years in the past, and the twentieth-century eye looks back astonished at the millennialist delusions rampant then."[43] It is clear that the Heywoods were idiosyncratic, with their New England Anti-Death League, or their championing of male continence as a birth control system and the spiritual approach to life. Still, their radical theories and activism significantly contributed to the advancement of social justice in the nineteenth century and influenced succeeding generations of social activists. Further, their lives of devotion to the betterment of humankind were exemplary in their own time and stand as examples and role models for those who follow them in history who seek to build a better world.

NOTES

1. Hal D. Sears, *The Sex Radicals: Free Love in High Victorian America* (Lawrence: Regents Press of Kansas), pp. 74–80, 107–17; *The Word*, August 1889, p. 2.

2. *Lucifer*, August 14, 1891, pp. 2–3; *The Word*, July 1884, p. 2; April 1887, p. 2; June 1889, p. 2.

3. New England Watch and Ward Society, *Annual Report: 1890–1891* (Boston: Office of the Society, 1891), p. 8.

4. *The Word*, May 1890, p. 2; June 1890, p. 2. For a general denunciation of the Republican party, see Heywood's "Press Censorship-Republicanism," *The Word*, September 1892, p. 2. For Barry's quote, see *Lucifer*, June 10, 1892, p. 3.

5. Sidney Warren, *American Freethought, 1860–1914* (New York: Gordian Press, 1966), pp. 196–97.

6. *The Word*, April 1890, p. 3; Sears, *The Sex Radicals*, pp. 110–12; *Lucifer*, March 21, 1890, p. 1.

7. *The Word*, March 1890, p. 3; Oswald Dawson, *Personal Rights and Sexual Wrongs* (London: Wm. Reeves, 1897), pp. 32–33.

8. *The Word*, April 1889, pp. 2–3; *Twentieth Century*, October 9, 1890, p. 5.

9. *The Word*, June 1890, p. 2; *The Truth Seeker*, May 28, 1892, p. 841; Edward W. Chamberlain, "United States vs. Heywood—Why the Defendant Should Be Released. Mr. Chamberlain's Letter to Mr. Harrison" (New York: National Defense Association, 1891), p. 6.

10. Mordechai E. Liebling, "Ezra Heywood: Intransigent Individualist," research paper, Brandeis University, Waltham, Mass., 1970, pp. 45–46.

11. Liebling, "Ezra Heywood," p. 46; *United States v. Heywood*, United States Circuit Court of Massachusetts, May term, 1890 (handwritten, no publisher), criminal case # 980, p. 16.

12. *United States v. Heywood*, pp. 17–25; Liebling, "Ezra Heywood," p. 47.

13. See *United States v. Heywood*.

14. *Lucifer*, July 18, 1890, p. 2; Chamberlain, "United States vs. Heywood," pp. 9–10; *The Truth Seeker*, June 28, 1890, p. 405.

15. Ibid.; for Slenker's series, see *Lucifer*, May 22, 1891, p. 4; June 5, 1891, p. 1; July 31, 1891, p. 1; September 4, 1891, p. 1; October 16, 1891, p. 1; October 30, 1891, p. 1; November 13, 1891, p. 1.

16. Liebling, "Ezra Heywood," p. 49; Dawson, *Personal Rights and Sexual Wrongs*, pp. 34–35.

17. *Lucifer*, November 7, 1890, p. 3; June 5, 1891, p. 2; October 30, 1891, p. 3; November 21, 1890, p. 3; November 13, 1891, p. 1; *The Truth Seeker*, August 16, 1890, p. 517; Julian Hawthorne, *In Behalf of Personal Liberty* (New York: Twentieth Century Publishing, 1891), p. 1; *The Word*, August 1892, p. 3.

18. Ezra Heywood to Mrs. Elizabeth M. F. Denton, April 18, 1892, Denton Family Papers, Labadie Collection, University of Michigan, Ann Arbor; *Lucifer*, February 6, 1891, p. 2; February 13, 1891, p. 2; April 3, 1891, p. 3; February 27, 1891, p. 3.

19. Ezra Heywood to Mrs. Elizabeth M. F. Denton, April 18, 1892; *Lucifer*, December 11, 1891, p. 3; June 5, 1891, pp. 2–3; for Tucker's comments on Heywood and Harman, see *Liberty*, August 16, 1890, p. 4; May 24, 1890, p. 6; June 21, 1890, pp. 4–5; August 30, 1890, p. 5; George E. Macdonald, *Fifty Years of Free Thought: Being the Story of "The Truth Seeker" with the Natural History of Its Editor* (New York: Truth Seeker, 1929), pp. 530–31.

20. Ezra Heywood to George Schumm, undated, George Schumm Papers, Labadie Collection, University of Michigan, Ann Arbor.

21. *Lucifer*, March 13, 1891, pp. 1, 3; September 4, 1891, p. 3; March 18, 1892, p. 1; April 3, 1891, pp. 1–2; *Foote's Health Monthly*, May 1891, p. 10; Chamberlain, "United States vs. Heywood," pp. 17–21; *Lucifer*, February 6, 1891, p. 3; March 6, 1891, p. 1.

22. *Lucifer*, August 21, 1891, p. 2; *The Truth Seeker*, January 16, 1892, p. 38.

23. Ezra Heywood to Elizabeth M. F. Denton, April 18, 1892; *The Truth Seeker*, August 29, 1891, p. 547; *Lucifer*, November 13,1891, p. 4; *Foote's Health Monthly*, December 1890, p. 11.

24. *Lucifer*, May 27, 1892, p. 2; *The Word*, July 1892, pp. 1–2; *The Truth Seeker*, May 21, 1892, p. 328; May 28, 1892, p. 340.

25. Ezra Heywood to A. G. Pope, April 4, 1893, bound in Volume 3 of the copy of *The Word*, Rare Book Collection, the State Historical Society of Wisconsin, Madison; *The Word*, March 1893, p. 1; *The Truth Seeker*, May 7, 1892, p. 292; May 21, 1892, p. 328.

26. *Lucifer*, June 9, 1893, p. 2; A. E. Giles to Professor Poland, June 11, 1893, Hay Library, Brown University, Providence, R.I.

27. *The Truth Seeker* was cited in *Lucifer*, June 9, 1893, p. 3; A. E. Giles to Professor Poland, June 11, 1893.

28. *The Truth Seeker*, June 10, 1893, p. 358; Josephine S. Tilton to W. C. Poland, June 11, 1893, Hay Library, Brown University, Providence, R.I.

29. *Lucifer*, June 25, 1893, p. 3; *The Truth Seeker*, June 10, 1893, pp. 358–59.

30. Ibid.

31. Ibid.

32. *The Word*, June 1890, p. 1; Probate Record of Ezra H. Heywood, Case 16159, May 24, 1894, Registry of Probate, Worcester County Court House; "Samuel R. Heywood Estate of $800,000 Goes to Relatives," undated newspaper clipping, Princeton, Mass. Public Library.

33. Marguerite Davis to Zechariah Chafee, September 30, 1929, Hay Library, Brown University, Providence, R.I.; Ceres Heywood Bradshaw to Agnes Inglis, November 15, 1947, Agnes Inglis Papers, Labadie Collection, University of Michigan, Ann Arbor.

34. Kenneth S. Davis, "Ezra Heywood" (Princeton, Mass.: Princeton Historical Society), p. 15; interview with Dee Heywood, October 2, 1981; *The Laborer's Friend*, Princeton, Mass., November 6, 1908, p. 1.

35. Ceres Heywood Bradshaw to Mrs. Bailie, May 30, 1947, Bradshaw to Agnes Inglis, November 15, 1947, April 10, 1948, June 18, 1949, Agnes Inglis Papers, Labadie Collection, University of Michigan, Ann Arbor; *The Indianapolis News*, December 10, 1963; press release, DePauw University News Bureau, December 10, 1963.

36. Autograph Album of Josephine S. Tilton, Denton Family Papers, Labadie Collection, University of Michigan, Ann Arbor; Ceres Heywood Bradshaw to Mrs. Bailie, May 30, 1947; "Services for Joan Flora Tilton," unidentified newspaper clipping, November 25, 1918, Labadie Collection, University of Michigan, Ann Arbor.

37. Eric Foner, "Radical Individualism in America: Revolution to Civil War," *Literature of Liberty* 1 (July–September 1978):26–27.

38. Lewis Perry, *Childhood, Marriage, and Reform: Henry Clarke Wright, 1797–1870* (Chicago: University of Chicago Press, 1980), p. 290.

39. In a history of individualist anarchism in the United States, the anarcho-syndicalist Rudolf Rocker included Jefferson, Emerson, Thoreau, Garrison, and Wendell Phillips, Rocker, *Pioneers of American Freedom* (Los Angeles: Rocker Publications Committee, 1949). In her essay "Anarchism and American Traditions," Voltairine deCleyre declared: "Among the fundamental likenesses between the revolutionary Republicans and the Anarchists is the recognition that the little must precede the great; that the local must be the basis of the general; that there can be a free federation only when there are free communities to federate. . . . the sin our fathers sinned was that they did not trust liberty wholly. They thought it possible to compromise between liberty and government. . . ," *Selected Works of Voltairine deCleyre*, ed. Alexander Berkman (New York: Mother Earth Publishing Association, 1914), pp. 121, 131; Avrich, "Preface," *An American Anarchist*, pp. xiv-xv.

40. Avrich, "Preface," *An American Anarchist*, pp. xvi-xvii.

41. Emma Goldman, *Living My Life*, vol. 2 (New York: Dover, 1970), p. 533. Several historians have noted Heywood's central role in birth control agitation. See the following: Victor Robinson, *Pioneers of Birth Control in England and America* (New York: Voluntary Parenthood League, 1919), pp. 58–62; Linda Gordon, *Woman's Body, Woman's Right: A Social History of Birth Control in America* (New York: Penguin Books, 1977), pp. 65–66, 97–109; Peter Fryer, *The Birth Controllers* (London: Secker and Warburg, 1965), pp. 193–96; "Marriage and Love" in *Red Emma Speaks: An Emma Goldman Reader* (New York: Schocken Books, 1983), p. 211; "Anarchism: What It Really Stands For" in *Red Emma Speaks*, p. 77. For further information on Goldman, see Richard Drinnon, *Rebel in Paradise: A Biography of Emma Goldman* (1961. reprint, New York: Bantam, 1973); Candace Falk, *Love, Anarchy, and Emma Goldman: A Biography* (New York:

Holt, Rinehart, and Winston, 1984); Alice Wexler, *Emma Goldman: An Intimate Life* (New York: Pantheon, 1984).

42. Gordon, *Woman's Body, Woman's Right*, p. 415.

43. Celia Morris Eckhardt, *Fanny Wright: Rebel in America* (Cambridge: Harvard University Press, 1984), p. 281.

Bibiliography

I. PRIMARY SOURCES

A. Manuscripts

1. Labadie Collection, Hatcher Library, University of Michigan, Ann Arbor:
   Organizational Papers: National Defense Association, New England Free Love League, New England Labor Reform League, Union Reform League
   Personal Papers: Stephen Pearl Andrews, Ceres Heywood Bradshaw, Denton Family, Angela Tilton Heywood, Ezra Heywood, Agnes Inglis, Archibald H. Simpson, George Schumm, Joan Flora Tilton, Josephine S. Tilton, Benjamin R. Tucker, Josiah Warren, Alfred B. Westrup
2. Boston Public Library, Boston, Mass.:
   Personal Papers: William Lloyd Garrison, Samuel May
3. Houghton Library, Harvard University, Cambridge, Mass.:
   Personal Papers: Wendell Phillips
4. Rutherford B. Hayes Presidential Center, Fremont, Ohio:
   Personal Papers: Rutherford B. Hayes
5. Anti-Slavery Collection, Department of Rare Books, John M. Olin Library, Cornell University, Ithaca, N.Y.:
   Personal Papers: Ezra Heywood
6. Rare Book Collection, State Historical Society of Wisconsin, Madison
7. Manuscript Department, The New York Historical Society:
   Personal Papers: William Lloyd Garrison
8. Special Collections: Henry W. and Albert A. Berg Collection, Astor, Lenox and Tilden Foundations, New York Public Library:
   Personal Papers: Walt Whitman
   Rare Books and Manuscripts Division:
   Personal Papers: Benjamin R. Tucker
9. Archives, Princeton Public Library, Princeton, Mass.
10. Hay Library, Brown University, Providence, R.I.:
    Archives: Student Records.
    Personal Papers: Alfred E. Giles, Ezra Heywood
11. Manuscript Division, George Arents Research Library, Syracuse University, Syracuse, N.Y.:
    Personal Papers: Gerrit Smith
12. National Archives Center, National Archives-Boston Branch, Waltham, Mass.:
    United States v. Heywood. Circuit Court Federal Records, vol. 78, 1877-78, District Court of United States of America, for District of Massachusetts at Boston. Handwritten volume, no publisher.

United States vs. Ezra Heywood, United States District Court of Massachusetts, March Term, 1883.
United States v. Heywood, United State Circuit Court of Massachusetts, May Term, 1890. Handwritten, no publisher.
13. Worcester, Mass.: Registry of Probate, Worcester County Court House; Worcester District Registry of Deeds; Worcester Historical Museum Archives; American Antiquarian Society

B. Journals and Newspapers

American Workman, The Boston Commonwealth, Boston Investigator, Daily Evening Voice, Foote's Health Monthly, The Index, Kansas Liberal, The Laborer's Friend, The Liberator, Liberty, Lucifer, The Providence Journal, The Radical Review, The Revolution, The Truth Seeker, Twentieth Century, Weekly American Workman, Woodhull and Claflin's Weekly, The Word, Workingman's Advocate

C. Works by Ezra Heywood

Constitution and By-Laws of the Mountain Home Corporation. Princeton, Mass.: Co-Operative Publishing, 1882.
Cupid's Yokes, or, The Binding Forces of Conjugal Life: An Essay to Consider Some Moral and Physiological Phases of Love and Marriage, Wherein Is Asserted the Natural Right and Necessity of Sexual Self-Government. Princeton, Mass.: Co-Operative Publishing, 1876.
Declaration of Sentiments and Constitution of the New England Labor Reform League. Boston: Weekly American Workman, 1869. (with William B. Greene)
The Evolutionists: Being a Condensed Report of the Principles, Purposes, and Methods of the Union Reform League. Princeton, Mass.: Co-Operative Publishing, 1882.
Free Speech: Report of Ezra Hervey Heywood's Defense Before the United States Court in Boston, April 10, 11, and 12, 1883. Princeton, Mass.: Co-Operative Publishing, n.d.
Free Trade: Showing the Medieval Barbarism, Cunningly Termed "Protection to Home Industry," Tariff Delusion Invades Enterprise, Defrauds Labor, Plunders Trade, and Postpones Industrial Emancipation. Princeton, Mass.: Co-Operative Publishing, n.d.
The Great Strike: Its Relations to Labor, Property and Government. Suggested by the Memorable Events Which, Originating in the Tyrannous Extortion of Railway Masters, and the Execution of Eleven Labor Reformers, Called "Mollie Maguires," June 21, 1877, Culminating in Burning the Corporation Property, in Pittsburgh, July 22, Following; This Essay Carefully Defines the Relative Claims of Work and Wealth, Involved in the Irresistible Conflict Between Capital and Labor, Which Engages Increasingly the Attention of Thoughtful People the World Over. Princeton, Mass.: Co-Operative Publishing, 1878.
Hard Cash: An Essay to Show That Financial Monopolies Hinder Enterprise and Defraud Both Labor and Capital; That Panics and Business Revulsions, Caused

by Arbitrary Interference with Production and Exchange, Will Be Effectually Prevented Only Through Free Money. Princeton, Mass.: Co-Operative Publishing, 1874.

The Labor Party: A Speech Delivered Before the Labor Reform League, of Worcester, Massachusetts, Explaining the Ideas and Objects of the Labor Movement— What Workingmen Want—Whom It Concerns—And How to Get It. New York: Journeymen Printers' Co-Operative Association, 1868.

Social Ethics: An Essay to Show the Right of Private Judgment Must Be Respected in Morals, as Well as in Religion, Free Rum, the Conceded Right of Choice in Beverages, and Required Power to Decline Intoxicants Promotes Rational Sobriety and Assures Temperance. Princeton, Mass.: Co-Operative Publishing, n.d.

Uncivil Liberty: An Essay to Show the Injustice and Impolicy of Ruling Woman without Her Consent. Princeton, Mass.: Co-Operative Publishing, 1870.

Yours or Mine: An Essay to Show the True Basis of Property and the Causes of Its Inequitable Distribution. Princeton, Mass.: Co-Operative Publishing, 1877.

II. SECONDARY SOURCES

Andrews, Stephen Pearl. *The Science of Society.* Edited by Charles Shively. Weston, Mass.: M and S Press, 1970.

Apter, David, and James Joll, eds., *Anarchism Today.* New York: Doubleday, 1972.

Arieli, Yehoshua. *Individualism and Nationalism in American Ideology.* Cambridge, Mass.: Harvard University Press, 1964.

Asfar, Denise, ed. *The Journal of William Dearth (November 2, 1854–September 5, 1855).* Providence, R.I.: Brown University, 1980.

Avrich, Paul. *An American Anarchist: The Life of Voltairine deCleyre.* Princeton, N.J.: Princeton University Press, 1978.

———. *Anarchist Portraits.* Princeton, N.J.: Princeton University Press, 1988.

———. *The Haymarket Tragedy.* Princeton, N.J.: Princeton University Press, 1984.

———. *The Modern School Movement: Anarchism and Education in the United States.* Princeton, N.J.: Princeton University Press, 1980.

Bailie, William. *Josiah Warren: The First American Anarchist.* Boston: Small, Maynard, 1906.

Barker-Benfield, G. J. *The Horrors of the Half-Known Life: Male Attitudes Toward Women and Sexuality in Nineteenth-Century America.* New York: Harper and Row, 1976.

Barnett, Redmond J. "The Movement Against Imprisonment for Debt in Massachusetts, 1811–1834," senior honor's thesis, Harvard University, Cambridge, Mass., 1965.

Bennett, D. M. *The Champions of the Church: Their Crimes and Persecutions.* New York: Liberal and Scientific Publishing House, 1878.

Blake, Francis E. *History of the Town of Princeton, 1759–1915.* Princeton, Mass.: Published by the town, 1915.

Blatt, Martin, ed. *The Collected Works of Ezra Heywood.* Weston, Mass.: M and S Press, 1985.

———, Uri Davis, and Paul Kleinbaum. *Dissent and Ideology in Israel: Resistance to the Draft, 1948-1973.* London: Ithaca Press, 1975.

———. "Ezra Heywood and Benjamin R. Tucker." In *Benjamin R. Tucker and the Champions of "Liberty": A Centenary Anthology,* edited by Mark Sullivan, Charles Hamilton, and Michael Coughlin. St. Paul: Michael Coughlin, Publisher, 1987.

———. "Ezra Heywood and the Chicago Martyrs." In *Haymarket Scrapbook,* edited by Dave Roediger and Franklin Rosemont. Chicago: Charles H. Kerr, Publishing, 1986.

———. "Noam Chomsky." In *The Sixties—Without Apology,* edited by Sohnya Sayres, Anders Stephanson, Stanley Aronowitz, and Fredric Jameson. Minneapolis: University of Minnesota Press, 1984.

———. "Why I Am an Anarchist." *Black Rose Magazine,* no. 3 (Fall 1979): 2–7.

Bookchin, Murray. *The Ecology of Freedom.* Palo Alto, Calif.: Cheshire Books, 1982.

———. *The Limits of the City.* New York: Harper and Row, 1974.

———. *The Modern Crisis.* Philadelphia: New Society Publishers, 1986.

———. *Toward an Ecological Society.* Montreal: Black Rose Books, 1980.

Bouley, Charles Henry. *Biographical Sketches of the Pioneer Settlers of New England and Their Descendants in Worcester, Massachusetts.* Barre, Mass.: Barre Publishers, 1964.

Brecher, Jeremy. *Strike!* San Francisco: Straight Arrow Books, 1972.

Brock, Peter. *Pacifism in the United States: From the Colonial Era to the First World War.* Princeton, N.J.: Princeton University Press, 1968.

Bronson, Walter C. *The History of Brown University, 1764–1914.* Providence, R.I.: Brown University, 1914.

Broun, Heywood, and Margaret Leech. *Anthony Comstock: Roundsman of the Lord.* New York: Albert and Charles Boni, 1927.

Bruce, Robert V. *1877: Year of Violence.* Indianapolis: Bobbs-Merrill, 1959.

Buber, Martin. *Paths in Utopia.* Boston: Beacon Press, 1971.

Buhle, Paul. "Anarchism and American Labor." *International Labor and Working Class History,* no. 23 (Spring 1983): 21–34.

———, and Alan Dawley. *Working for Democracy: American Workers from the Revolution to the Present.* Urbana: University of Illinois Press, 1985.

Buhle, Mari Jo, and Paul Buhle, eds. *The Concise History of Woman Suffrage: Selections from the Classic Works of Stanton, Anthony, Gage, and Harper.* Urbana: University of Illinois Press, 1978.

Bumgardner, George H. *Princeton and the High Roads, 1775–1975.* Princeton, Mass.: Princeton Bicentennial Commission, 1975.

Butler, Ann C. "Josiah Warren: Peaceful Revolutionist." Ph.D. diss., Ball State University, Muncie, Ind., 1978.

Callenbach, Ernest. *Ecotopia.* Berkeley, Calif.: Banyon Tree Books, 1975.

Campbell, Rachel. *The Prodigal Daughter; or, The Price of Virtue.* Valley Falls, Ks.: Lucifer Publishing, 1888.

Carden, Maren Lockwood. *Oneida: Utopian Community to Modern Corporation.* New York: Harper and Row, 1969.

Celebration of the One Hundredth Anniversary of the Incorporation of the Town of Princeton, Massachusetts, October 20, 1859. Worcester, Mass.: William R. Hooper, 1860.

Chafee, Zechariah, Jr. "Biographical Sketch of Ezra Heywood." In *Dictionary of American Biography,* edited by Dumas Malone. New York: Charles Scribner's Sons, 1932.

Chamberlain, Edward W. "United States vs. Heywood-Why the Defendant Should Be Released. Mr. Chamberlain's Letter to Mr.Harrison." New York: National Defense Association, 1891.

Commager, Henry Steele. *Theodore Parker.* Boston: Beacon Press, 1947.

Comstock, Anthony. *Traps for the Young.* New York: Funk and Wagnalls, 1883.

Cook, J. H. "Sexual Science and Dress Reform," parts 1 and 2. *Lucifer,* April 8 and 15, 1892.

Cooney, Robert, and Helen Michalowski. *The Power of the People: Active Nonviolence in the United States.* Culver City, Calif.: Peace Press, 1977.

Cott, Nancy F. *The Bonds of Womanhood: "Woman's Sphere" in New England, 1780–1835.* New Haven, Conn.: Yale University Press, 1977.

———, and Elizabeth H. Pleck, eds. *A Heritage of Her Own.* New York: Simon and Schuster, 1979.

Coughlin, Michael, Charles Hamilton, and Mark Sullivan, eds. *Benjamin R. Tucker and the Champions of "Liberty": A Centenary Anthology.* St. Paul: Michael Coughlin, Publisher, 1987.

Curti, Merle. *Peace or War: The American Struggle, 1636–1936.* New York: W. W. Norton, 1936.

David, Henry. *The History of the Haymarket Affair.* 1936. Reprint. New York: Collier, 1963.

Davis, Kenneth S. "Ezra Heywood." Princeton, Mass.: Princeton Historical Society, 1967.

Dawson, Oswald. *Personal Rights and Sexual Wrongs.* London: Wm. Reeves, 1897.

Dearth, William Griswold. *The Diary of William Griswold Dearth: Preateria, Journal of Acts and Thoughts, a Portion (September 6–November 1, 1854),* edited by Timothy Nolan. Providence, R.I.: Brown University Press, 1979.

———. *The Journal of William Griswold Dearth (November 2, 1854–September 5, 1855),* edited by Denise Asfar. Providence, R.I.: Brown University Press, 1980.

deCleyre, Voltairine. "Anarchism and American Traditions." In *Selected Works of Voltairine deCleyre,* edited by Alexander Berkman. New York: Mother Earth Publishing Association, 1914.

Degler, Carl N. *At Odds: Women and the Family in America from the Revolution to the Present.* New York: Oxford University Press, 1980.

Destler, Chester M. *American Radicalism, 1865–1901.* New London: Connecticut College, 1946.

DeWitt, Francis, ed. *Statistical Information Relating to Branches of Industry in Massachusetts, for the Year Ending June 1, 1855.* Boston: William White Printer, 1856.

Ditzion, Sidney. *Marriage, Morals, and Sex in America.* New York: W. W. Norton, 1978.

Doherty, Robert W. "Alfred H. Love and the Universal Peace Union." Ph.D. diss., University of Pennsylvania, Philadelphia, 1962.

Dolgoff, Sam, ed. *Bakunin on Anarchy.* New York: Vintage Books, 1972.

———. *Bakunin on Anarchism,* rev. ed. Montreal: Black Rose Books, 1980.

Drinnon, Richard. *Rebel in Paradise: A Biography of Emma Goldman.* 1961. Reprint. New York: Bantam Books, 1973.

Duberman, Martin, ed. *The Antislavery Vanguard: New Essays on the Abolitionists.* Princeton, N.J.: Princeton University Press, 1965.

———. *The Uncompleted Past.* New York: E. P. Dutton, 1971.

DuBois, Ellen Carol, ed. *Elizabeth Cady Stanton/Susan B. Anthony: Correspondence, Writings, Speeches.* New York: Schocken Books, 1981.

———. *Feminism and Suffrage: The Emergence of an Independent Woman's Movement in America, 1848–1869.* Ithaca, N.Y.: Cornell University Press, 1978.

———, ed. "On Labor and Free Love: Two Unpublished Speeches of Elizabeth Cady Stanton." *Signs* 1 (Autumn 1975):257–68.

———, and Linda Gordon. "Seeking Ecstasy on the Battlefield: Danger and Pleasure in Nineteenth-Century Feminist Sexual Thought." *Feminist Studies* 9 (Spring 1983):7–25.

Dubovsky, Melvyn. *We Shall Be All: A History of the Industrial Workers of the World.* New York: Quadrangle Books, 1969.

Eckhardt, Celia Morris. *Fanny Wright: Rebel in America.* Cambridge, Mass.: Harvard University Press, 1984.

Ehrenreich, Barbara, and Deirdre English. *For Her Own Good: 150 Years of the Experts' Advice to Women.* New York: Doubleday, 1979.

Ehrlich, Carol, Howard Ehrlich, David DeLeon, and Glenda Morris, eds. *Reinventing Anarchy.* London: Routledge and Kegan Paul: 1979.

Falk, Candace. *Love, Anarchy, and Emma Goldman.* New York: Holt, Rinehart, and Winston, 1984.

Feuerlicht, Roberta Strauss. *Justice Crucified: The Story of Sacco and Vanzetti.* New York: McGraw-Hill, 1977.

Fogarty, Robert S. *Dictionary of American Communal and Utopian History.* Westport, Conn.: Greenwood Press, 1980.

Foner, Eric. *Free Soil, Free Labor, Free Men: The Ideology of the Republican Party Before the Civil War.* New York: Oxford University Press, 1970.

———. *Politics and Ideology in the Age of the Civil War.* New York: Oxford University Press, 1980.

———. "Radical Individualism in America." *Literature of Liberty* 1 (July–September 1978):5–31.

Foote, Edward Bliss. *Reply to the Alphites.* New York: Murray Hill, 1882.

Foster, Lawrence. "Free Love and Feminism: John Humphrey Noyes and the Oneida Community." *Journal of the Early Republic* 1 (Summer 1981):165–83.

Foucault, Michel. *The History of Sexuality.* Vol. 1, *An Introduction.* New York: Pantheon, 1978.

Fredrickson, George M. *The Inner Civil War: Northern Intellectuals and the Crisis of the Union.* New York: Harper and Row, 1965.

Fryer, Peter. *The Birth Controllers.* London: Secker and Warburg, 1965.

Gandhi, Mohandas K. "The Origins of *Satyagraha* Doctrine." In *The Quiet Battle: Writings on the Theory and Practice of Non-Violent Resistance*, edited by Mulford Q. Sibley. Boston: Beacon Press, 1963.

Gattey, Charles Neilson. *The Bloomer Girls.* New York: Coward-McCann, 1968.

Goldman, Emma. *Living My Life.* New York: Dover Publications, 1970.

Goodman, Paul. "The Black Flag of Anarchism." In *Drawing the Line: Political Essays by Paul Goodman*, edited by Taylor Stoehr. New York: Free Life Editions, 1977.

Goodman, Paul, and Percival Goodman. *Communitas: Means of Livelihood and Ways of Life.* 2d rev. ed. New York: Random House, 1960.

Gordon, Ann D., Mari Jo Buhle, and Nancy Schrom Dye. *Women in American Society.* Somerville, Mass.: New England Free Press, 1972.

Gordon, Linda, and Allen Hunter. *Sex, Family, and the New Right.* Somerville, Mass.: New England Free Press, 1978.

———. *Woman's Body, Woman's Right: A Social History of Birth Control in America.* New York: Penguin Books, 1977.

Green, James R. *The World of the Worker: Labor in Twentieth-Century America.* New York: Hill and Wang, 1980.

———, and Hugh Carter Donahue. *Boston's Workers: A Labor History.* Boston: Boston Public Library, 1979.

Greene, William B. *Mutual Banking: Showing the Radical Deficiency of the Present Circulating Medium and the Advantage of a Free Currency.* Worcester, Mass.: New England Labor Reform League, 1870.

Greven, Phillip J., Jr. *Four Generations: Population, Land and Family in Colonial Andover, Massachusetts.* Ithaca, N.Y.: Cornell University Press, 1970.

Grob, Gerald. "Mental Illness, Indigency, and Welfare: The Mental Hospital in Nineteenth-Century America." In *Anonymous Americans: Explorations in Nineteenth-Century Social History*, edited by Tamara Hareven. Englewood Cliffs, N.J.: Prentice-Hall, 1971.

———. *Workers and Utopia: A Study of Ideological Conflict in the American Labor Movement 1865-1900.* Chicago: Quadrangle Books, 1961.

Gross, Alex, and Ilene Gross. Letter to the author, undated.

Gutman, Herbert G. Introduction to *Liberty.* Westport, Conn.: Greenwood Press, 1970.

———, ed. *Work, Culture and Society in Industrializing America.* New York: Vintage Books, 1977.

Hareven, Tamara, ed. *Anonymous Americans: Explorations in Nineteenth-Century Social History.* Englewood Cliffs, N.J.: Prentice-Hall, 1971.

Hawthorne, Julian. *In Behalf of Personal Liberty.* New York: Twentieth Century Publishing, 1891.

Hayden, Dolores. *The Grand Domestic Revolution: A History of Feminist Designs for American Homes, Neighborhoods, and Cities.* Cambridge, Mass.: MIT Press, 1981.

Heilbroner, Robert L. *The Worldly Philosophers.* 3d rev. ed. New York: Simon and Schuster, 1967.

Hess, John L. "The Compleat Adam Smith." *The Nation* 232 (May 16, 1981): 596–97.

Heywood, William Sweetzer. *History of Westminster, 1728–1893.* Lowell, Mass.: Vox Populi Press, 1893.

Hibben, Paxton. *Henry Ward Beecher: An American Portrait.* New York: George H. Doran, 1927.

Hiskes, Richard P. "Community in the Anarcho-Individualist Society: The Legacy of Benjamin Tucker." *Social Anarchism* 1 (Winter 1980):41–52.

Hoare, Daniel W. *Digest of Ancestry and Early History of the Hoare Family and Descent of the New Brunswick Family from Charles Hoare of Gloucester, England.* Typescript, 1976.

Hoare, Edward. *Some Accounts of the Early History and Genealogy with Pedigrees from 1330, Unbroken to the Present Time of the Families of Hoare and Hore with All Their Branches.* London: Alfred Russell Smith, 1883.

Holloway, Mark. *Heavens on Earth: Utopian Communities in America, 1680–1880.* New York: Dover Publications, 1966.

Horowitz, Irving L., ed. *The Anarchists.* New York: Dell Publishing, 1964.

Hull, Moses. *The General Judgment. Or Great Overturning.* Boston: Moses Hull, 1875.

Hunter, William B., Jr., ed. *A Milton Encyclopedia.* Lewisburgh, Pa.: Bucknell University Press, 1979.

Hyams, Edward. *Pierre-Joseph Proudhon: His Revolutionary Life, Mind, and Works.* New York: Taplinger, 1979.

Jackson, Helen Hunt. "Hide and Seek Town." *Scribner's Monthly* 12 (August 1876):449–62.

James, Edward T., ed. *Notable American Women, 1670–1950: A Biographical Dictionary.* Cambridge, Mass.: Harvard University Press, 1971.

Kern, Louis J. *An Ordered Love: Sex Roles and Sexuality in Victorian Utopias—the Shakers, the Mormons, and the Oneida Community.* Chapel Hill: University of North Carolina Press, 1981.

Kett, Joseph F. "Growing Up in Rural New England." In *Anonymous Americans: Explorations in Nineteenth-Century Social History*, edited by Tamara Hareven. Englewood Cliffs, N.J.: Prentice-Hall, 1971.

Kinsey, Alfred, Wendell Pomeroy, and Clyde Martin. *Sexual Behavior in the Human Male.* Philadelphia: W.B. Saunders, 1948.

Larson, Orvin. *American Infidel: Robert G. Ingersoll.* New York: Citadel Press, 1962.

Lasch, Christopher. "Life in the Therapeutic State." *New York Review of Books*, June 12, 1980, pp. 24–32.

Leach, William. *True Love and Perfect Union: The Feminist Reform of Sex and Society.* New York: Basic Books, 1980.

Leighton, Marion. "Victoria Woodhull Meets Karl Marx." *Liberation Magazine* 20 (Fall 1977):15–21.

Lerner, Gerda. *The Majority Finds Its Past: Placing Women in History.* New York: Oxford University Press, 1979.

Lerner, Michael. "Anarchism and the American Counter-Culture." In *Anarchism Today,* edited by David Apter and James Joll. New York: Doubleday, 1972.

Liebling, Mordechai E. "Ezra Heywood: Intransigent Individualist." Research paper, Brandeis University, Waltham, Mass., 1970.

Lynd, Staughton. *Intellectual Origins of American Radicalism.* London: Wildwood House, 1973.

Mabee, Carleton. *Black Freedom: The Nonviolent Abolitionists from 1830 Through the Civil War.* New York: Macmillan, 1970.

Macdonald, Geroge E. *Fifty Years of Free Thought: Being the Story of "The Truth Seeker," with the Natural History of Its Editor.* New York: Truth Seeker, 1929.

Mandel, Ernest. *An Introduction to Marxist Economic Theory.* New York: Pathfinder, 1969.

Marsh, Margaret. *Anarchist Women, 1870-1920.* Philadelphia: Temple University Press, 1981.

Martin, James J. *Men Against the State: The Expositors of Individualist Anarchism in America, 1827-1908.* Colorado Springs: Ralph Myles Publisher, 1970.

———, ed. *State Socialism and Anarchism and Other Essays by Benjamin R. Tucker.* Colorado Springs: Ralph Myles Publisher, 1972.

Marx, Leo. *The Machine in the Garden: Technology and the Pastoral Ideal in America.* New York: Oxford University Press, 1964.

Mason, Atherton P. "Wachusett Mountain and Princeton." *Granite Monthly,* May–June 1886.

Massachusetts Soldiers and Sailors of the Revolutionary War. Boston: Wright and Potter, 1901.

McCoy, Ralph E. "Banned in Boston: The Development of Literary Censorship in Massachusetts." Ph.D. diss., University of Illinois, Urbana, 1956.

McElroy, Wendy, ed. *Freedom, Feminism, and the State.* Washington, D.C.: Cato Institute, 1982.

Melder, Keith E. *Beginnings of Sisterhood: The American Woman's Rights Movement, 1800-1850.* New York: Schocken Books, 1977.

Meltzer, Milton. *Bread and Roses: The Struggle of American Labor, 1865–1915.* New York: Random House, 1973.

Miller, Edwin H., ed. *Walt Whitman: The Correspondence.* Vol. 3, *1876–1885.* New York: New York University Press, 1964.

Minutes of the Thirteenth Annual Meeting of the Women's Christian Temperance Union of Rhode Island, Held in Newport, September 27, 28, and 29. Providence, R.I.: E. L. Freeman and Sons, 1887.

Mohr, James C. *Abortion in America.* New York: Oxford University Press, 1978.

Montgomery, David. *Beyond Equality: Labor and the Radical Republicans, 1862–1872.* Urbana: University of Illinois Press, 1981.

Moore, R. Laurence. *In Search of White Crows: Spiritualism, Parapsychology, and American Culture.* New York: Oxford University Press, 1977.

Morgan, H. Wayne, ed. *The Gilded Age.* Syracuse, N.Y.: Syracuse University Press, 1970.

Morse, Sidney H. "Chips from My Studio." *The Radical Review* 1 (1877–78):821.

Mumford, Lewis. *The Culture of Cities.* New York: Harcourt, Brace, Jovanovich, 1938.

Murphy, Marion F. "The Princeton Story." n.p., n.d.

Nelson, Geoffrey K. *Spiritualism and Society.* London: Routledge and Kegan Paul, 1969.

New England Watch and Ward Society. *Annual Report, 1890–1891.* Boston: Office of the Society, 1891.

Nissenbaum, Stephen. *Sex, Diet, and Debility in Jacksonian America: Sylvester Graham and Health Reform.* Westport, Conn.: Greenwood Press, 1980.

Nolan, Timothy, ed. *The Diary of William Griswold Dearth: Praeteria, Journal of Acts and Thoughts, a Portion (September 6–November 1,1854).* Providence, R.I.: Brown University, 1979.

Nourse, Henry Steadman. "The Hoare Family in America and Its English Ancestry: A Compilation from the Collections Made by the Honorable George Frisbie Hoar." *New England Historical and Genealogical Register,* April 1899.

Noyes, John Humphrey. *Essay on Scientific Propagation.* Oneida, N.Y.: Oneida Community, 1875.

——. *Male Continence.* Oneida, N.Y.: Oneida Community, 1872.

O'Neill, William L. *Everyone Was Brave: A History of Feminism in America.* New York: Quadrangle Books, 1969.

Perry, Lewis. *Childhood, Marriage and Reform: Henry Clarke Wright, 1797–1870.* Chicago: University of Chicago Press, 1980.

——, and Leonard Krimerman, eds. *Patterns of Anarchy: A Collection of Writings on the Anarchist Tradition.* Garden City, N.Y.: Anchor Books, 1966.

——. *Radical Abolitionism: Anarchy and the Government of God in Antislavery Thought.* Ithaca, N.Y.: Cornell University Press, 1973.

Pillsbury, Parker. *"Cupid's Yokes" and the Holy Scriptures Contrasted in a Letter from Parker Pillsbury to Ezra H. Heywood.* Princeton, Mass.: Co-Operative Publishing, 1878.

Pinney, Lucien V. "The Man and the Woman of Princeton," *The Word,* June 1890.

Pivar, David. *Purity Crusade: Sexual Morality and Social Control, 1868–1900.* Westport, Conn.: Greenwood Press, 1973.

Pleck, Joseph H., and Elizabeth Pleck, eds. *The American Man.* Englewood Cliffs, N.J.: Prentice-Hall, 1980.

Pomeroy, Sarah B. *Goddesses, Whores, Wives, and Slaves: Women in Classial Antiquity.* New York: Schocken Books, 1976.

Proceedings of the First Anniversary of the Universal Peace Society, Masonic Hall, New York, May 8 and 9, 1867. Philadelphia: Universal Peace Society, 1867.

Proceedings of the Indignation Meeting Held in Faneuil Hall, Thursday Evening, August 1, 1878, to Protest Against the Injury Done to the Freedom of the Press by the Conviction and Imprisonment of Ezra H. Heywood. Boston: Benjamin R. Tucker, Publisher, 1878.

Proceedings of the Peace Convention Held in Boston, March 14 and 15, 1866, and in Providence. May 16, 1866. Philadelphia: Universal Peace Society, 1866.

"Program of the Eighty-Seventh Annual Commencement of Brown University," September 3, 1856. Brown University, Providence, R.I., 1856.

Putnam, Samuel P. *400 Years of Freethought.* New York: Truth Seeker, 1894.

Reich, Wilhelm. *The Function of the Orgasm.* New York: World Publishing, 1971.

———. *The Sexual Revolution.* New York: Farrar, Straus, and Giroux, 1974.

Reichert, William O. *Partisans of Freedom: A Study in American Anarchism.* Bowling Green, Ohio: Bowling Green University Popular Press, 1976.

Remini, Robert V. *Andrew Jackson.* New York: Harper and Row, 1969.

Reverby, Susan, and David Rosner, eds. *Health Care in America: Essays in Social History.* Philadelphia: Temple University Press, 1979.

Riegel, Robert E. Women's Clothes and Women's Rights." *American Quarterly* 15 (Fall 1963):392–401.

Robinson, Victor. *Pioneers of Birth Control in England and America.* New York: Voluntary Parenthood League, 1919.

Rocker, Rudolf. *Pioneers of American Freedom.* Los Angeles: Rocker Publications Committee, 1949.

Roediger, David. "Ira Steward and the Anti-Slavery Origins of American Eight-Hour Theory." *Labor History* 27 (Summer 1986):410–26.

Roediger, David, and Franklin Rosemont. *Haymarket Scrapbook.* Chicago: Charles Kerr, 1986.

Rosenberg, Charles E. "Sexuality, Class and Role in Nineteenth-Century America." In *The American Man,* edited by Joseph H. Pleck and Elizabeth Pleck. Englewood Cliffs, N.J.: Prentice-Hall, 1980.

Russell, Francis. *Tragedy in Dedham.* New York: McGraw-Hill, 1971.

Sachs, Emanie. *"The Terrible Siren": Victoria Woodhull.* New York: Harper and Brothers, 1928.

Sale, Kirkpatrick. *Human Scale.* New York: Coward, McCann, and Geoghegan, 1980.

Schlesinger, Arthur M., Jr. *The Age of Jackson.* Boston: Little, Brown, 1945.

Schuster, Eunice. *Native American Anarchism: A Study of Left-Wing American Individualism.* Northampton, Mass.: Smith College, 1932.

Sears, Hal D. *The Sex Radicals: Free Love in High Victorian America.* Lawrence: Regents Press of Kansas, 1977.

Sennett, Richard. "The Desire to Know." *The New Yorker,* July 16, 1979, pp. 101–6.

Shakespeare, William. *Henry IV, Part One.* New York: New American Library, 1965.

Shaplen, Robert. *Free Love and Heavenly Sinners: The Great Henry Ward Beecher Scandal.* New York: Alfred A. Knopf, 1954.

Shively, Charles, ed. *Love, Marriage and Divorce and the Sovereignty of the Individual: A Discussion Between Henry James, Horace Greeley, and Stephen Pearl Andrews.* Weston, Mass.: M and S Press, 1975.

———. "Josiah Warren, The First American Anarchist." Paper delivered at the Anarchos Institute Conference, Montreal, June 5, 1982.

Shulman, Alix Kates, ed. *Red Emma Speaks: Selected Writings and Speeches by Emma Goldman*. New York: Vintage, 1972.
———. *Red Emma Speaks: An Emma Goldman Reader*. New York: Schocken Books, 1983.
Sibley, Mulford Q., ed. *The Quiet Battle: Writings on the Theory and Practice of Non-Violent Resistance*. Boston: Beacon Press, 1963.
Sinclair, Upton. *Boston*. New York: Albert and Charles Boni, 1928.
Sklar, Kathryn Kish. *Catherine Beecher: A Study in American Domesticity*. New York: W. W. Norton, 1976.
Smith, Daniel Scott. "Family Limitation, Sexual Control and Domestic Feminism in Victorian America." In *A Heritage of Her Own*, edited by Nancy F. Cott and Elizabeth H. Pleck. New York: Simon and Schuster, 1979.
Smith, Howard, and Lin Harris. "The New Sex: Come Again Some Other Day." *Village Voice*, December 31–January 6, 1981, p. 18.
Smith, Timothy L. *Revivalism and Social Reform: American Protestantism on the Eve of the Civil War*. New York: Harper and Row, 1965.
Snitow, Ann, Christine Stansell, and Sharon Thompson, eds. *Powers of Desire: The Politics of Sexuality*. New York: Monthly Review Press, 1983.
Sorin, Gerald. *Abolitionism: A New Perspective*. New York: Praeger Publishers, 1972.
Spooner, Lysander. *The Collected Works of Lysander Spooner*. 6 vols. Biography and Introduction by Charles Shively. Weston, Mass.: M and S Press, 1971.
Stern, Madeleine B. *Heads and Headliners: The Phrenological Fowlers*. Norman: University of Oklahoma Press, 1971.
———. *The Pantarch: A Biography of Stephen Pearl Andrews*. Austin: University of Texas Press, 1968.
———, ed. *The Victoria Woodhull Reader*. Weston, Mass.: M and S Press, 1974.
Stevens, Elizabeth. "Victoria Woodhull." Research paper, Brown University, Providence, R.I., 1981.
Stirner, Max. *The Ego and His Own*. New York: Libertarian Book Club, 1963.
Stoehr, Taylor, ed. *Drawing the Line: Political Essays by Paul Goodman* (New York: Free Life Editions, 1977).
———, ed. *Free Love in America: A Documentary History*. New York: AMS Press, 1979.
———. *Hawthorne's Mad Scientists: Psuedoscience and Social Science in Nineteenth-Century Life and Letters*. Hamden, Conn.: The Shoe String Press, 1978.
———. *Nay-Saying in Concord: Emerson, Alcott, and Thoreau*. Hamden, Conn.: Shoe String Press, 1979.
Swedberg, Richard. "The Individual and the Group: A Study of Nineteenth-Century Anarchist Communes." Research paper, Harvard University, Cambridge, Mass., 1973.
Symes, Lillian, and Travers Clement. *Rebel America: The Story of Social Revolt in the United States*. 1934. Reprint. Boston: Beacon Press, 1972.
Thomas, Robert David. *The Man Who Would Be Perfect: John Humphrey Noyes and the Utopian Impulse*. Philadelphia: University of Pennsylvania Press, 1977.

Tillotson, Mary E. *An Essay on the Sanitary and Social Influences of Woman's Dress.* Vineland, N.J.: Self-published, 1873.

Trall, R. T. *Sexual Physiology.* New York: Wood and Holbrook, Hygienic Institute, 1866.

Traubel, Horace. *With Walt Whitman in Camden,* vol. 1. Boston: Small, Maynard, 1906.

———. *With Walt Whitman in Camden,* vol. 2. New York: Mitchell Kennedy, 1915.

Tucker, Benjamin R. *Individual Liberty.* New York: Vanguard Press, 1926.

———. "The Life of Benjamin R. Tucker—Disclosed by Himself in the Principality of Monaco at the Age of 74." Handwritten manuscript, n.d. Benjamin R. Tucker Papers, Rare Books and Manuscript Division, The New York Public Library.

———. *State Socialism and Anarchism and Other Essays.* Colorado Springs: Ralph Myles Publisher, 1972.

———. "Walt Whitman and Anthony Comstock." *New York Herald,* Paris edition, November 23, 1930.

Veysey, Laurence. *The Communal Experience: Anarchist and Mystical Counter-Cultures in America.* New York: Harper and Row, 1973.

Walters, Ronald G. *American Reformers, 1815–1860.* New York: Hill and Wang, 1978.

Ware, Norman. *The Industrial Worker, 1840–1860.* New York: Quadrangle Books, 1964.

———. *The Labor Movement in the United States, 1860–1890.* 1929. Reprint. New York: Vintage Books, 1964.

Warren, Josiah. *True Civilization.* New York: Burt Franklin, 1967.

Warren, Sidney. *American Freethought, 1860–1914.* New York: Gordian Press, 1966.

Watner, Carl. *Voluntaryism in the Libertarian Tradition.* Baltimore: The Voluntaryists, 1982.

———. *A Voluntaryist Bibliography, Annotated.* Baltimore: The Voluntaryists, 1982.

Wexler, Alice. *Emma Goldman: An Intimate Life.* New York: Pantheon, 1984.

Wilder, Harris Hawthorne. *The Early Years of a Zoologist: The Story of a New England Boyhood.* Northampton, Mass.: Smith College, 1930.

Wilentz, Sean. *Chants Democratic: New York City and the Rise of the American Working Class, 1788-1850.* New York: Oxford University Press, 1984.

"Will of Charles Hoare of Gloucester, England, with Notes by George F. Hoar." Boston: David Clapp and Son, 1891.

Williams, Charles Richard, ed. *Diary and Letters of Rutherford B. Hayes.* Columbus: Ohio State Archeological and Historical Society, 1924.

Woodcock, George. *Anarchism: A History of Libertarian Ideas and Movements.* New York: World Publishing, 1971.

Zinn, Howard, "Anarchist Features of the Radical Movements of the 1960s and 1980s." Paper delivered at the Conference on Anarchism in America, Boston Public Library, December 4, 1982.

———. *A People's History of the United States.* New York: Harper and Row, 1980.

———. *The Politics of History.* Boston: Beacon Press, 1970.

Index

Abbot, Francis E., 127
Abolitionist movement, E. H.'s
    involvement in, 15–40, 175, 176;
    influence of, on Angela Heywood, 69;
    as model for Labor Reform League, 50;
    on pacifism, 35; and roots of
    anarchism, 36–37; on violence, 25–27.
    See also Garrisonian abolitionists
Abortion, 148, 149
Adams, Robert C., 5–6, 170
Alcott, A. Bronson, 45
Allen, District Attorney Frank D., 164
Almy, Charles, Jr., 115, 144
American Anti-Slavery Society, 30
American Equal Rights Association, 103
American Federation of Labor, 62
American Free Dress League, 87
American Workman, The, on eight-hour
    day, 46
Anarchism, 175–76, 177; E. H.'s
    development of, in 1860s, 31; as
    Emersonian notion, 30; and influence
    of Josiah Warren, 34; and labor reform,
    41, 52–53, 54–63; roots of, 36–37; and
    spiritualism, 86; versus collectivist
    social movements, 54–55; and women's
    suffrage, 135. *See also* Individualism
Andrews, Reverend Elisha, 7
Andrews, Stephen Pearl, 34, 50; and
    E. H.'s second trial, 147; and National
    Defense Association, 128, 130; on
    Angela Heywood, 85, 89; on Angela
    Heywood's background 68, 69; on free
    love, 72; on Heywood family, 91, 92,
    93–94; on marriage, 156; on Mountain
    Home Resort, 90, 125; and
    Pantarchism, 88; and social reform, 7;
    and Union Reform League, 87–88; and
    Victoria Woodhull, 71
Anthony, Susan B., on marriage and
    suffrage, 101, 102, 135

Anti-Death League, 178; founding of, 86,
    See also Spiritualism
Anti-Monopoly and Settlers' Rights
    Association, 91
Appleton, Henry, 90
Arieli, Yehoshua (historian), on labor
    reform, 62
Arrests, of D. M Bennett, 118–19; E. H's,
    114, 142, 147, 148, 164; of Josephine
    Tilton, 113, 118; of Moses Harman,
    163; of W. S. Bell, 118
Artisan republicanism, 61–62
Avrich, Paul (historian), on anarchism,
    176; on labor movement, 55

Babcock, Reverend J. M. L., 90
Bailie, William (historian), on Josiah
    Warren, 58
Bakunin, Michael, 56–57, 71
Ballou, Adin, 35
Baltimore Congress, 43, 44
Barry, Francis, 162
Beaman, Harry C., 92
Beaman, P. A., 147
Beecher, Catherine, on Victoria Woodhull,
    73, 74
Beecher, Reverend Henry Ward and
    Elizabeth Tilton, 73–74, 79, 80–81,
    110
Beeney, Henry, 50
Bell, W. S., 118
Bennett, D. M., and Anthony Comstock,
    78, 110; arrest and imprisonment of,
    118, 119, 128, 133; effect of conviction
    of, 165; on E. H.'s release from prison,
    132
Benson, Helen (Garrison), 15
Berkman, Alexander, 57
Birth control, *See* Comstock, Act;
    Sexuality
Blanchard, Joshua, 35
Blatchford, Judge Samuel, 119, 133

Low, Thomas, 157
Lynd, Staughton (historian), on natural rights, 21

Mcdonald, George E., 133, 168
Mann, Reverend Cyrus, of Westminster Academy, 7
Manufacturing, in Princeton, Mass., 3–4; of Samuel Heywood, 3, 6, 90, 91; after Civil War, 41–42
Markland, W. G., 161, 162
Marriage, E. H.'s views on, 79, 81; E. H.'s writings on, 103–5; Emma Goldman on, 177; and eugenics, 155; and free love movement, 82–83, 109; and obscenity charges, 132; and sexuality, 149, 150; and social purity movement, 112; Victoria Woodhull on, 81; and women's suffrage, 100–1, 102–3. *See also Cupid's Yokes*; Free love
Marsh, F. H., 155
Martin, James J. (historian), on *Uncivil Liberty*, 100
Marx, Karl, and Victoria Woodhull, 71
Marxism, contrasted with individualist anarchism, 53, 55, 56, 57. *See also* International Workingmen's Association; Socialism
Masquerier, Lewis, 50
Massachusetts Anti-Slavery Society, and E. H.'s views on free speech, 29; E. H.'s work with, 24
May, Samuel, 22–23; E. H.'s comments to, 24; and E. H.'s finances, 25
McCoy, Ralph (historian), on Anthony Comstock, 74; on urban life, 75–76
McKay, David, 142
McNeill, George, 43, 45, 46
McPherson, James M. (historian), on E. H.'s thinking in 1850s, 23
Mental illness, of Angelo Tilton Heywood, 174; of Ezra Hoar, 4–5
Merriam, C. L., and Anthony Comstock, 78
Millennium, E. H.'s lecturing on, 29; and pantarchism, 88; and Protestant evangelicalism, 18, 19, 20; and spiritualism, 84–85
"Monadnock from Wachusett" (John Greenleaf Whittier), 3

Montgomery, David (historian), on E. H.'s labor reform work, 62; on radicalism, 44, 46
Moore, Laurence R. (historian), on spiritualism, 85
Morse, Sidney, H., 49; on E. H.'s obscenity trial, 115, 116–17; on Victoria Woodhull, 81
Most, Johann, 57
Mountain Home Resort, 88–89, 90, 94; destruction of, 174; and E. H.'s finances, 123–26; and E. H.'s last imprisonment, 167; and Princeton community, 92, 93

National Defense Association. *See* Defense Association, National
National Labor Union (NLU), 42, 43, 44, 53, 54; and suffrage movement, 101
National Liberal League, 126–27, 129; and new dating system, 121
National Spiritualist Association, and Victoria Woodhull, 74
National Women's Rights Convention, 102
Natural rights. *See* Rights, natural
Nelson, Judge T.L., 144, 145, 147, 148, 164
New England, E. H.'s roots in, 1–11
New England and American Mutual Life Relief Association, 87
New England Anti-Slavery Convention, 27
New England Free Love League (NEFLL), 121, 149, 155, 156; and E.H.'s arrest, 114, 143; founding of, 82–83
New England Non-Resistance Society, 33
New England Non-Resistants, 30
Nichols, Mary Gove, 157
Nichols, Thomas, 109
Nissenbaum, Stephen (historian), on free love advocates, 157
Nonresistance, of Garrisonian abolitionists, 19–20, 22, 26–27, 30, 33, 35–36. *See also* Garrisonian abolitionists; Pacifism, Violence
North, and abolitionist movement in, 15, 26–27, 28
Noyes, John Humphrey, 19; philosophy of, 151–52, 154, 155

Obscenity, and Anthony Comstock, 75, 76–79; and charges against free speech

Note on the Author

Martin Blatt received his Ph.D. in American and New England Studies from Boston University in 1983. A labor educator living in Cambridge, Massachusetts, he has written extensively on labor and social history and has also worked on a number of documentary film projects.